MLA Directory of
Scholarly Presses in
Language and Literature

Second Edition

Edited by James L. Harner

The Modern Language Association of America
New York 1996

ISBN 87352-680-5 (cloth)
ISBN 87352-681-3 (paper)
ISSN 1057-2899

Contents

Introduction

The *MLA Directory of Scholarly Presses in Language and Literature*, a companion to the *MLA Directory of Periodicals*, describes the fields of interest, submission requirements, contract provisions, and editorial procedures of scholarly publishers of book-length literary and linguistic studies. In addition to offering authors a systematic guide to identifying and assessing publishers who might be interested in a manuscript or proposal on a particular topic, the *Directory* seeks to answer such common questions as

> To whom should I address an inquiry?
> Should I send a letter, a prospectus, sample chapters, or the full manuscript?
> Will the publisher consider a proposal or manuscript that other publishers are considering?
> How long should I expect to wait for a decision?
> Does the publisher require an electronic manuscript if my book is accepted?
> Will I be expected to provide a subvention?
> How selective is the publisher?
> What royalty can I expect?
> How many copies does the publisher typically print?
> How many review copies will be sent out?

Scope

This second edition of the *Directory* includes entries on 315 scholarly publishers from 34 countries. It excludes vanity presses, most publishers that issue only a very few books in language and literature, and firms that publish only textbooks or original poetry, drama, or fiction. Data on submissions, acceptances, and titles published are for a typical calendar year; all other information dates from 1995. (Of the 41 publishers listed in the first edition who did not return the questionnaire for this edition, some have merged with other firms, and some are out of business. Entries for the others repeat information from the first edition; these entries are marked by an asterisk.)

Sources of information

A questionnaire was mailed to all university presses as well as to all other publishers that have a list in language or literature. Of the more than one thousand publishers initially queried, several had ceased publishing or had merged with other firms; some that responded published only textbooks or original fiction, plays, or poems and thus were ineligible for inclusion; a few requested that they not be included; and others, despite additional letters or telephone calls, did not respond. (With the exception of merged firms, publishers that were sent questionnaires but not included in the *Directory* are listed in the appendix.)

The information in each entry is derived from the questionnaire and checked, when possible, against the publisher's standard contract form, current catalog, and guide for authors or style manual (all of which publishers were requested to submit along with the completed questionnaire).

Organization

Entries are listed alphabetically by publisher. To avoid a clump of entries beginning with *University* (or the equivalent in another language) and to avoid the difficulty of locating a publisher when one is uncertain whether the official name is "University of X Press" or "University Press of X," all university presses are alphabetized by the state, city, or other proper name in their titles (thus, University of Illinois Press is alphabetized by "Illinois," Presses de l'Université de Montréal by "Montréal"). Imprints and subsidiary firms must be located through the imprint and subsidiary-firm index.

A full entry consists of forty-one parts organized into six sections:

GENERAL INFORMATION

Entry number (to which the indexes are keyed)
Name of publisher
Editorial office address
Imprints or subsidiary firms
Person(s) to whom inquiries or proposals should be addressed
Year established
Telephone number
Fax number
Electronic-mail address

SCOPE

Publishing interests (publishers were asked to identify as precisely as possible national literatures, periods, genres, topics, regions, theoretical approaches, languages, specific authors, and linguistic topics in which they are especially interested). This section indicates only a publisher's special interests and must be consulted in concert with the next three parts as well as with the list of current series.

Indication whether the publisher is willing to consider proposals on virtually all literary and linguistic topics.

Topics in which the publisher has no interest.

Types of works not published (publishers were asked whether they were willing to consider dissertations [revised and unrevised], bibliographies, critical editions, collections of letters, biographies, textbooks, readers, collections of original essays, Festschriften, literary handbooks or encyclopedias, or other reference-type works).

Prizes or competitions intended to encourage submissions.

Language(s) of publication.

Series published (in language or literature). Only active series are included here. Because many series have separate editorial boards and submission requirements, subject entries have not been created from series titles for inclusion in the index of publishing interests. The publishing interests and submission requirements for many series are described in the *MLA Directory of Periodicals.*

SUBMISSION REQUIREMENTS

Restrictions on authors (e.g., whether an author must be a member of a particular professional organization).

Preferred form of initial contact (letter of inquiry only; letter and prospectus; letter, outline, and sample chapter[s]; letter and full manuscript [including number of copies required]).

Policy on simultaneous submissions (publishers were asked if they would consider a proposal or manuscript simultaneously submitted to another firm).

Contract prerequisites (publishers were asked if they would issue a contract on the basis of a proposal, prospectus, or sample chapter rather than a complete manuscript).

Style manual preferred.

Manuscript restrictions (publishers were asked if they impose any length restrictions and if they accept or expect dot-matrix printout, photocopies, camera-ready copy, or electronic manuscripts).

Subvention requirements.

EDITORIAL INFORMATION

Number of manuscripts or proposals on literature and language typically received during a calendar year. (Users must exercise considerable care in interpreting the responses in this part. Most are estimates—and are identified as such—since many publishers do not log the number of letters of inquiry, proposals, or unsolicited manuscripts received. Some estimates are more conservative than others.)

Number of manuscripts on literature and language typically sent to outside readers in a calendar year.

Number of manuscripts on literature and language typically accepted during a calendar year.

Number of outside readers who evaluate a manuscript.

Author-anonymous submission (publishers were asked if they deleted an author's name before sending a manuscript to outside readers).

Approximate time between receipt of a manuscript and decision to publish. (Responses in this and the next two parts must, of course, be approximate since the actual time that elapses depends on such factors as time of year, an editor's workload, the condition and length of the manuscript [especially the extent and nature of revisions that it requires], timely responses by outside readers, and production schedules.)

Approximate time between decision and return of copyedited manuscript.

Approximate time between decision and publication.

Time allowed for reading proof.

CONTRACT PROVISIONS

Copyright ownership
Typical royalty provisions

PUBLICATION AND DISTRIBUTION INFORMATION

Forms of publication (cloth, paper, electronic media)
Titles in literature and language published during 1994
Typical print run
Number of review copies distributed for each title
Distribution area (e.g., only in country of origin; worldwide)
Typical number of years a scholarly book is kept in print
Miscellaneous

No entry actually includes all forty-one parts. Although the questionnaire requested all the above information, some publishers indicated that their practices varied too much to allow for generalizations about editorial practices or contract provisions; some treated contract provisions, print runs, and other details as confidential information; some do not keep statistics on submissions or acceptances or did not have them available in the form requested; and still others simply chose, for whatever reason, not to complete parts of the questionnaire.

Indexes

Five indexes conclude the *Directory*: publishing interests, imprints and subsidiary firms, series titles, editorial personnel, languages of publication other than English. The index of publishing interests follows, insofar as possible, the information provided by respondents. Because the index of publishing interests does not include any entries derived solely from titles of series, users should also skim the series titles index. In the indexes, numbers are entry numbers, not page numbers.

Future editions

Scholars and publishers with suggestions for additional kinds of information that might be desirable in the next edition and publishers wishing to be included in the *Directory* should write the editor at Dept. of English, Texas A&M Univ., College Station 77843-4227.

Selected bibliography

The following publications offer useful advice to both novice and seasoned authors:

Harman, Eleanor, and Ian Montagnes, eds. *The Thesis and the Book.* Toronto: U of Toronto P, 1976. [The classic guide to transforming a dissertation into a publishable book.]

Henson, Kenneth T. "When Signing Book Contracts, Scholars Should Be Sure to Read the Fine Print." *Chronicle of Higher Education* 24 Oct. 1990: B2-3. [On royalty provisions and hidden expenses.]

Luey, Beth. *Handbook for Academic Authors.* 3rd ed. Cambridge: Cambridge UP, 1995. [A practical guide addressed to the publish-or-perish American academic, with advice on revising a dissertation into a book, finding and working with a publisher, and understanding the mechanics and economics of publishing.]

Parsons, Paul. *Getting Published: The Acquisition Process at University Presses.* Knoxville: U of Tennessee P, 1989. [Explains how American university presses build lists, how editors decide what to publish, and how the peer-review process works.]

Acknowledgments

The *Directory* could not have been prepared without the generous assistance of the editors and publishers who responded—frequently in detail and with encouraging notes—to a lengthy questionnaire. They will, I hope, be rewarded if their responses encourage the submission of important manuscripts or proposals they might otherwise not have seen (and, similarly, reduce the number of submissions on topics outside their publishing programs).

In constructing the original questionnaire, I benefited from the advice of Harrison T. Meserole, Willard Fox III, Paul J. Klemp, Joe Hollander, Danielle Uchitelle, Kathleen Kent, and several anonymous readers of the original proposal. Danielle Uchitelle unselfishly shared her expertise (gained from editing the *MLA Directory of Periodicals*) in designing the database, editing entries, and creating the indexes. Andrew LaCroix, who deftly interpreted heavily marked printouts, also made an important contribution to this edition. Each in some way made this a better directory than it would otherwise have been, but the responsibility for errors and omissions remains mine alone.

MLA Directory of Scholarly Presses in Language and Literature

(1)
AARHUS UNIVERSITY PRESS

Bldg. 170
Aarhus University
8000 Aarhus C, Denmark

Contact: Tønnes Bekker-Nielsen
Established: 1985
Telephone: (86) 197033
Fax: (86) 198433

SCOPE

Publishing interests: Classical philology;
 Greek (classical) literature; Greek
 (classical) language; Latin (classical)
 literature; Latin (classical) language;
 English literature (modern); American
 literature (modern); Scandinavian
 literature; translation studies; media
 studies
*Considers all literary and linguistic
 topics:* No
Types of works not published: Dissertations; critical editions; collections of
 letters; bibliographies; readers
Languages published: English; Spanish;
 German; Danish
Series title(s): The Dolphin; Acta
 Jutlandica

SUBMISSION REQUIREMENTS

Initial contact: Letter, outline, and sample
 chapter
Considers simultaneous submissions: No
*Will issue contract on the basis of
 proposal, prospectus, and/or sample
 chapter:* No
Style: Cambridge
Special requirements: Requires electronic
 manuscript
Subvention: Yes

EDITORIAL INFORMATION

*Manuscripts or proposals submitted each
 year:* 15 (estimate)
Manuscripts sent to readers each year:
 10 (estimate)
Manuscripts accepted each year: 8
Number of outside readers: 1-2
Author-anonymous submission: No
*Time between submission and publication
 decision:* 3-6 months
*Time between decision and return of copy-
 edited manuscript:* 3-12 months
Time between decision and publication: 6
 months
Time allotted for reading proof: 2-6
 weeks

CONTRACT PROVISIONS

Copyright: Publisher
Royalty provisions: No royalties on first
 printing; 15% of net thereafter

PUBLICATION AND DISTRIBUTION
INFORMATION

Forms of publication: Cloth, paper
Titles published each year: 4
Print run: 600
Number of review copies: 30-50
Distribution area: Worldwide
Time in print: 5-10 years

(2)
*ABLEX PUBLISHING CORP.

355 Chestnut St.
Norwood, NJ 07648

Contact: Barbara Bernstein, Managing
 Editor
Established: 1976
Telephone: 201 767-8450
Fax: 201 767-6717

SCOPE

Publishing interests: Linguistics; sociolinguistics; psycholinguistics; neurolinguistics; discourse processes; rhetoric;
bilingualism; second language acqui-
sition; literacy
*Considers all literary and linguistic
topics:* Yes (linguistics); no (literature)
Types of works not published: Bibli-
ographies; critical editions; collections
of letters; biographies; literary encyclo-
pedias
Languages published: English
Series title(s): Advances in Discourse
Processes; Delaware Symposium on
Language Studies; Language and
Educational Processes; Language and
Learning for Human Service
Professions; Second Language
Learning; Thematic Studies in Second
Language Acquisition and Learning;
Cognition and Literacy; Writing
Research

SUBMISSION REQUIREMENTS

Initial contact: Letter and prospectus
(with table of contents)
Style: MLA; Chicago; American Psychological Association; Linguistic Society
of America
Special requirements: Length: 350 pages
maximum for monographs, 500 pages
maximum for edited volumes; accepts
photocopies, dot-matrix printout, and
electronic manuscripts
Subvention: No

EDITORIAL INFORMATION

*Manuscripts or proposals submitted each
year:* 15 (estimate)
Manuscripts sent to readers each year: 8-
10 (estimate)
Manuscripts accepted each year: 6-7
(estimate)

Number of outside readers: 1-3
*Time between submission and publication
decision:* 4-6 weeks
*Time between decision and return of copy-
edited manuscript:* 6 weeks
Time between decision and publication:
10 months

CONTRACT PROVISIONS

Copyright: Publisher
Royalty provisions: 10-12%

PUBLICATION AND DISTRIBUTION
INFORMATION

Forms of publication: Cloth, paper
Titles published each year: 10 (estimate)
Print run: 1,000-1,500
Number of review copies: 20
Distribution area: Worldwide
Time in print: 10 years

(3)
ACADEMIA SCIENTIARUM
FENNICA

FF Communications
PO Box 14
20501 Turku, Finland

Imprint(s) and subsidiary firm(s):
Folklore Fellows' Communications
Established: 1910
Telephone: (358) 21 4443091
Fax: (358) 21 2442505

SCOPE

Publishing interests: Folklore (especially
oral literature, belief systems, myth and
ritual, and methodology and history of
folklore)
*Considers all literary and linguistic
topics:* No

Types of works not published: Critical editions; collections of letters; biographies; textbooks; collections of essays; Festschriften; literary reference works

Languages published: English; French; German

SUBMISSION REQUIREMENTS

Initial contact: Letter of inquiry or manuscript

Considers simultaneous submissions: Prefers single submission

Will issue contract on the basis of proposal, prospectus, and/or sample chapter: No

Style: House

Special requirements: Length: 50-300 pages; prefers electronic copy; sometimes requires camera-ready copy

Subvention: Yes (if manuscript is over 300 pages)

EDITORIAL INFORMATION

Manuscripts or proposals submitted each year: 10-12

Manuscripts sent to readers each year: 5-6

Manuscripts accepted each year: 4-5

Number of outside readers: 2

Author-anonymous submission: No

Time between submission and publication decision: 2-6 months

Time between decision and publication: 3-4 months

Time allotted for reading proof: 3-4 weeks

CONTRACT PROVISIONS

Copyright: Publisher or both author and publisher

Royalty provisions: 0

PUBLICATION AND DISTRIBUTION INFORMATION

Forms of publication: Cloth, paper

Titles published each year: 4

Print run: 800

Number of review copies: 50

Distribution area: Worldwide

Time in print: Indefinitely

(4)
ACADEMIC PRESS

525 B St., Suite 1900
San Diego, CA 92101-4495

Contact: J. Scott Bentley (linguistics); Nikki Fine (psycholinguistics)

Established: 1942

Telephone: 619 699-6387

Fax: 619 699-6715

E-mail: jbentley@acad.com

SCOPE

Publishing interests: Phonetics; phonology; syntax; semantics; patterns of language

Considers all literary and linguistic topics: No

Types of works not published: Dissertations; Festschriften

Languages published: English

Series title(s): Syntax and Semantics

SUBMISSION REQUIREMENTS

Initial contact: Detailed proposal or full manuscript

Considers simultaneous submissions: Yes

Will issue contract on the basis of proposal, prospectus, and/or sample chapter: Yes

Style: Prefers Chicago; accepts others

Special requirements: Prefers electronic copy

Subvention: No

EDITORIAL INFORMATION

Number of outside readers: 4-6
Author-anonymous submission: No
Time between submission and publication decision: 2 months
Time between decision and publication: 6-10 months
Time allotted for reading proof: Varies

CONTRACT PROVISIONS

Copyright: Publisher
Royalty provisions: Varies

PUBLICATION AND DISTRIBUTION INFORMATION

Forms of publication: Cloth, paper, electronic media
Titles published each year: 20
Number of review copies: 40
Distribution area: Worldwide
Time in print: Varies

Prospective authors should consult the press's catalogs, as well as volumes in the Syntax and Semantics series, before submission.

(5)
ACADEMIC PRINTING AND PUBLISHING

PO Box 4218
South Edmonton, AB T6E 4T2, Canada

Established: 1975
Telephone: 403 435-5898
Fax: 403 435-5852

SCOPE

Publishing interests: Eighteenth-century studies; comparative literature; literary theory
Considers all literary and linguistic topics: No
Types of works not published: Dissertations; bibliographies; critical editions; collections of letters; biographies; readers; literary reference works
Languages published: English; French

SUBMISSION REQUIREMENTS

Restrictions on authors: Prefers Canadian residents because of availability of subventions
Initial contact: Letter and prospectus (2 copies)
Style: House
Special requirements: Accepts photocopies and dot-matrix printout; may require electronic manuscript
Subvention: No

EDITORIAL INFORMATION

Manuscripts or proposals submitted each year: 5 (estimate)
Manuscripts sent to readers each year: 1
Manuscripts accepted each year: 2
Number of outside readers: 1-2
Author-anonymous submission: Yes
Time between submission and publication decision: 6 months
Time between decision and return of copy-edited manuscript: 2 months
Time between decision and publication: 6 months

CONTRACT PROVISIONS

Copyright: Author (monographs); publisher (collections of essays)
Royalty provisions: 10%

PUBLICATION AND DISTRIBUTION INFORMATION

Forms of publication: Cloth, paper
Titles published each year: 1
Print run: 750
Number of review copies: 20-25
Distribution area: Worldwide
Time in print: Indefinitely

(6) *ACADEMY CHICAGO PUBLISHERS

213 West Institute Place
Chicago, IL 60610

Contact: Anita Miller, Editorial Director
Established: 1975
Telephone: 312 751-7302
Fax: 312 751-7306

SCOPE

Publishing interests: English literature
(especially nineteenth- and twentieth-
century); American literature; Pre-
Raphaelites; decadents; novel (in
English); women's studies; Latin
American literatures; English-language
translations of European novels
*Considers all literary and linguistic
topics:* Yes
Types of works not published:
Festschriften; literary encyclopedias
Languages published: English
Series title(s): Cassandra Editions;
Academy Travel Classics

SUBMISSION REQUIREMENTS

Initial contact: Letter of inquiry
Style: MLA
Special requirements: Does not accept
electronic manuscripts or dot-matrix
printout

Subvention: Sometimes

EDITORIAL INFORMATION

*Manuscripts or proposals submitted each
year:* 150 (estimate)
Manuscripts accepted each year: 10-15
Number of outside readers: 1-2
*Time between submission and publication
decision:* 6-16 weeks
*Time between decision and return of copy-
edited manuscript:* 1 year
Time between decision and publication:
2 years

CONTRACT PROVISIONS

Copyright: Author
Royalty provisions: 5-10% of net

PUBLICATION AND DISTRIBUTION INFORMATION

Forms of publication: Cloth, paper
Titles published each year: 10-15
Print run: 2,500 cloth, 5,000 paper
Number of review copies: 150
Distribution area: United States; Canada;
United Kingdom; Europe
Time in print: 8-10 years minimum

(7) ACCO PUBLISHERS

Tiensestr. 134-136
3000 Leuven, Belgium

Contact: Rob Berrevoets, General
Manager
Established: 1960
Telephone: (016) 291100
Fax: (016) 207389

SCOPE

Publishing interests: Linguistics; general
literature; Netherlandic literature

Considers all literary and linguistic topics: Yes
Types of works not published: Bibliographies; literary encyclopedias
Languages published: Dutch; English

SUBMISSION REQUIREMENTS

Initial contact: Letter and manuscript
Considers simultaneous submissions: Yes
Will issue contract on the basis of proposal, prospectus, and/or sample chapter: No
Style: House
Special requirements: Prefers electronic manuscripts or camera-ready copy
Subvention: No

EDITORIAL INFORMATION

Manuscripts or proposals submitted each year: 15 (estimate)
Manuscripts accepted each year: 8 (estimate)
Number of outside readers: 0
Author-anonymous submission: No
Time between submission and publication decision: 1 month
Time between decision and return of copy-edited manuscript: 3 months
Time between decision and publication: 3 months

CONTRACT PROVISIONS

Copyright: Author
Royalty provisions: 0-10%

PUBLICATION AND DISTRIBUTION INFORMATION

Forms of publication: Paper
Titles published each year: 8 (estimate)
Print run: 1,000
Number of review copies: 25
Distribution area: Belgium; Netherlands
Time in print: 4 years

(8)
AJANTA BOOKS INTERNATIONAL

1 U.B., Jawahar Nagar
Bungalow Rd.
Delhi 110007, India

Imprint(s) and subsidiary firm(s): Ajanta Publications
Contact: S. Balwant; Amit Atwal
Established: 1975
Telephone: (91) 11 2926182; (91) 11 7258630
Fax: (91) 11 7249664

SCOPE

Publishing interests: Literature; language learning; women's studies
Considers all literary and linguistic topics: Yes
Types of works not published: Dissertations; collections of letters
Languages published: English; Hindi; Sanskrit; Punjabi

SUBMISSION REQUIREMENTS

Initial contact: Letter and sample chapter
Considers simultaneous submissions: No
Will issue contract on the basis of proposal, prospectus, and/or sample chapter: Possibly
Special requirements: Prefers camera-ready copy or electronic copy

EDITORIAL INFORMATION

Manuscripts or proposals submitted each year: 12-48
Manuscripts sent to readers each year: 6-12
Manuscripts accepted each year: 6-12
Number of outside readers: 3
Author-anonymous submission: Yes
Time between submission and publication decision: 3-6 months

Time between decision and publication:
  6-12 months
Time allotted for reading proof: Varies

CONTRACT PROVISIONS

Copyright: Author
Royalty provisions: Varies

**PUBLICATION AND DISTRIBUTION
INFORMATION**

Forms of publication: Cloth, paper
Titles published each year: 12
Print run: Varies
Time in print: Varies

**(9)
ALA EDITIONS**

American Library Association
50 East Huron St.
Chicago, IL 60611

Contact: Marlene R. Chamberlain, Senior
  Acquisitions Editor
Established: 1886
Telephone: 312 280-1544
Fax: 312 440-9374

SCOPE

Publishing interests: Reference books;
  children's literature; bibliographies
*Considers all literary and linguistic
  topics:* No
Not interested in proposals on: Literary
  theory; linguistics
Types of works not published: Dissertations; collections of letters; most
  biographies; textbooks (unless library-
  related)
Languages published: English

SUBMISSION REQUIREMENTS

Initial contact: Letter of inquiry

Considers simultaneous submissions:
  Prefers single submission
*Will issue contract on the basis of
  proposal, prospectus, and/or sample
  chapter:* Yes
Style: Chicago
Special requirements: Prefers electronic
  manuscripts; provides guidelines for
  submitting proposals and for manuscript
  preparation
Subvention: No

EDITORIAL INFORMATION

*Manuscripts or proposals submitted each
  year:* 20 (estimate)
Manuscripts sent to readers each year: 4
  (estimate)
Manuscripts accepted each year: 5
  (estimate)
Number of outside readers: 1-2
Author-anonymous submission: No
*Time between submission and publication
  decision:* 2-3 months
*Time between decision and return of copy-
  edited manuscript:* 2 years
Time between decision and publication:
  30 months
Time allotted for reading proof: 2 weeks

CONTRACT PROVISIONS

Copyright: Publisher
Royalty provisions: 10%

**PUBLICATION AND DISTRIBUTION
INFORMATION**

Forms of publication: Cloth, paper, elec-
  tronic media
Titles published each year: 5
Print run: 1,500-3,000
Number of review copies: 40-50
Distribution area: Worldwide
Time in print: 5 years

(10)
UNIVERSITY OF ALABAMA PRESS

Box 870380
Tuscaloosa, AL 35487-0380

Contact: Nicole F. Mitchell, Acquisitions
Editor; Malcolm M. MacDonald,
Director
Established: 1945
Telephone: 205 348-5180
Fax: 205 348-9201
E-mail: nmitchel@va1vm.ua.edu

SCOPE

Publishing interests: American literature;
southern American literature; women's
studies; African American studies;
British literature; dialectology; Judaic
studies
*Considers all literary and linguistic
topics:* Yes
Types of works not published: Bibli-
ographies; critical editions; readers;
Festschriften; literary encyclopedias
Prizes and competitions: Elizabeth Agee
Prize ($1,000 for best manuscript in
American literature accepted during the
calendar year)
Languages published: English
Series title(s): Studies in Rhetoric and
Communication

SUBMISSION REQUIREMENTS

Initial contact: Letter and prospectus
(indicate length of manuscript)
*Will issue contract on the basis of
proposal, prospectus, and/or sample
chapter:* Occasionally
Style: Chicago; MLA; others acceptable
Special requirements: Length: reasonable
length (although no strict limit); accepts
photocopies and dot-matrix printout;
sometimes requests electronic manuscript or camera-ready copy

Subvention: Rarely

EDITORIAL INFORMATION

*Manuscripts or proposals submitted each
year:* 150 (estimate)
Manuscripts sent to readers each year: 30
(estimate)
Manuscripts accepted each year: 10
Number of outside readers: 2
Author-anonymous submission: No
*Time between submission and publication
decision:* 2-4 months
*Time between decision and return of copy-
edited manuscript:* 6-8 weeks
Time between decision and publication:
10-12 months

CONTRACT PROVISIONS

Copyright: Negotiable
Royalty provisions: Negotiable: authors
are asked to forgo royalties on some
copies of specialized scholarly books;
otherwise, 10% of net

**PUBLICATION AND DISTRIBUTION
INFORMATION**

Forms of publication: Cloth, paper
Titles published each year: 14
Print run: 1,000-2,000
Number of review copies: 50-150
Distribution area: Worldwide
Time in print: 7-20 years

(11)
UNIVERSITY OF ALASKA PRESS

Gruening Bldg., 1st fl.
University of Alaska
PO Box 756240
Fairbanks, AK 99775-6240

Contact: Pamela Odom, Acquisitions
Editor

Established: 1967
Telephone: 907 474-6389
Fax: 907 474-5502

SCOPE

Publishing interests: Alaskan literature; Alaskan languages; north Pacific Rim literature; north Pacific Rim languages; circumpolar literature; circumpolar languages
Considers all literary and linguistic topics: No

SUBMISSION REQUIREMENTS

Initial contact: Letter and full manuscript
Considers simultaneous submissions: No
Will issue contract on the basis of proposal, prospectus, and/or sample chapter: No
Style: Chicago
Subvention: No

EDITORIAL INFORMATION

Manuscripts or proposals submitted each year: 3-5
Manuscripts sent to readers each year: 3
Manuscripts accepted each year: 1-2
Number of outside readers: 1-2
Author-anonymous submission: No
Time between submission and publication decision: 3-6 months
Time between decision and publication: 8-10 months

CONTRACT PROVISIONS

Copyright: Usually publisher
Royalty provisions: 7.5-10%

PUBLICATION AND DISTRIBUTION INFORMATION

Forms of publication: Cloth, paper
Titles published each year: 2
Print run: 1,500-3,000

Number of review copies: 60-100
Distribution area: Worldwide

Currently publishes few titles in language and literature

(12)
UNIVERSITY OF ALBERTA PRESS

141 Athabasca Hall
Edmonton, AB T6G 2E8, Canada

Imprint(s) and subsidiary firm(s): Pica Pica Press
Contact: Mary Mahoney-Robson, Acting Director
Established: 1969
Telephone: 403 492-3662
Fax: 403 492-0719
E-mail: mmahoney@gpu.srv.ualberta.ca

SCOPE

Publishing interests: Canadian literature; Native American languages (Cree and Ojibwa); Slavic literature; William Wordsworth
Considers all literary and linguistic topics: No
Types of works not published: Dissertations; readers; collections of original essays; Festschriften; literary reference works
Languages published: English; French
Series title(s): AB Nature and Culture Series

SUBMISSION REQUIREMENTS

Restrictions on authors: Prefers Canadian scholars; low priority given to authors outside Canada whose manuscripts are not on a Canadian subject

Initial contact: Letter, outline, and sample chapter
Considers simultaneous submissions: Prefers single submission
Will issue contract on the basis of proposal, prospectus, and/or sample chapter: No
Style: Chicago
Special requirements: Expects electronic manuscript
Subvention: Usually

EDITORIAL INFORMATION

Manuscripts or proposals submitted each year: 20 (estimate)
Manuscripts sent to readers each year: 6
Manuscripts accepted each year: 2
Number of outside readers: 2-3
Author-anonymous submission: Yes
Time between submission and publication decision: 8 months
Time between decision and return of copy-edited manuscript: 6-9 months
Time between decision and publication: 12-18 months
Time allotted for reading proof: 2-3 weeks

CONTRACT PROVISIONS

Copyright: Publisher
Royalty provisions: 10% of list

PUBLICATION AND DISTRIBUTION INFORMATION

Forms of publication: Cloth, paper
Titles published each year: 1
Print run: 1,000
Number of review copies: 20-30
Distribution area: Worldwide
Time in print: Indefinitely

**(13)
AMERICAN UNIVERSITY IN CAIRO PRESS**

113 Sharia Kasr el Aini
Cairo, Egypt

Contact: Arnold C. Tovell, Director
Established: 1960
Telephone: (02) 3576888
Fax: (02) 3557565
E-mail: atovell@auc-acs.eun.eg

SCOPE

Publishing interests: Arabic literature; translations of Arabic literature
Considers all literary and linguistic topics: No
Languages published: English

SUBMISSION REQUIREMENTS

Initial contact: Letter and prospectus
Considers simultaneous submissions: Yes, if notified
Will issue contract on the basis of proposal, prospectus, and/or sample chapter: No
Style: Chicago
Special requirements: Prefers electronic manuscripts; provides guidelines for manuscript preparation
Subvention: No

EDITORIAL INFORMATION

Manuscripts or proposals submitted each year: 10
Manuscripts sent to readers each year: 3-5
Manuscripts accepted each year: 2-3
Number of outside readers: 2
Author-anonymous submission: No
Time between submission and publication decision: 3-4 months

Time between decision and publication:
6-9 months
Time allotted for reading proof: 1-3
weeks

CONTRACT PROVISIONS

Copyright: Publisher

**PUBLICATION AND DISTRIBUTION
INFORMATION**

Forms of publication: Cloth, paper
Titles published each year: 3
Print run: 1,000
Number of review copies: 15-20
Distribution area: Worldwide
Time in print: 5-10 years

**(14)
AMS PRESS**

56 East 13th St.
New York, NY 10003

Contact: John Hopper, Editor in Chief
Established: 1962
Telephone: 212 777-4700
Fax: 212 995-5413

SCOPE

Publishing interests: Literary criticism;
bibliography; biography; comparative
literature; English literature; American
literature; Romance literature;
medieval literature; Renaissance
literature; linguistics
*Considers all literary and linguistic
topics:* Yes
Types of works not published: Unrevised
dissertations; textbooks; Festschriften
Languages published: English
Series title(s): AMS Studies in the Middle
Ages; AMS Studies in the Renaissance;
AMS Studies in the Seventeenth

Century; AMS Studies in the
Eighteenth Century; AMS Studies in
the Nineteenth Century; AMS Studies
in Modern Literature; AMS Ars Poetica;
Georgia State Literary Studies; AMS
Studies in the Emblem; AMS Studies in
Cultural History; AMS Studies in
German Literature and Culture;
Conference on Editorial Problems;
AMS Ancient and Classical Studies;
AMS Henry James Studies

SUBMISSION REQUIREMENTS

Initial contact: Letter, outline, and sample
chapter
Considers simultaneous submissions: Yes
*Will issue contract on the basis of
proposal, prospectus, and/or sample
chapter:* No
Style: Chicago; MLA
Special requirements: Requires camera-
ready copy; accepts dot-matrix printout
for initial reading
Subvention: No

EDITORIAL INFORMATION

*Manuscripts or proposals submitted each
year:* 100 (estimate)
Manuscripts sent to readers each year: 25
(estimate)
Manuscripts accepted each year: 12
(estimate)
Number of outside readers: 1 minimum
Author-anonymous submission: Yes
*Time between submission and publication
decision:* 2-3 months
*Time between decision and return of copy-
edited manuscript:* 2-3 months
Time between decision and publication:
1 year
Time allotted for reading proof: 1 month

CONTRACT PROVISIONS

Copyright: Publisher

PUBLICATION AND DISTRIBUTION
INFORMATION

Forms of publication: Cloth
Titles published each year: 40 (estimate)
Number of review copies: 20-30
Distribution area: Worldwide
Time in print: 25 years

(15)
*EL ANCORA EDITORES

Apartado Aereo 56882
Bogotá, Colombia

Contact: Felipe Escobar, Director
  Editorial
Established: 1980
Telephone: 2839040; 2839235
Fax: 2121826

SCOPE

Publishing interests: Colombian
  literature; Latin American literature;
  Spanish-language literature
Types of works not published: Bibli-
  ographies; literary encyclopedias
Languages published: Spanish
Series title(s): Colección de literatura
  colombiana

SUBMISSION REQUIREMENTS

Initial contact: Letter and manuscript
Special requirements: Accepts photo-
  copies
Subvention: No

EDITORIAL INFORMATION

*Manuscripts or proposals submitted each
  year:* 25 (estimate)
Manuscripts sent to readers each year:
  15
Manuscripts accepted each year: 3
Number of outside readers: 2

*Time between submission and publication
  decision:* 3-6 months
*Time between decision and return of copy-
  edited manuscript:* 2 months
Time between decision and publication: 3
  months

CONTRACT PROVISIONS

Copyright: Author and publisher
Royalty provisions: 10%

PUBLICATION AND DISTRIBUTION
INFORMATION

Forms of publication: Cloth, paper
Titles published each year: 9
Print run: 2,000-3,000
Number of review copies: 100
Distribution area: Colombia; Argentina;
  Peru; Ecuador; Venezuela; Dominican
  Republic; Spain

(16)
APPLAUSE THEATRE AND CINEMA
BOOKS

1841 Broadway, Suite 1100
New York, NY 10023

Contact: Glenn Young, Publisher
Established: 1980
Telephone: 212 765-7880
Fax: 212 765-7875

SCOPE

Publishing interests: Performing arts
*Considers all literary and linguistic
  topics:* No
Types of works not published: Disser-
  tations; bibliographies
Languages published: English

SUBMISSION REQUIREMENTS

Initial contact: Letter, outline, and sample chapter(s)
Considers simultaneous submissions: No
Will issue contract on the basis of proposal, prospectus, and/or sample chapter: No
Style: Chicago; house
Special requirements: Requires electronic manuscript
Subvention: No

EDITORIAL INFORMATION

Manuscripts or proposals submitted each year: 700
Manuscripts sent to readers each year: 50
Manuscripts accepted each year: 25
Number of outside readers: 2
Author-anonymous submission: No
Time between submission and publication decision: 3-6 months
Time between decision and publication: 6-12 months
Time allotted for reading proof: 3 weeks

CONTRACT PROVISIONS

Copyright: Author
Royalty provisions: 5-9%

PUBLICATION AND DISTRIBUTION INFORMATION

Forms of publication: Cloth, paper, electronic media
Titles published each year: 24
Print run: 5,000
Number of review copies: 50-200
Distribution area: United States and United Kingdom
Time in print: Indefinitely

(17)
ARDIS PUBLISHERS

15 Monarch Bay Pl., 394
Dana Point, CA 92629

Contact: Ellendea Proffer, Publisher; Mary Ann Szporluk, Editor; Ronald Meyer, Editor
Established: 1971
Telephone: 714 499-0926
Fax: 714 499-0926
E-mail: 75664.1043@compuserve.com

SCOPE

Publishing interests: Russian literature; Soviet literature; Russian language; Russian culture; Soviet culture
Considers all literary and linguistic topics: No
Languages published: English; Russian

SUBMISSION REQUIREMENTS

Initial contact: Letter and prospectus
Style: Chicago
Special requirements: Prefers electronic manuscripts
Subvention: Sometimes

EDITORIAL INFORMATION

Manuscripts or proposals submitted each year: 50 (estimate)
Manuscripts sent to readers each year: 10 (estimate)
Manuscripts accepted each year: 15-20 (estimate)

CONTRACT PROVISIONS

Copyright: Varies
Royalty provisions: Varies

PUBLICATION AND DISTRIBUTION
INFORMATION

Forms of publication: Cloth, paper
Titles published each year: 25 (estimate)
Print run: 1,000
Number of review copies: 30
Distribution area: Worldwide

**(18)
ARIADNE PRESS**

270 Goins Court
Riverside, CA 92507

Contact: Donald G. Daviau; Jorun B.
  Johns
Established: 1989
Telephone: 909 684-9202
Fax: 909 684-9202

SCOPE

Publishing interests: Austrian literature
  and culture (nineteenth- and twentieth-
  century)
*Considers all literary and linguistic
  topics:* No
Types of works not published: Textbooks
Languages published: English; German
Series title(s): Studies in Austrian
  Literature, Culture, and Thought

SUBMISSION REQUIREMENTS

Initial contact: Letter and prospectus
Considers simultaneous submissions: No
*Will issue contract on the basis of
  proposal, prospectus, and/or sample
  chapter:* No
Style: Chicago; MLA
Subvention: No

EDITORIAL INFORMATION

Manuscripts accepted each year: 16-20
Number of outside readers: 2

Author-anonymous submission: Yes
*Time between submission and publication
  decision:* 3-6 months
Time between decision and publication:
  1 year
Time allotted for reading proof: 2 weeks

CONTRACT PROVISIONS

Copyright: Publisher
Royalty provisions: 6%

PUBLICATION AND DISTRIBUTION
INFORMATION

Forms of publication: Cloth, paper
Titles published each year: 18
Print run: 500
Number of review copies: 10-20
Distribution area: Worldwide
Time in print: Indefinitely

**(19)
*ARIS & PHILLIPS**

Teddington House
Warminster, Wiltshire BA12 8PQ
England

Contact: Lucinda Phillips
Established: 1972
Telephone: (0985) 213409
Fax: (0985) 212910

SCOPE

Publishing interests: Spanish literature;
  Portuguese literature; Catalan literature;
  bilingual annotated editions of the best
  works of Hispanic literature
*Considers all literary and linguistic
  topics:* Only if related to Iberian literatures and languages
Languages published: English
Series title(s): Hispanic Classics; Rereading Hispanic Studies

SUBMISSION REQUIREMENTS

Restrictions on authors: Translators must
have English as first language
Initial contact: Letter, outline, and sample
chapters or translated passages
Style: Cambridge; house; *Bulletin of
Hispanic Studies*
Special requirements: Length: prefers
fewer than 240 pages
Subvention: Varies; publisher is usually
successful at securing subsidies from
the Spanish Ministry of Culture or other
agencies.

EDITORIAL INFORMATION

*Manuscripts or proposals submitted each
year:* 10-12 (estimate)
Manuscripts sent to readers each year: 8-
10 (estimate)
Manuscripts accepted each year: 4
Number of outside readers: 1-2
*Time between submission and publication
decision:* 1-2 months
*Time between decision and return of copy-
edited manuscript:* 6 months
Time between decision and publication:
1 year

CONTRACT PROVISIONS

Copyright: Author
Royalty provisions: 10% of net

PUBLICATION AND DISTRIBUTION
INFORMATION

Forms of publication: Cloth, paper
Titles published each year: 16
Print run: 750-1,000
Number of review copies: 10-20
Distribution area: Worldwide
Time in print: 10 years minimum

(20)
UNIVERSITY OF ARIZONA PRESS

1230 North Park Ave., 102
Tuscon, AZ 85719

Contact: Joanne O'Hare, Senior Editor
Established: 1959
Telephone: 602 621-1441
Fax: 602 621-8899

SCOPE

Publishing interests: Native American
literature; Chicano literature; Latin
American literature; ethnic literature;
minority literature; women's literature;
linguistics (especially involving Native
American languages); lexicography
(especially involving Native American
languages); Native American languages;
bilingualism
Languages published: English

SUBMISSION REQUIREMENTS

Initial contact: Letter and prospectus
Style: Chicago
Special requirements: Accepts electronic
manuscripts
Subvention: No

EDITORIAL INFORMATION

Number of outside readers: 2 minimum
Author-anonymous submission: No
Time between decision and publication:
1 year

CONTRACT PROVISIONS

Copyright: Publisher

PUBLICATION AND DISTRIBUTION
INFORMATION

Forms of publication: Cloth, paper
Titles published each year: 2

Print run: 800-2,000
Number of review copies: 150-200
Distribution area: Worldwide
Time in print: Indefinitely

(21)
UNIVERSITY OF ARKANSAS PRESS

201 Ozark Ave.
Fayetteville, AR 72701-1201

Contact: Kevin Brock, Acquisitions
  Editor
Established: 1980
Telephone: 501 575-3246
Fax: 501 575-6044
E-mail: ehudgens@saturn.uark.edu

SCOPE

Publishing interests: General literature;
  linguistics; southern American literature
  (especially ethnic, minority, and women
  writers); biography
*Considers all literary and linguistic
  topics:* Yes
Types of works not published: Textbooks;
  unsolicited Festschriften
Languages published: English

SUBMISSION REQUIREMENTS

Initial contact: Letter and prospectus
Considers simultaneous submissions: No
*Will issue contract on the basis of
  proposal, prospectus, and/or sample
  chapter:* No
Style: Chicago
Special requirements: Requires sample
  before accepting dot-matrix printout;
  expects electronic manuscript
Subvention: Only in special cases

EDITORIAL INFORMATION

*Manuscripts or proposals submitted each
  year:* 1,500 (estimate)
Manuscripts sent to readers each year: 75
  (estimate)
Manuscripts accepted each year: 7
Number of outside readers: 2
Author-anonymous submission: No
*Time between submission and publication
  decision:* 3 months
*Time between decision and return of copy-
  edited manuscript:* 2 months
Time between decision and publication:
  10 months
Time allotted for reading proof: 2 weeks

CONTRACT PROVISIONS

Copyright: Negotiable
Royalty provisions: Varies (usually 10%
  of net for cloth, 6% of net for paper and
  electronic media)

PUBLICATION AND DISTRIBUTION INFORMATION

Forms of publication: Cloth, paper, elec-
  tronic media
Titles published each year: 7
Print run: 1,200-3,500
Number of review copies: Less than 2%
  of print run
Distribution area: Worldwide
Time in print: 10 years

(22)
EDWARD ARNOLD

338 Euston Rd.
London NW1 3BH, England

Contact: Christopher Wheeler (literature);
  Lesley Riddle (modern languages);
  Naomi Meredith (linguistics)
Established: 1890

Telephone: (0171) 8736330
Fax: (0171) 8736325
E-mail:
  i35cxw@hodder.mhs.compuserve.com

SCOPE

Publishing interests: English literature;
  American literature; women and
  literature; literary theory; theoretical
  linguistics; applied linguistics; second
  language acquisition; literary reference
  works (for English, French, German,
  Spanish, and Italian literature); cultural
  theory
*Considers all literary and linguistic
  topics:* Yes
Types of works not published: Disser-
  tations; Festschriften
Languages published: English
Series title(s): Interrogating Texts;
  Writing in History; Second-Language
  Acquisition; Understanding Linguistics

SUBMISSION REQUIREMENTS

Initial contact: Letter and prospectus
Considers simultaneous submissions:
  Yes, if informed
*Will issue contract on the basis of
  proposal, prospectus, and/or sample
  chapter:* Yes
Style: House
Special requirements: Accepts photo-
  copies and electronic manuscripts;
  provides guidelines for manuscript
  preparation
Subvention: No

EDITORIAL INFORMATION

*Manuscripts or proposals submitted each
  year:* 150 (estimate)
Manuscripts sent to readers each year: 45
  (estimate)
Manuscripts accepted each year: 30
  (estimate)

Number of outside readers: 3-4
Author-anonymous submission: Only
  under special circumstances
*Time between submission and publication
  decision:* 3 months
*Time between decision and return of copy-
  edited manuscript:* 2 months
Time between decision and publication:
  7-8 months
Time allotted for reading proof: 2 weeks
  minimum

CONTRACT PROVISIONS

Copyright: Author

**PUBLICATION AND DISTRIBUTION
INFORMATION**

Forms of publication: Cloth, paper, elec-
  tronic media
Titles published each year: 20
Print run: 350 cloth; 2,500-5,000 paper
Number of review copies: 20-30
Distribution area: Worldwide
Time in print: 3 years minimum

(23)
ARTE PUBLICO PRESS

University of Houston
Houston, TX 77204-2090

Imprint(s) and subsidiary firm(s): Piñata
  Books
Contact: Nicolás Kanellos, Publisher
Established: 1979
Telephone: 713 749-4768
Fax: 713 743-2847

SCOPE

Publishing interests: Hispanic American
  literature; Mexican American literature;
  Puerto Rican literature; Cuban

American literature; Hispanic women's literature
Considers all literary and linguistic topics: No
Types of works not published: Bibliographies; collections of letters; biographies; literary handbooks
Languages published: English; Spanish

SUBMISSION REQUIREMENTS

Initial contact: Letter, outline, and sample chapters
Considers simultaneous submissions: No
Will issue contract on the basis of proposal, prospectus, and/or sample chapter: No
Style: MLA
Special requirements: Requires typed or laser-printed copy; expects electronic manuscript
Subvention: No

EDITORIAL INFORMATION

Manuscripts or proposals submitted each year: 20 (estimate)
Manuscripts sent to readers each year: 9
Manuscripts accepted each year: 1
Number of outside readers: 2
Author-anonymous submission: Yes
Time between submission and publication decision: 4 months
Time between decision and return of copy-edited manuscript: 18 months
Time between decision and publication: 2 years

CONTRACT PROVISIONS

Copyright: Author
Royalty provisions: Negotiable

PUBLICATION AND DISTRIBUTION INFORMATION

Forms of publication: Paper
Titles published each year: 2

Print run: 3,000
Number of review copies: 100
Distribution area: Worldwide
Time in print: Indefinitely

(24)
ATHLONE PRESS

1 Park Dr.
London NW11 7SG, England

Contact: Brian Southam, Chairman
Established: 1950
Telephone: (081) 4580888
Fax: (081) 2018115

SCOPE

Publishing interests: Critical editions; collections of letters; literary theory; English literature; American literature; Japanese literature; linguistics
Considers all literary and linguistic topics: Yes
Types of works not published: Readers
Languages published: English
Series title(s): Women in Context

SUBMISSION REQUIREMENTS

Initial contact: Letter, outline, and sample chapter
Considers simultaneous submissions: No
Will issue contract on the basis of proposal, prospectus, and/or sample chapter: Sometimes
Style: House
Special requirements: Provides guidelines for manuscript preparation
Subvention: Sometimes

EDITORIAL INFORMATION

Manuscripts or proposals submitted each year: 150 (estimate)

Manuscripts sent to readers each year: 40 (estimate)
Manuscripts accepted each year: 12
Number of outside readers: 1-2
Author-anonymous submission: No
Time between submission and publication decision: 2-3 months
Time between decision and return of copy-edited manuscript: 2-3 months
Time between decision and publication: 7-9 months

CONTRACT PROVISIONS

Copyright: Author
Royalty provisions: 10% of list (cloth); 5-7.5% of list (paper)

PUBLICATION AND DISTRIBUTION INFORMATION

Forms of publication: Cloth, paper
Titles published each year: 12 (estimate)
Print run: 2,000
Number of review copies: 25-30
Distribution area: Worldwide
Time in print: 5-7 years

Originally the publishing house of the University of London, Athlone Press is now an independent publisher, but it maintains, through its academic advisory board, a relationship with the university.

(25)
*ATTIC PRESS

44 East Essex St.
Dublin 2, Ireland

Contact: Ailbhe Smyth, Editor
Established: 1984
Telephone: (01) 716367
Fax: (01) 6793754

SCOPE

Publishing interests: Sexual politics; general literature; Irish studies; women's studies
Types of works not published: Bibliographies; critical editions; Festschriften; literary reference works; unrevised dissertations
Languages published: English; Irish Gaelic

SUBMISSION REQUIREMENTS

Restrictions on authors: Does not publish male authors
Initial contact: Letter, outline, and sample chapters
Style: House
Special requirements: Prefers electronic manuscripts
Subvention: Depends on topic

EDITORIAL INFORMATION

Manuscripts or proposals submitted each year: 12 (estimate)
Manuscripts sent to readers each year: 8
Manuscripts accepted each year: 2
Number of outside readers: 2
Time between submission and publication decision: 6 months
Time between decision and return of copy-edited manuscript: 10-12 months
Time between decision and publication: 1 year

CONTRACT PROVISIONS

Copyright: Author
Royalty provisions: 7.5%

PUBLICATION AND DISTRIBUTION INFORMATION

Forms of publication: Paper
Titles published each year: 3
Print run: 2,000-30,000

Number of review copies: 50
Distribution area: Ireland; United
   Kingdom; Australia; New Zealand;
   North America

Specializes in books for and about women

(26)
AUCKLAND UNIVERSITY PRESS

University of Auckland
Private Bag
92019 Auckland, New Zealand

Contact: Elizabeth Caffin, Managing
   Editor
Established: 1966
Telephone: (09) 373-7528
Fax: (09) 373-7465

SCOPE

Publishing interests: New Zealand
   literature; Maori literature; Polynesian
   literature; Maori language (dictionaries
   and reference works); Polynesian
   languages (dictionaries and reference
   works)
*Considers all literary and linguistic
   topics:* No
Prizes and competitions: Keith Sinclair
   Prize in New Zealand History
Languages published: English; Maori;
   Polynesian languages

SUBMISSION REQUIREMENTS

Initial contact: Letter, outline, and sample
   chapter(s)
Considers simultaneous submissions;
   Prefers single submission
*Will issue contract on the basis of
   proposal, prospectus, and/or sample
   chapter:* Rarely
Style: House

Special requirements: Provides guidelines
   for manuscript preparation
Subvention: No

EDITORIAL INFORMATION

*Manuscripts or proposals submitted each
   year:* 50 (estimate)
Manuscripts sent to readers each year: 20
   (estimate)
Manuscripts accepted each year: 5
Number of outside readers: 1
Author-anonymous submission: No
*Time between submission and publication
   decision:* 6 weeks
*Time between decision and return of copy-
   edited manuscript:* 2 months
Time between decision and publication:
   3-12 months

CONTRACT PROVISIONS

Copyright: Author
Royalty provisions: 10%

PUBLICATION AND DISTRIBUTION
INFORMATION

Forms of publication: Cloth, paper
Titles published each year: 11
Print run: 1,000
Number of review copies: 20-25
Distribution area: New Zealand; United
   Kingdom; United States; Australia
Time in print: 1-10 years

(27)
AUSTIN & WINFIELD

7831 Woodmont Ave., Suite 345
Bethesda, MD 20814

PO Box 2590
San Francisco, CA 94126

Contact: Robert West, Editor in Chief

Established: 1992
Telephone: 415 981-5144
Fax: 415 981-6313

SCOPE

Publishing interests: Politics and
literature; politics and language;
language policy; Latin American liter-
atures; central European literatures;
eastern European literatures; Pacific
Basin postcolonial literature
*Considers all literary and linguistic
topics:* Yes
Not interested in proposals on: Neo-
Marxist, feminist, or gender studies
Languages published: English; Spanish;
German

SUBMISSION REQUIREMENTS

Initial contact: Letter, prospectus, 2
sample chapters, and curriculum vitae;
provides manuscript proposal form
Considers simultaneous submissions: Yes
*Will issue contract on the basis of
proposal, prospectus, and/or sample
chapter:* Yes
Style: MLA; Chicago
Special requirements: Expects camera-
ready copy
Subvention: No

EDITORIAL INFORMATION

*Manuscripts or proposals submitted each
year:* 18
Manuscripts sent to readers each year:
10
Manuscripts accepted each year: 8
Number of outside readers: 1
Author-anonymous submission: Yes
*Time between submission and publication
decision:* 3 months
Time between decision and publication:
6-8 months
Time allotted for reading proof: 2 weeks

CONTRACT PROVISIONS

Copyright: Author
Royalty provisions: 8% of net

PUBLICATION AND DISTRIBUTION
INFORMATION

Forms of publication: Cloth, paper
Titles published each year: 3 (1993); 8
(1994)
Print run: 300
Number of review copies: 50
Distribution area: Worldwide
Time in print: Indefinitely

**(28)
EDITIONS DE LA BACONNIERE**

Case postale 185
2017 Boudry, Switzerland

Contact: Marie-Christine Hauser
Established: 1927
Telephone: (41) 38 421004

SCOPE

Publishing interests: Literary history;
philosophy; literature
*Considers all literary and linguistic
topics:* Yes
Not interested in proposals on:
Linguistics; language teaching
Types of works not published: Textbooks;
literary handbooks; literary encyclo-
pedias
Languages published: French; other
Romance languages, German, and
English in collections of essays only
Series title(s): Langages; Cahiers du
Rhône; Etudes baudelairiennes

SUBMISSION REQUIREMENTS

Initial contact: Letter and outline
Considers simultaneous submissions: No

*Will issue contract on the basis of
proposal, prospectus, and/or sample
chapter:* No
Style: House
Special requirements: Length restrictions;
prefers electronic copy
Subvention: Yes

EDITORIAL INFORMATION

*Manuscripts or proposals submitted each
year:* 5
Manuscripts sent to readers each year: 5
Manuscripts accepted each year: 1-2
Number of outside readers: 1-2
Author-anonymous submission: No
*Time between submission and publication
decision:* 1-2 years
Time between decision and publication:
1 year
Time allotted for reading proof: Varies

CONTRACT PROVISIONS

Copyright: Publisher
Royalty provisions: 10% maximum

PUBLICATION AND DISTRIBUTION
INFORMATION

Forms of publication: Paper
Titles published each year: 2
Print run: 1,000
Number of review copies: 50
Distribution area: French-speaking
countries; Italy; Germany; United States
Time in print: Indefinitely

(29)
*MOTILAL BANARSIDASS

41-UA Bungalow Rd.
Jawahar Nagar
Delhi 110007, India

Contact: R. P. Jain, Director

Established: 1903
Telephone: (011) 2911985; (011)
2918335
Fax: (011) 2926803 Attn: MLBD

SCOPE

Publishing interests: Indian literature;
Indian languages; oriental literature;
oriental languages
*Considers all literary and linguistic
topics:* Yes
Types of works not published: Unrevised
dissertations; collections of letters
Languages published: English; Sanskrit;
Pali; Prakrit
Series title(s): MLBD Series in
Linguistics

SUBMISSION REQUIREMENTS

Initial contact: Letter of inquiry
Style: Chicago
Special requirements: Prefers camera-
ready copy
Subvention: Yes

EDITORIAL INFORMATION

*Manuscripts or proposals submitted each
year:* 50 (estimate)
Manuscripts sent to readers each year: 20
(estimate)
Manuscripts accepted each year: 10
Number of outside readers: 2
*Time between submission and publication
decision:* 1 month
*Time between decision and return of copy-
edited manuscript:* 1 month
Time between decision and publication:
1 year

CONTRACT PROVISIONS

Copyright: Publisher
Royalty provisions: No royalties on first
edition, 10% thereafter

PUBLICATION AND DISTRIBUTION
INFORMATION

Forms of publication: Cloth, paper
Titles published each year: 15 (estimate)
Print run: 1,000
Number of review copies: 75-100
Distribution area: Worldwide
Time in print: 10 years minimum

(30)
*BAYLOR UNIVERSITY PRESS

CSB 547
Baylor University
Waco, TX 76798

PUBLICATION AND DISTRIBUTION
INFORMATION

Publishes few literature titles

(31)
BEACON PRESS

25 Beacon St.
Boston, MA 02108

Contact: Deb Chasman
Established: 1854
Telephone: 617 742-2110
Fax: 617 723-3097

SCOPE

Publishing interests: African American
  women writers; South African literature;
  gay literature; lesbian literature;
  women's studies
*Considers all literary and linguistic
  topics:* Possibly
Types of works not published: Literary
  reference books
Languages published: English

Series title(s): Black Women Writers;
  Asian Voices Series

SUBMISSION REQUIREMENTS

Initial contact: Letter and prospectus
Considers simultaneous submissions: Yes
*Will issue contract on the basis of
  proposal, prospectus, and/or sample
  chapter:* Rarely
Style: Chicago

EDITORIAL INFORMATION

Number of outside readers: 2
*Time between submission and publication
  decision:* 6-8 weeks
*Time between decision and return of copy-
  edited manuscript:* Varies
Time between decision and publication:
  1 year

CONTRACT PROVISIONS

Copyright: Negotiable

PUBLICATION AND DISTRIBUTION
INFORMATION

Forms of publication: Cloth, paper
Print run: 5,000
Number of review copies: 20-100
Distribution area: United States;
  Australasia; United Kingdom

(32)
C. H. BECK

Wilhelmstr. 9
80801 Munich, Germany

Imprint(s) and subsidiary firm(s):
  Biederstein Verlag; Verlag Franz Vahlen
Contact: Susanne Simer
Established: 1763
Telephone: (089) 38189228
Fax: (089) 38189402

SCOPE

Publishing interests: German literature;
Asian literature; Islamic literature;
linguistics; literary history
*Considers all literary and linguistic
topics:* No
Types of works not published: Disser-
tations; bibliographies; readers;
Festschriften
Languages published: German
Series title(s): Orientalische Bibliothek;
Bibliothek des 18. Jahrhunderts

SUBMISSION REQUIREMENTS

Initial contact: Letter and outline
Considers simultaneous submissions: Yes
*Will issue contract on the basis of
proposal, prospectus, and/or sample
chapter:* Yes
Subvention: Sometimes

EDITORIAL INFORMATION

*Manuscripts or proposals submitted each
year:* 200
Manuscripts sent to readers each year: 20
Manuscripts accepted each year: 10
Number of outside readers: 5
Author-anonymous submission:
Sometimes
*Time between submission and publication
decision:* 1-3 months
*Time between decision and return of copy-
edited manuscript:* 6 months
Time between decision and publication:
1 year

CONTRACT PROVISIONS

Copyright: Publisher
Royalty provisions: 7-10% of retail

PUBLICATION AND DISTRIBUTION
INFORMATION

Forms of publication: Cloth, paper

Titles published each year: 25-30
Print run: 4,000-6,000
Number of review copies: 100
Distribution area: Worldwide
Time in print: 10 years

**(33)
JOHN BENJAMINS PUBLISHING
CO.**

Amsteldijk 44
Postbus 75577
1070 AN Amsterdam, Netherlands

John Benjamins North America, Inc.
PO Box 27519
Philadelphia, PA 19118-0519

Imprint(s) and subsidiary firm(s): B. R.
Grüner Publishing Co.
Contact: Yola de Lusenet
Established: 1972
Telephone: (020) 6762325 (Amsterdam);
215 836-1200 (Philadelphia)
Fax: (020) 6739773 (Amsterdam); 215
836-1204 (Philadelphia)
E-mail: kees.vaes@benjamins.nl
(Amsterdam);
7046.123@compuserve.com
(Philadelphia)

SCOPE

Publishing interests: Linguistics;
semiotics; translation; cultural history;
bilingualism
*Considers all literary and linguistic
topics:* Yes (linguistics); no (literature)
Types of works not published: Literary
handbooks or encyclopedias
Languages published: English
Series title(s): Amsterdam Classics in
Linguistics, 1800-1925; Actes sémio-
tiques; Current Issues in Linguistic
Theory; Classics in Psycholinguistics;

Creole Language Library; Foundations of Semiotics; Language Acquisition and Language Disorders; Lingvisticae Investigationes Supplementa; Library and Information Sources in Linguistics; Linguistic and Literary Studies in Eastern Europe; Pragmatics and Beyond; Semiotic Crossroads; Studies in Bilingualism; Studies in Discourse and Grammar; Studies in the History of the Language Sciences; Studies in Language Companion Series; Studies in the Sciences of Language Series; Studies in Speech Pathology and Clinical Linguistics; Studia Uralo-Altaica; Typological Studies in Language; Utrecht Publications in General and Comparative Literature; Varieties of English around the World; American Translators Monograph Series; Case and Grammatical Relations across Languages; Comparative History of Literatures in European Languages; *Linguistik Aktuell* / Linguistics Today; London Oriental and African Language Library; Studies in Written Language and Literacy

SUBMISSION REQUIREMENTS

Initial contact: Letter, outline, and table of contents
Considers simultaneous submissions: Yes
Will issue contract on the basis of proposal, prospectus, and/or sample chapter: Yes
Style: Chicago; house
Special requirements: Length: prefers less than 450 pages; prefers electronic manuscripts or camera-ready copy; accepts photocopies; provides guidelines for manuscript preparation
Subvention: No

EDITORIAL INFORMATION

Manuscripts or proposals submitted each year: 100-150
Manuscripts sent to readers each year: 60
Manuscripts accepted each year: 60
Number of outside readers: 2
Author-anonymous submission: No
Time between submission and publication decision: 2-3 months
Time between decision and return of copy-edited manuscript: 8 months
Time between decision and publication: 5-6 months
Time allotted for reading proof: 3 weeks

CONTRACT PROVISIONS

Copyright: Publisher
Royalty provisions: 10% (after 200 copies if camera-ready copy is provided or after 300 copies if an electronic manuscript is provided)

PUBLICATION AND DISTRIBUTION INFORMATION

Forms of publication: Cloth, paper
Titles published each year: 60
Print run: 600
Number of review copies: 25
Distribution area: Worldwide
Time in print: 7 years

(34)
BERGHAHN BOOKS

165 Taber Ave.
Providence, RI 02906

Contact: Marion Berghahn
Established: 1994
Telephone: 401 861-9330
Fax: 401 521-0046

SCOPE

Publishing interests: German literature;
French literature; Russian literature;
Spanish literature; English literature;
American literature; biography
*Considers all literary and linguistic
topics:* Yes
Languages published: English
Series title(s): Monographs on German
Literature; Contemporary France

SUBMISSION REQUIREMENTS

Initial contact: Letter of inquiry or letter
and prospectus
Considers simultaneous submissions: No
*Will issue contract on the basis of
proposal, prospectus, and/or sample
chapter:* Yes
Style: Chicago; house
Special requirements: Provides guidelines
for manuscript preparation
Subvention: No

EDITORIAL INFORMATION

*Manuscripts or proposals submitted each
year:* 40 (estimate)
Manuscripts sent to readers each year: 20
(estimate)
Manuscripts accepted each year: 10
Number of outside readers: 1-2
Author-anonymous submission: Yes
*Time between submission and publication
decision:* 2-3 months
*Time between decision and return of copy-
edited manuscript:* 1-2 months
Time between decision and publication:
7-9 months
Time allotted for reading proof: 2 weeks

CONTRACT PROVISIONS

Copyright: Author
Royalty provisions: 10% of net

PUBLICATION AND DISTRIBUTION INFORMATION

Forms of publication: Cloth, paper
Titles published each year: 2
Print run: 400 cloth and 2,000 paper or
800 cloth
Number of review copies: 15
Distribution area: Worldwide
Time in print: Indefinitely

(35)
BLACKWELL PUBLISHERS

108 Cowley Rd.
Oxford OX1 4JF, England

Imprint(s) and subsidiary firm(s): Shake-
speare Head Press
Contact: Andrew McNeillie
Established: 1921
E-mail: blkwell@world.std.com

SCOPE

Publishing interests: Literary theory;
cultural theory; biography; literary
history; feminist theory; linguistics
(general and applied); sociolinguistics;
history of language; linguistic theory;
phonetics; phonology; computational
linguistics
*Considers all literary and linguistic
topics:* Yes
Languages published: English
Series title(s): Rereading Literature;
Bucknell Lecture Series; Manifestos;
Critical Issues; The Language Library;
Language in Society; Applied Language
Studies

SUBMISSION REQUIREMENTS

Initial contact: Letter and prospectus
Considers simultaneous submissions: Yes

Will issue contract on the basis of proposal, prospectus, and/or sample chapter: Yes
Style: House
Special requirements: Provides guidelines for manuscript preparation
Subvention: No

EDITORIAL INFORMATION

Manuscripts or proposals submitted each year: 150 (estimate)
Manuscripts sent to readers each year: 60 (estimate)
Manuscripts accepted each year: 30 (estimate)
Number of outside readers: 2-3
Author-anonymous submission: No
Time between submission and publication decision: 1 month
Time between decision and return of copy-edited manuscript: 2 months
Time between decision and publication: 9 months

CONTRACT PROVISIONS

Copyright: Author
Royalty provisions: 6-10%

PUBLICATION AND DISTRIBUTION INFORMATION

Forms of publication: Cloth, paper
Titles published each year: 45 (estimate)
Number of review copies: 50
Distribution area: Worldwide
Time in print: 4 years

(36)
BOLCHAZY-CARDUCCI PUBLISHERS

1000 Brown St.
Unit 101
Wauconda, IL 60084

Contact: Ladislaus Bolchazy, President; S. Casey Fredericks, Editor
Established: 1978
Telephone: 708 526-4344
Fax: 708 526-2867
E-mail: bolchazy@delphi.com

SCOPE

Publishing interests: Near Eastern literature; Near Eastern languages; Greek literature; Greek language; Latin literature; Neo-Latin literature; Latin language (including Neo-Latin); Slovak language; Slovak literature; Slavic languages; Slavic literature
Considers all literary and linguistic topics: Yes
Types of works not published: Collections of letters; biographies; collections of essays
Languages published: English; Latin; Greek; Slovak

SUBMISSION REQUIREMENTS

Initial contact: Letter and prospectus
Considers simultaneous submissions: Yes
Will issue contract on the basis of proposal, prospectus, and/or sample chapter: No
Style: Chicago
Subvention: No

EDITORIAL INFORMATION

Manuscripts or proposals submitted each year: 10 (estimate)
Manuscripts sent to readers each year: 2
Manuscripts accepted each year: 11
Number of outside readers: 2
Author-anonymous submission: Yes
Time between submission and publication decision: 1 month
Time between decision and return of copy-edited manuscript: 15 months

Time between decision and publication:
  18 months
Time allotted for reading proof: 1 month

CONTRACT PROVISIONS

Copyright: Publisher
Royalty provisions: 10% of gross

PUBLICATION AND DISTRIBUTION
INFORMATION

Forms of publication: Cloth, paper
Titles published each year: 11
Print run: 2,000
Number of review copies: 50 (approxi-
  mately)
Distribution area: Worldwide
Time in print: Indefinitely

(37)
BOREALIS PRESS

9 Ashburn Dr.
Ottawa, ON K2E 6N4, Canada

Imprint(s) and subsidiary firm(s):
  Tecumseh Press
Contact: W. Glenn Clever, Publisher;
  Frank M. Tierney, Publisher
Established: 1970
Telephone: 613 224-6837
Fax: 613 829-7783

SCOPE

Publishing interests: Canadian literature
Considers all literary and linguistic
  topics: No
Not interested in proposals on:
  Linguistics
Languages published: English
Series title(s): Early Canadian Women
  Writers Series

SUBMISSION REQUIREMENTS

Initial contact: Letter and prospectus or
  letter, outline, and sample chapter
Considers simultaneous submissions:
  No
Will issue contract on the basis of
  proposal, prospectus, and/or sample
  chapter: No
Style: MLA
Subvention: No

EDITORIAL INFORMATION

Manuscripts or proposals submitted each
  year: 20
Manuscripts sent to readers each year:
  10
Manuscripts accepted each year: 5
Number of outside readers: 3
Author-anonymous submission: No
Time between submission and publication
  decision: 3-9 months
Time between decision and return of copy-
  edited manuscript: 1 month
Time between decision and publication: 6
  months
Time allotted for reading proof: 2 months

CONTRACT PROVISIONS

Copyright: Negotiable
Royalty provisions: 10% of gross

PUBLICATION AND DISTRIBUTION
INFORMATION

Forms of publication: Cloth, paper
Titles published each year: 12
Print run: 500-1,500
Number of review copies: 40
Distribution area: North America
Time in print: 15 years

(38)
BORGO PRESS

PO Box 2845
San Bernardino, CA 92406

Imprint(s) and subsidiary firm(s):
Brownstone Books; Burgess and
Wickizer; Emeritus Enterprises;
Sidewinder Press; St. Willibrord's Press;
Unicorn and Son
Contact: Robert Reginald; Mary A.
Burgess
Established: 1975
Telephone: 909 884-5813
Fax: 909 888-4942

SCOPE

Publishing interests: Modern literature;
twentieth-century literature; science
fiction; fantasy fiction; mystery fiction;
bibliographies; literary reference works;
literary theory
*Considers all literary and linguistic
topics:* Yes (literature); no (linguistics)
Not interested in proposals on:
Linguistics; literature before 1800
Types of works not published: Readers;
textbooks
Languages published: English
Series title(s): Borgo Literary Guides;
Milford Series: Popular Writers of
Today; Bibliographies of Modern
Authors; I. O. Evans Studies in the
Philosophy and Criticism of Literature;
Essays on Fantastic Literature

SUBMISSION REQUIREMENTS

Initial contact: Letter of inquiry
Considers simultaneous submissions:
Prefers single submission
*Will issue contract on the basis of
proposal, prospectus, and/or sample
chapter:* Yes
Style: Chicago

Special requirements: Accepts electronic
manuscripts; provides guidelines for
manuscript preparation
Subvention: No

EDITORIAL INFORMATION

*Manuscripts or proposals submitted each
year:* 50 +
Manuscripts accepted each year: 20
Number of outside readers: Series editor
Author-anonymous submission: No
*Time between submission and publication
decision:* 2 months minimum
*Time between decision and return of copy-
edited manuscript:* 2 years
Time between decision and publication:
2-3 years

CONTRACT PROVISIONS

Copyright: Author
Royalty provisions: 10% of list

PUBLICATION AND DISTRIBUTION
INFORMATION

Forms of publication: Cloth, paper
Titles published each year: 25 (estimate)
Print run: 200-300 (but reprints
frequently)
Number of review copies: 20
Distribution area: Worldwide
Time in print: Indefinitely

(39)
**BOUSTANY'S AL-ARAB
PUBLISHING HOUSE**

29 Faggalah St.
PO Box 32–Faggalah
Cairo, Egypt

Contact: Saladin Boustany; Fadwa
Boustany
Established: 1900

Telephone: (00202) 908025
Fax: (00202) 3404905

SCOPE

Publishing interests: Egyptian literature;
Middle Eastern literature; Arabic
language
*Considers all literary and linguistic
topics:* Yes
Languages published: Arabic; English;
German

SUBMISSION REQUIREMENTS

Initial contact: Letter of inquiry or letter
and prospectus
Considers simultaneous submissions: Yes
*Will issue contract on the basis of
proposal, prospectus, and/or sample
chapter:* No

EDITORIAL INFORMATION

*Manuscripts or proposals submitted each
year:* 10 (estimate)
Manuscripts accepted each year: 10
(estimate)
Number of outside readers: 3
Author-anonymous submission: No
*Time between submission and publication
decision:* 3 months
*Time between decision and return of copy-
edited manuscript:* 6 months
Time between decision and publication: 6
months
Time allotted for reading proof: 1 month

CONTRACT PROVISIONS

Copyright: Negotiable

PUBLICATION AND DISTRIBUTION INFORMATION

Forms of publication: Paper
Titles published each year: 10
Number of review copies: 20

Distribution area: Worldwide
Time in print: Indefinitely

(40)
*BOWKER-SAUR

60 Grosvenor St.
London W1, England

Imprint(s) and subsidiary firm(s): Hans
Zell
Contact: Publisher
Telephone: (071) 6371571
Fax: (071) 5804089

SCOPE

Publishing interests: Bibliographies (with
international coverage); biographical
reference works (with international
coverage); literary reference works
(with international coverage); film
reference works (with international
coverage)
*Considers all literary and linguistic
topics:* No
Types of works not published: Dissertations; critical editions; collections of
letters; readers
Languages published: English
Series title(s): Bibliographies on African
Writers; Bibliographies on German
Writers; Bibliographies on European
Writers

SUBMISSION REQUIREMENTS

Initial contact: Letter, outline, and sample
chapters
Style: House
Subvention: No

EDITORIAL INFORMATION

Number of outside readers: 1-2

Time between submission and publication decision: 4-6 months
Time between decision and return of copy-edited manuscript: 2-6 months
Time between decision and publication: 6-18 months

CONTRACT PROVISIONS

Copyright: Publisher

PUBLICATION AND DISTRIBUTION INFORMATION

Forms of publication: Cloth, electronic media
Print run: 1,000
Number of review copies: 25
Distribution area: Worldwide
Time in print: 10 years

**(41)
BOWLING GREEN STATE UNIVERSITY POPULAR PRESS**

Bowling Green State University
Bowling Green, OH 43403

Contact: Pat Browne, Director
Established: 1967
Telephone: 419 372-7867
Fax: 419 372-8095
E-mail: abrowne@andy.bgsu.edu

SCOPE

Publishing interests: Mass culture; popular culture; popular literature
Types of works not published: Dissertations; bibliographies; critical editions; collections of essays
Languages published: English

SUBMISSION REQUIREMENTS

Initial contact: Letter and manuscript
Considers simultaneous submissions: No

Will issue contract on the basis of proposal, prospectus, and/or sample chapter: Yes
Style: MLA
Special requirements: Accepts photocopies and dot-matrix printout; does not accept electronic manuscripts
Subvention: No

EDITORIAL INFORMATION

Manuscripts or proposals submitted each year: 350
Manuscripts sent to readers each year: 50
Manuscripts accepted each year: 28
Number of outside readers: 3
Author-anonymous submission: No
Time between submission and publication decision: 3-6 months
Time between decision and return of copy-edited manuscript: 3 months
Time between decision and publication: 9-12 months

CONTRACT PROVISIONS

Copyright: Publisher
Royalty provisions: Varies

PUBLICATION AND DISTRIBUTION INFORMATION

Forms of publication: Cloth, paper
Titles published each year: 21
Print run: 1,000-1,500
Number of review copies: 30-40
Distribution area: Worldwide
Time in print: Indefinitely

**(42)
BOYDELL & BREWER**

PO Box 9
Woodbridge, Suffolk IP12 3DF, England

Imprint(s) and subsidiary firm(s): D. S.
Brewer; Boydell Press; University of
Rochester Press
Established: 1970
Telephone: (0394) 411320
Fax: (0394) 411477
E-mail: 100317.477@compuserve.com

SCOPE

Publishing interests: English literature
(Old English, Middle English,
Renaissance); English language (Old
English, Middle English, early modern
English); Arthurian literature
Languages published: English
Series title(s): Arthurian Studies; Chaucer
Studies; Piers Plowman Studies; Tudor
Interludes; Publications of the John
Gower Society

SUBMISSION REQUIREMENTS

Initial contact: Letter and prospectus
Special requirements: Prefers electronic
manuscripts
Subvention: Only in special circumstances

EDITORIAL INFORMATION

Manuscripts accepted each year: 30
(estimate)
Number of outside readers: Varies
*Time between submission and publication
decision:* 2 months

CONTRACT PROVISIONS

Copyright: Author

**PUBLICATION AND DISTRIBUTION
INFORMATION**

Forms of publication: Cloth, paper
Titles published each year: 30 (estimate)
Distribution area: Worldwide
Time in print: Varies

**(43)
BRANDEN PUBLISHING CO.**

17 Station St.
Box 843
Brookline, MA 02147

Contact: Adolph Caso
Established: 1965
Telephone: 617 734-2045

SCOPE

Publishing interests: Biography; autobiography
*Considers all literary and linguistic
topics:* Yes
Types of works not published: Dissertations; Festschriften; literary
handbooks
Languages published: English; Italian

SUBMISSION REQUIREMENTS

Initial contact: Letter of inquiry with
SASE; no phone queries
Considers simultaneous submissions: No
*Will issue contract on the basis of
proposal, prospectus, and/or sample
chapter:* No
Style: MLA
Subvention: No

EDITORIAL INFORMATION

*Manuscripts or proposals submitted each
year:* 600
Manuscripts accepted each year: very
few
Number of outside readers: 5
Author-anonymous submission: No
*Time between submission and publication
decision:* 2 months
Time between decision and publication: 6
months
Time allotted for reading proof: 2 weeks

CONTRACT PROVISIONS

Copyright: Author or publisher
Royalty provisions: 10%

PUBLICATION AND DISTRIBUTION INFORMATION

Forms of publication: Cloth, paper
Print run: 3,000
Number of review copies: 50
Distribution area: Worldwide

**(44)
WILHELM BRAUMÜLLER
UNIVERSITÄTS-
VERLAGSBUCHHANDLUNG**

Servitengasse 5
1092 Vienna, Austria

Contact: Brigitte Pfeifer, Geschäfts-
führerin
Established: 1783
Telephone: (0222) 3191159
Fax: (0222) 3192805

SCOPE

Publishing interests: Linguistics;
Austrian literature; German language
*Considers all literary and linguistic
topics:* No
Languages published: German; English;
French; Italian
Series title(s): Schriften zur deutschen
Sprache in Österreich; Schriftenreihe
der Franz-Kafka-Gesellschaft; Unter-
suchungen zur österreichischen
Literatur des 20. Jahrhunderts; Wiener
Arbeiten zur deutschen Literatur;
Wiener Beiträge zur englischen
Philologie; Wiener romanistische
Arbeiten

SUBMISSION REQUIREMENTS

Initial contact: Letter, outline, and sample
chapter
Considers simultaneous submissions: No
*Will issue contract on the basis of
proposal, prospectus, and/or sample
chapter:* No
Special requirements: Prefers camera-
ready copy
Subvention: Yes (except for textbooks)

EDITORIAL INFORMATION

Number of outside readers: 1 minimum

CONTRACT PROVISIONS

Copyright: Publisher
Royalty provisions: 9% of net

PUBLICATION AND DISTRIBUTION INFORMATION

Forms of publication: Paper
Print run: 600-2,000
Number of review copies: Varies
Distribution area: Worldwide

**(45)
GEORGE BRAZILLER**

60 Madison Ave.
New York, NY 10010

Contact: George Braziller, President;
Caroline Baumann, Editor; Adrienne
Baxter, Editor
Established: 1955
Telephone: 212 889-0909
Fax: 212 689-5405

SCOPE

Publishing interests: French literature
(contemporary, avant-garde); African
literature (contemporary); Jewish

literature (contemporary); Spanish
literature (contemporary); belles lettres
*Considers all literary and linguistic
topics:* Yes
Types of works not published: Bibliographies; literary handbooks; literary
encyclopedias
Languages published: English; French

SUBMISSION REQUIREMENTS

Initial contact: Letter and prospectus
Considers simultaneous submissions: Yes
*Will issue contract on the basis of
proposal, prospectus, and/or sample
chapter:* No
Style: Chicago; Cambridge
Subvention: No

EDITORIAL INFORMATION

*Manuscripts or proposals submitted each
year:* 200 (estimate)
Manuscripts sent to readers each year:
10-20 (estimate)
Manuscripts accepted each year: 5
(estimate)
Number of outside readers: 1-3
*Time between submission and publication
decision:* 1-3 months
*Time between decision and return of copy-
edited manuscript:* 1-2 months
Time between decision and publication:
9-15 months

CONTRACT PROVISIONS

Copyright: Varies
Royalty provisions: Negotiable

**PUBLICATION AND DISTRIBUTION
INFORMATION**

Forms of publication: Cloth, paper
Titles published each year: 10-20
(estimate)
Print run: 7,000-15,000
Number of review copies: 50-75

Distribution area: Worldwide
Time in print: Varies

**(46)
E. J. BRILL**

PO Box 9000
2300 PA Leiden, Netherlands

24 Hudson St.
Kinderhook, NY 12106

Contact: M. G. Elisabeth Venekamp,
Editorial Director (Netherlands); F.
Lankhof, Managing Director (United
States)
Established: 1683
Telephone: (3171) 312624 (Netherlands);
518 758-1411 or 800 962-4406 (United
States)
Fax: (3171) 317532 (Netherlands);
518 758-1959 (United States)

SCOPE

Publishing interests: Classical studies;
oriental languages
*Considers all literary and linguistic
topics:* No
Types of works not published: Unrevised
dissertations; collections of letters;
readers; Festschriften
Languages published: English; German;
French
Series title(s): Mnemosyne Supplements

SUBMISSION REQUIREMENTS

Initial contact: Letter and outline;
completion of questionnaire used in
evaluation of manuscript
Considers simultaneous submissions: No
*Will issue contract on the basis of
proposal, prospectus, and/or sample
chapter:* No
Style: Chicago

Special requirements: Length: 160 pages minimum; accepts electronic manuscripts or camera-ready copy; provides guidelines for manuscript preparation
Subvention: Sometimes (depends whether author supplies camera-ready copy or electronic manuscripts)

EDITORIAL INFORMATION

Manuscripts or proposals submitted each year: 20 (estimate)
Manuscripts sent to readers each year: 20 (estimate)
Manuscripts accepted each year: 10 (estimate)
Number of outside readers: 1-2
Time between submission and publication decision: 3 months
Time between decision and return of copyedited manuscript: Does not copyedit manuscript
Time between decision and publication: 6-8 months

CONTRACT PROVISIONS

Copyright: Publisher
Royalty provisions: 0-10% of net

PUBLICATION AND DISTRIBUTION INFORMATION

Forms of publication: Cloth, paper, electronic media
Titles published each year: 15 (estimate)
Print run: 400-900
Number of review copies: 25
Distribution area: Worldwide
Time in print: 20 years minimum

(47)
UNIVERSITY OF BRITISH COLUMBIA PRESS (UBC PRESS)

6344 Memorial Rd.
Vancouver, BC V6T 1Z2, Canada

Contact: Jean Wilson, Senior Editor
Established: 1971
Telephone: 604 822-3259
Fax: 604 822-6083
E-mail: wilson@ubcpress.ubc.ca

SCOPE

Publishing interests: Chinese languages; Native American languages
Considers all literary and linguistic topics: No
Not interested in proposals on: Literary criticism
Types of works not published: Dissertations; Festschriften; literary reference works; bibliographies
Languages published: English
Series title(s): First Nations Language Series

SUBMISSION REQUIREMENTS

Restrictions on authors: Gives priority to Canadian authors because of subvention requirement
Initial contact: Letter of inquiry and outline
Considers simultaneous submissions: Yes
Will issue contract on the basis of proposal, prospectus, and/or sample chapter: No
Style: Chicago; house
Special requirements: Accepts photocopies; requires electronic manuscript
Subvention: Yes

EDITORIAL INFORMATION

Manuscripts or proposals submitted each year: 10 (estimate)
Manuscripts sent to readers each year: 1
Manuscripts accepted each year: 0-1
Number of outside readers: 2 minimum
Author-anonymous submission: No
Time between submission and publication decision: 3-5 months
Time between decision and return of copy-edited manuscript: 1-2 months
Time between decision and publication: 3-4 months
Time allotted for reading proof: 1-2 weeks

CONTRACT PROVISIONS

Copyright: Publisher
Royalty provisions: 5% of net (usually after first 500 copies)

PUBLICATION AND DISTRIBUTION INFORMATION

Forms of publication: Cloth, paper
Titles published each year: 2
Print run: 1,000
Number of review copies: 30-40
Distribution area: Worldwide
Time in print: 5-10 years

**(48)
BROWN UNIVERSITY PRESS**

c/o University Press of New England
23 South Main St.
Hanover, NH 03755

Contact: Philip Pochoda, Humanities Editor
Established: 1932
Telephone: 603 643-7110
Fax: 603 643-1540

SCOPE

Publishing interests: General literature; linguistics
Types of works not published: Unrevised dissertations; literary reference works
Languages published: English

SUBMISSION REQUIREMENTS

Initial contact: Letter and prospectus
Considers simultaneous submissions: No
Will issue contract on the basis of proposal, prospectus, and/or sample chapter: No
Special requirements: Accepts photocopies and dot-matrix printout
Subvention: No

EDITORIAL INFORMATION

Manuscripts or proposals submitted each year: 15 (estimate)
Manuscripts sent to readers each year: 6
Manuscripts accepted each year: 0-10
Number of outside readers: 2

**(49)
BRUCCOLI CLARK LAYMAN**

2006 Sumter St.
Columbia, SC 29201

Contact: Matthew J. Bruccoli, President; Richard Layman, Vice President
Established: 1976
Telephone: 803 771-4642
Fax: 803 799-6953

SCOPE

Publishing interests: Literary history; literary biography; bibliography; social history
Types of works not published: Dissertations; critical editions; Festschriften
Languages published: English

Series title(s): Dictionary of Literary Biography; Bibliography of American Fiction

SUBMISSION REQUIREMENTS

Initial contact: Letter and prospectus
Style: Chicago; house
Special requirements: Accepts electronic manuscripts
Subvention: No

EDITORIAL INFORMATION

Manuscripts or proposals submitted each year: 75 (estimate)
Number of outside readers: 0

CONTRACT PROVISIONS

Copyright: Publisher, generally
Royalty provisions: Flat fee for work for hire

PUBLICATION AND DISTRIBUTION INFORMATION

Forms of publication: Cloth
Titles published each year: 30 (estimate)
Print run: 2,000 (approximate)

Bruccoli Clark Layman is an editorial center that specializes in producing camera-ready reference books for other publishers such as Gale, Omnigraphics, and Facts on File. The publisher normally commissions authors.

(50)
BUCKNELL UNIVERSITY PRESS

Bucknell University
Lewisburg, PA 17837

Contact: Mills F. Edgerton, Jr., Director
Established: 1968
Telephone: 717 524-3674

Fax: 717 524-3760
E-mail: medgertn@bucknell.edu

SCOPE

Publishing interests: Literary criticism; literary theory; English literature; American literature; Irish literature; German literature; Hispanic literature
Considers all literary and linguistic topics: Yes
Types of works not published: Textbooks; literary handbooks
Languages published: English

SUBMISSION REQUIREMENTS

Initial contact: Letter and prospectus
Considers simultaneous submissions: Yes (proposals); no (manuscripts)
Will issue contract on the basis of proposal, prospectus, and/or sample chapter: No
Style: Chicago
Special requirements: Prefers not to receive dot-matrix printout
Subvention: No

EDITORIAL INFORMATION

Manuscripts or proposals submitted each year: 40 (estimate; manuscripts only)
Manuscripts sent to readers each year: 30
Manuscripts accepted each year: 20
Number of outside readers: 1-3
Author-anonymous submission: No
Time between submission and publication decision: 3-6 months
Time between decision and return of copy-edited manuscript: 4-6 months
Time between decision and publication: 14-18 months
Time allotted for reading proof: 2-4 weeks

CONTRACT PROVISIONS

Copyright: Negotiable

Royalty provisions: 10% of list

PUBLICATION AND DISTRIBUTION INFORMATION

Forms of publication: Cloth, occasionally paper
Titles published each year: 20
Print run: 600-1,000
Number of review copies: 20-50
Distribution area: Worldwide
Time in print: Indefinitely

(51)
CALDER PUBLICATIONS

179 Kings Cross Rd.
London WC1X 9BZ, England

Riverrun
1170 Broadway
New York, NY 10001

Imprint(s) and subsidiary firm(s):
  Riverrun Press
Contact: John Calder (Calder)
Established: 1949 (Calder), 1978
  (Riverrun)
Telephone: (0171) 8331300 (Calder);
  212 889-6850 (Riverrun)

SCOPE

Publishing interests: General literature
  (especially since the seventeenth
  century); literary criticism; biography;
  reference books
*Considers all literary and linguistic
  topics:* Yes
Languages published: English
Series title(s): German Expressionism;
  French Surrealism; Scottish Library;
  European Classics

SUBMISSION REQUIREMENTS

Initial contact: Letter and prospectus
  (with SASE)
Considers simultaneous submissions: No
*Will issue contract on the basis of
  proposal, prospectus, and/or sample
  chapter:* No
Style: House
Subvention: Sometimes

EDITORIAL INFORMATION

*Manuscripts or proposals submitted each
  year:* 300-400 (estimate)
Manuscripts accepted each year: 1
Number of outside readers: 0
*Time between submission and publication
  decision:* 1-6 months
Time between decision and publication:
  2 years
Time allotted for reading proof: 2 weeks

CONTRACT PROVISIONS

Copyright: Author
Royalty provisions: 10% (cloth); 7.5%
  (paper)

PUBLICATION AND DISTRIBUTION INFORMATION

Forms of publication: Cloth, paper
Titles published each year: 10
Print run: 3,000-5,000
Number of review copies: 150
Distribution area: Worldwide
Time in print: Indefinitely

(52)
UNIVERSITY OF CALGARY PRESS

2500 University Dr., NW
Calgary, AB T2N 1N4, Canada

Contact: Shirley A. Onn, Director
Established: 1981

Telephone: 403 220-7578
Fax: 403 282-0085
E-mail:
 sonn@ucdasvm1.admin.ucalgary.ca

SCOPE

*Considers all literary and linguistic
 topics:* Yes
Types of works not published: Unrevised
 dissertations; collections of letters;
 readers; Festschriften; literary
 handbooks
Languages published: English; French
Series title(s): Canadian Archival
 Inventory Series

SUBMISSION REQUIREMENTS

Initial contact: Letter, prospectus, and
 sample chapter; provides guidelines for
 preparation of prospectus
Style: Chicago
Special requirements: Accepts photocopies and dot-matrix printout; prefers
 electronic manuscripts
Subvention: Yes

EDITORIAL INFORMATION

*Manuscripts or proposals submitted each
 year:* 12 (estimate)
Manuscripts sent to readers each year: 6
 (estimate)
Manuscripts accepted each year: 3
 (estimate)
Number of outside readers: 2
*Time between submission and publication
 decision:* 2-3 months
*Time between decision and return of copy-
 edited manuscript:* 2-4 weeks
Time between decision and publication:
 6-9 months

CONTRACT PROVISIONS

Copyright: Author

Royalty provisions: Negotiable, but
 payment begins only after production
 costs have been met

PUBLICATION AND DISTRIBUTION INFORMATION

Forms of publication: Cloth, paper
Titles published each year: 3
Print run: 1,000
Number of review copies: 24-50
Distribution area: Worldwide
Time in print: Indefinitely

(53) UNIVERSITY OF CALIFORNIA PRESS

2120 Berkeley Way
Berkeley, CA 94720

Contact: William Murphy, Editor
Established: 1893
Telephone: 510 643-9793
Fax: 415 643-7127
E-mail: will.murphy@ucop.edu

SCOPE

Publishing interests: English literature;
 American literature; American studies;
 literary theory; cultural studies; ethnic
 studies; gender studies; French studies;
 Asian literature in translation; Middle
 Eastern literature in translation;
 European literature in translation; Latin
 American literature in translation
*Considers all literary and linguistic
 topics:* Yes
Not interested in proposals on: Spanish,
 Italian, German, Latin American,
 Middle Eastern, Asian, and African
 literatures
Types of works not published:
 Festschriften; bibliographies
Languages published: English

Series title(s): Contraversions: Critical
Studies in Jewish Literature, Culture,
and Society; Voices from Asia

SUBMISSION REQUIREMENTS

Initial contact: Letter and prospectus
Considers simultaneous submissions: Yes
*Will issue contract on the basis of
proposal, prospectus, and/or sample
chapter:* Yes
Style: Chicago; MLA
Special requirements: Prefers not to
receive dot-matrix printout; provides
guidelines for manuscript preparation
Subvention: Sometimes

EDITORIAL INFORMATION

*Manuscripts or proposals submitted each
year:* 150 (estimate)
Manuscripts sent to readers each year: 40
(estimate)
Manuscripts accepted each year: 29
Number of outside readers: 2 minimum
Author-anonymous submission: No
*Time between submission and publication
decision:* 4 months
*Time between decision and return of copy-
edited manuscript:* 2 months
Time between decision and publication:
1 year
Time allotted for reading proof: 4 weeks

CONTRACT PROVISIONS

Copyright: Negotiable
Royalty provisions: 7% of net on first
5,000 copies (cloth; often results in no
royalties); 5% of net (paper)

**PUBLICATION AND DISTRIBUTION
INFORMATION**

Forms of publication: Cloth, paper, some
electronic media
Titles published each year: 20 (estimate)
Print run: 750-1,250

Number of review copies: 20-30
Distribution area: Worldwide
Time in print: 7 years

**(54)
CALIFORNIA STATE UNIVERSITY
PRESS**

California State University
Maples and Shaw Aves.
Fresno, CA 93740

**PUBLICATION AND DISTRIBUTION
INFORMATION**

Has a four-year moratorium on new
manuscripts

**(55)
CAMBRIDGE UNIVERSITY PRESS**

**for American, Latin American, and
Hispanic literatures**
40 West 20th St.
New York, NY 10011

all other inquiries
The Edinburgh Bldg.
Shaftesbury Rd.
Cambridge CB2 2RU, England

Contact: T. Susan Chang (New York:
American, Latin American, and
Hispanic literatures); Josie Dixon
(Cambridge: English, African, and
Caribbean literatures; literary theory);
Katharina Brett (Cambridge: French,
German, Russian, and Arabic liter-
atures); Judith Aylir (Cambridge:
linguistics); Sarah Stanton (Cambridge:
drama and Anglo-Saxon)
Established: 1534
Telephone: 212 924-3900 (New York);
(01223) 312393 (Cambridge)

Fax: 212 691-3239 (New York); (01223)
315052 (Cambridge)

SCOPE

Publishing interests: English literature;
American literature; Latin American
literature; Hispanic literature; French
literature; German literature; Russian
literature; African literature; Caribbean
literature; Arabic literature; literary
theory; interdisciplinary studies (e.g.,
literature and religion, literature and
science, literature and philosophy,
literature and anthropology, literature
and psychology); drama; theater; bibliography; publishing and printing
history; linguistics; theoretical
linguistics; sociolinguistics; philosophy
of language; descriptive linguistics;
applied linguistics; computational
linguistics; anthropological linguistics;
phonetics; phonology
Considers all literary and linguistic
topics: No
Languages published: English
Series title(s): British and Irish Authors:
Introductory Critical Studies;
Cambridge English Prose Texts;
Landmarks of World Literature;
Cambridge Medieval Classics;
Cambridge Studies in Medieval
Literature; Cambridge Studies in
Renaissance Literature and Culture;
Cambridge Studies in Eighteenth-
Century English Literature and
Thought; Cambridge Studies in Roman-
ticism; European Studies in English
Literature; Cambridge Studies in
African and Caribbean Literature;
Cambridge Studies in Latin American
and Iberian Literature; Cambridge
Studies in French; Cambridge Studies in
German; Cambridge Studies in Russian
Literature; Cambridge Studies in
American Literature and Culture;

The American Novel; American Critical
Archives; Cambridge Studies in
Publishing and Printing History;
Cambridge Studies in Paleography and
Codicology; Cambridge Studies in
Linguistics; Cambridge Language
Surveys; Studies in Natural Language
Processing; Studies in the Social and
Cultural Foundations of Language;
Cambridge Studies in Speech Science
and Communication; Studies in Interac-
tional Sociolinguistics; Studies in
English Language; Literature, Culture,
Theory; Cultural Margins; Cambridge
Studies in Nineteenth-Century
Literature and Culture; Cambridge
Studies in Modern Theatre; Cambridge
Studies in American Theatre and Drama

SUBMISSION REQUIREMENTS

Initial contact: Letter, prospectus, sample
chapter, and curriculum vitae
Considers simultaneous submissions:
Prefers single submission
Will issue contract on the basis of
proposal, prospectus, and/or sample
chapter: Yes
Style: Chicago; Cambridge
Special requirements: Accepts photocopies, electronic manuscripts, and
camera-ready copy; provides guidelines
for manuscript preparation
Subvention: No

EDITORIAL INFORMATION

Manuscripts or proposals submitted each
year: 500 (estimate)
Manuscripts sent to readers each year:
200 (estimate)
Manuscripts accepted each year: 120
Number of outside readers: 2-3
Author-anonymous submission: No
Time between submission and publication
decision: 4 months

Time between decision and return of copy-edited manuscript: 3-4 months
Time between decision and publication: 1 year
Time allotted for reading proof: 4-6 weeks

CONTRACT PROVISIONS

Copyright: Author
Royalty provisions: Varies

PUBLICATION AND DISTRIBUTION INFORMATION

Forms of publication: Cloth, paper, electronic media
Titles published each year: 120 (literature); 25 (linguistics)
Print run: Varies
Number of review copies: 50-100
Distribution area: Worldwide
Time in print: Varies

(56)
CAMDEN HOUSE

PO Box 2025
Columbia, SC 29202

Contact: James N. Hardin
Established: 1979
Telephone: 803 788-5633
Fax: 803 736-9455

SCOPE

Publishing interests: German literature; English literature; American literature; Austrian literature; Scandinavian literature; comparative literature; linguistics; biography; bibliography; literary criticism; medieval literature; baroque literature; age of Goethe; modern literature; descriptive bibliography; reference works

Considers all literary and linguistic topics: Yes
Types of works not published: Unrevised dissertations; Festschriften
Languages published: English; German
Series title(s): Studies in German Literature, Linguistics, and Culture; Studies in English and American Literature, Linguistics, and Culture; Studies in Scandinavian Literature and Culture; Literary Criticism in Perspective

SUBMISSION REQUIREMENTS

Initial contact: Letter, prospectus, table of contents, and curriculum vitae
Style: Chicago
Special requirements: Expects electronic manuscripts or camera-ready copy prepared according to the publisher's style sheet; length: 90-130 pages for Literary Criticism in Perspective series
Subvention: Depends on manuscript and series

EDITORIAL INFORMATION

Manuscripts or proposals submitted each year: 45 (estimate)
Manuscripts sent to readers each year: 25 (estimate)
Manuscripts accepted each year: 12 (estimate)
Number of outside readers: 2
Time between submission and publication decision: 6-8 weeks
Time between decision and return of copy-edited manuscript: Varies
Time between decision and publication: 1 year maximum
Time allotted for reading proof: 3 weeks

CONTRACT PROVISIONS

Copyright: Publisher usually

Royalty provisions: 5-8%; 5% for Literary Criticism in Perspective series

PUBLICATION AND DISTRIBUTION INFORMATION

Forms of publication: Cloth, paper
Titles published each year: 33
Print run: 500-600
Number of review copies: 40-60
Distribution area: United States; Germany; Great Britain
Time in print: Indefinitely

(57)
CARLETON UNIVERSITY PRESS

Paterson Hall, rm. 106
Carleton University
Ottawa, ON K1S 5B6, Canada

Contact: John Flood, Director
Established: 1982
Telephone: 613 788-3740
Fax: 613 788-2893

SCOPE

Publishing interests: General literature; Canadian literature; women's studies; media studies
Considers all literary and linguistic topics: Yes
Types of works not published: Unrevised dissertations
Languages published: English; French
Series title(s): Center for Editing Early Canadian Texts Series; Textual Analysis, Discourse, and Culture

SUBMISSION REQUIREMENTS

Initial contact: Letter of inquiry
Will issue contract on the basis of proposal, prospectus, and/or sample chapter: No

Style: MLA
Special requirements: Expects electronic manuscript
Subvention: Yes

EDITORIAL INFORMATION

Manuscripts or proposals submitted each year: 20
Manuscripts sent to readers each year: 5
Manuscripts accepted each year: 1
Number of outside readers: 2
Time between submission and publication decision: 6 months
Time between decision and return of copy-edited manuscript: 4 months
Time between decision and publication: 6-8 months

CONTRACT PROVISIONS

Copyright: Publisher and author
Royalty provisions: 10% of net

PUBLICATION AND DISTRIBUTION INFORMATION

Forms of publication: Cloth, paper
Titles published each year: 1
Print run: 1,000
Number of review copies: 50
Distribution area: Worldwide
Time in print: 5 years

(58)
CASTRUM PEREGRINI PRESSE

PO Box 645
1000 AP Amsterdam, Netherlands

Contact: M. R. Goldschmidt
Established: 1951
Telephone: (20) 6235287
Fax: (20) 6247096

SCOPE

Publishing interests: General literature; history of ideas; Stefan George
Considers all literary and linguistic topics: Yes
Languages published: German

SUBMISSION REQUIREMENTS

Will issue contract on the basis of proposal, prospectus, and/or sample chapter: No
Style: House

CONTRACT PROVISIONS

Copyright: Publisher

PUBLICATION AND DISTRIBUTION INFORMATION

Titles published each year: 12
Print run: 1,200
Distribution area: Worldwide

(59)
CATHOLIC UNIVERSITY OF AMERICA PRESS

620 Michigan Ave., NE
Washington, DC 20064

Contact: David J. McGonagle, Director
Established: 1939
Telephone: 202 319-5052
Fax: 202 319-5721
E-mail: mcgonagle@cua

SCOPE

Publishing interests: Western European literature; American literature; medieval studies; Irish studies
Considers all literary and linguistic topics: Yes (literature); no (linguistics)

Not interested in proposals on: German literature; linguistics
Types of works not published: Dissertations; Festschriften; literary encyclopedias; literary handbooks
Languages published: English

SUBMISSION REQUIREMENTS

Initial contact: Letter, prospectus, and curriculum vitae
Considers simultaneous submissions: Yes, if informed
Will issue contract on the basis of proposal, prospectus, and/or sample chapter: No
Style: Chicago
Special requirements: Accepts dot-matrix printout and electronic manuscripts; provides guidelines for manuscript preparation
Subvention: Sometimes

EDITORIAL INFORMATION

Manuscripts accepted each year: 10
Number of outside readers: 2 minimum
Author-anonymous submission: No
Time between submission and publication decision: 4-6 months
Time between decision and return of copy-edited manuscript: 3 months
Time between decision and publication: 1 year
Time allotted for reading proof: 4-6 weeks

CONTRACT PROVISIONS

Copyright: Publisher
Royalty provisions: No royalties for first 250 copies, 5% of net on next 250, and 10% thereafter (cloth)

PUBLICATION AND DISTRIBUTION INFORMATION

Forms of publication: Cloth, paper

Titles published each year: 4
Print run: 500
Number of review copies: 35-50
Distribution area: Worldwide
Time in print: 5 years maximum

(60)
CENTRAL INSTITUTE OF INDIAN LANGUAGES

Manasagangotri, Mysore 570006, India

Contact: Director
Established: 1969
Telephone: (0821) 515558; (0821) 515863; (0821) 515820
Fax: (0821) 515032

SCOPE

Publishing interests: Indian languages; linguistics (Indian languages); interdisciplinary studies involving Indian languages; folklore; lexicography
Considers all literary and linguistic topics: Yes
Not interested in proposals on: Non-Indian topics
Types of works not published: Collections of letters; biographies; unrevised dissertations; literary encyclopedias
Prizes and competitions: Prizes for manuscripts in Sanskrit, English, any Indian language other than Hindi, or the author's native language
Languages published: Indian languages; English
Series title(s): Grammar Series; Occasional Monographs Series; Folklore Series; Conferences and Seminars Series; Current Inquiries in Indian Languages; Sociolinguistic Series; Bilingual Hindi Series

SUBMISSION REQUIREMENTS

Initial contact: Letter and outline
Considers simultaneous submissions: No
Will issue contract on the basis of proposal, prospectus, and/or sample chapter: No
Style: House
Special requirements: Accepts photocopies, dot-matrix printout, camera-ready copy, or electronic manuscripts; provides guidelines for manuscript preparation
Subvention: No

EDITORIAL INFORMATION

Manuscripts or proposals submitted each year: 10-15
Manuscripts sent to readers each year: 10-15
Manuscripts accepted each year: 15-20
Number of outside readers: 1-2
Time between submission and publication decision: 4 months
Time between decision and return of copy-edited manuscript: 1 month
Time between decision and publication: 3 months
Time allotted for reading proof: 1-2 months

CONTRACT PROVISIONS

Copyright: Publisher
Royalty provisions: No royalties

PUBLICATION AND DISTRIBUTION INFORMATION

Forms of publication: Cloth, paper
Titles published each year: 25
Print run: 500-1,000
Number of review copies: 80
Distribution area: Worldwide
Time in print: 5 years

(61)
*EDITORIAL UNIVERSITARIA CENTROAMERICANA (EDUCA)

Apdo 64
Ciudad Universitaria Rodrigo Facio
2060 San José, Costa Rica

Contact: Carmen Naranjo, Directora
Established: 1969
Telephone: 258740

SCOPE

Publishing interests: General literature;
  linguistics
*Considers all literary and linguistic
  topics:* Yes
Types of works not published: Literary
  encyclopedias
Languages published: Spanish
Series title(s): Colección signo

SUBMISSION REQUIREMENTS

Initial contact: Letter and manuscript
Style: MLA
Subvention: Yes

EDITORIAL INFORMATION

*Manuscripts or proposals submitted each
  year:* 20
Manuscripts sent to readers each year: 20
Manuscripts accepted each year: 20
Number of outside readers: 3
*Time between submission and publication
  decision:* 1 month
*Time between decision and return of copy-
  edited manuscript:* 3 months
Time between decision and publication: 3
  months

CONTRACT PROVISIONS

Copyright: Author
Royalty provisions: 10%

PUBLICATION AND DISTRIBUTION INFORMATION

Forms of publication: Cloth
Titles published each year: 10
Number of review copies: 10
Distribution area: Worldwide
Time in print: 2 years

(62)
*CHADWYCK-HEALEY

1101 King St., Suite 380
Alexandria, VA 22314

Contact: Eric M. Calaluca, Director of
  Project Development
Established: 1974
Telephone: 703 683-4890
Fax: 703 683-7589

SCOPE

Publishing interests: General literature;
  classical studies; drama; African
  American studies; women's studies;
  Hispanic studies; Native American
  studies; bibliographies
*Considers all literary and linguistic
  topics:* Yes
Types of works not published: Disser-
  tations; readers; Festschriften; literary
  handbooks
Languages published: English; French;
  Spanish; German; Italian

SUBMISSION REQUIREMENTS

Initial contact: Letter and prospectus or
  letter and outline
Style: MLA
Special requirements: Expects electronic
  manuscript
Subvention: No

Manuscripts or proposals submitted each year: 100 (estimate)
Manuscripts accepted each year: 15 (estimate)
Number of outside readers: 2
Time between submission and publication decision: 2 months
Time between decision and return of copy-edited manuscript: 6 months
Time between decision and publication: 9 months

CONTRACT PROVISIONS

Copyright: Publisher

PUBLICATION AND DISTRIBUTION INFORMATION

Forms of publication: Cloth, paper, electronic media
Titles published each year: 3 (estimate)
Distribution area: Worldwide
Time in print: 10 years

(63)
*W. & R. CHAMBERS

43-45 Annandale St.
Edinburgh EH7 4AZ, Scotland

Contact: Min Lee (reference works); Catherine Schwarz (dictionaries)
Established: 1819
Telephone: (031) 5574571
Fax: (031) 5572936

SCOPE

Publishing interests: Reference works
Considers all literary and linguistic topics: No
Languages published: English

SUBMISSION REQUIREMENTS

Initial contact: Letter and outline or letter, outline, and manuscript
Style: House
Special requirements: Accepts electronic manuscripts
Subvention: No

EDITORIAL INFORMATION

Number of outside readers: 1
Time between submission and publication decision: 1 month
Time between decision and return of copy-edited manuscript: 4 months
Time between decision and publication: 9 months

CONTRACT PROVISIONS

Copyright: Negotiable
Royalty provisions: 7.5-10% of list

PUBLICATION AND DISTRIBUTION INFORMATION

Forms of publication: Cloth, paper
Titles published each year: 30
Print run: 7,500
Number of review copies: 100
Distribution area: United Kingdom; Australia; New Zealand; Canada; South Africa; Europe; Japan; Southeast Asia
Time in print: 5 years

(64)
UNIVERSITY OF CHICAGO PRESS

Editorial Department
5801 South Ellis Ave.
Chicago, IL 60637

Contact: Alan G. Thomas, Senior Editor
Established: 1891
Telephone: 312 702-7700
Fax: 312 702-9756

SCOPE

Publishing interests: Critical theory;
English literature; American literature;
French literature; gender studies;
African American studies; linguistics;
cognitive science; literary criticism;
cultural criticism; medieval studies;
Renaissance studies; Judaic studies;
German studies (twentieth-century);
East Asian studies (nineteenth- and
twentieth-century; cultural studies;
feminist criticism; psychoanalytic
criticism; literature and the visual arts;
religion and literature; science and
literature

*Considers all literary and linguistic
topics:* Yes

Types of works not published: Unrevised
dissertations; bibliographies;
Festschriften

Languages published: English

Series title(s): Black Literature and
Culture; Women in Culture and Society;
New Practices of Inquiry; Religion and
Postmodernism; Language and Legal
Discourse; Studies in Contemporary
Linguistics

SUBMISSION REQUIREMENTS

Initial contact: Letter, prospectus, and
sample chapter

Style: Chicago

Special requirements: Accepts electronic
manuscripts; provides guidelines for
manuscript standards and preparation

Subvention: No

EDITORIAL INFORMATION

*Manuscripts or proposals submitted each
year:* 1,200 (estimate)

Manuscripts sent to readers each year: 50
(estimate)

Manuscripts accepted each year: 25
(estimate)

Number of outside readers: 2 minimum

*Time between submission and publication
decision:* 3-4 months

*Time between decision and return of copy-
edited manuscript:* 6-8 weeks

Time between decision and publication:
11 month

CONTRACT PROVISIONS

Copyright: Publisher

PUBLICATION AND DISTRIBUTION INFORMATION

Forms of publication: Cloth, paper

Titles published each year: 30

Number of review copies: 4% of print run

Distribution area: Worldwide

Time in print: Varies

(65) CHINESE UNIVERSITY PRESS

Chinese University of Hong Kong
Shatin, N.T., Hong Kong

Contact: Paul S. L. Wong, Director

Established: 1977

Telephone: (852) 26096508

Fax: (852) 26036692

SCOPE

Publishing interests: Chinese literature;
Chinese linguistics; comparative
literature (Chinese-English)

*Considers all literary and linguistic
topics:* Yes

Types of works not published: Unrevised
dissertations; collections of letters

Languages published: English; Chinese
languages

Series title(s): Chinese Classics

SUBMISSION REQUIREMENTS

Initial contact: Letter of inquiry and/or 2 copies of manuscript
Style: Chicago
Special requirements: Accepts photo-copies or dot-matrix printout; expects electronic manuscript; provides guidelines for manuscript preparation
Subvention: No

EDITORIAL INFORMATION

Manuscripts or proposals submitted each year: 25 (estimate)
Manuscripts sent to readers each year: 20 (estimate)
Manuscripts accepted each year: 10 (estimate)
Number of outside readers: 1-2
Time between submission and publication decision: 3 months
Time between decision and return of copy-edited manuscript: 4 months
Time between decision and publication: 1 year

CONTRACT PROVISIONS

Copyright: Publisher
Royalty provisions: 10% of net

PUBLICATION AND DISTRIBUTION INFORMATION

Forms of publication: Cloth, paper
Titles published each year: 10 (estimate)
Print run: 1,000
Number of review copies: 20-30
Distribution area: Worldwide
Time in print: 5-10 years

(66)
COLGATE UNIVERSITY PRESS

302 Lawrence Hall
Colgate University
Hamilton, NY 13346

Contact: Wilbur T. Albrecht, Director
Established: 1964
Telephone: 315 824-1000, ext. 268

SCOPE

Publishing interests: John Cowper Powys; Powys family
Considers all literary and linguistic topics: No
Languages published: English

SUBMISSION REQUIREMENTS

Initial contact: Letter of inquiry
Style: MLA

PUBLICATION AND DISTRIBUTION INFORMATION

Forms of publication: Cloth, paper
Print run: 2,000

(67)
UNIVERSITY PRESS OF COLORADO

PO Box 849
Niwot, CO 80544

Contact: Luther Wilson, Director
Established: 1967
Telephone: 303 530-5337
Fax: 303 530-5306
E-mail: luther.wilson@colorado.edu

SCOPE

Publishing interests: Biography; literary theory; general literature; English

literature; American literature (twentieth-century); western American literature
Considers all literary and linguistic topics: Yes
Types of works not published: Bibliographies; collections of letters; readers; collections of essays; Festschriften; literary handbooks; literary encyclopedias
Prizes and competitions: Kayden Prize (best manuscript in the humanities)
Languages published: English

SUBMISSION REQUIREMENTS

Initial contact: Letter and prospectus
Considers simultaneous submissions: Yes
Will issue contract on the basis of proposal, prospectus, and/or sample chapter: Yes
Style: Chicago
Special requirements: Expects electronic manuscript; provides guidelines for manuscript preparation
Subvention: No

EDITORIAL INFORMATION

Manuscripts or proposals submitted each year: 150 (estimate)
Manuscripts sent to readers each year: 40 (estimate)
Manuscripts accepted each year: 10
Number of outside readers: 2 minimum
Author-anonymous submission: No
Time between submission and publication decision: 4 months
Time between decision and return of copyedited manuscript: 2 months
Time between decision and publication: 9 months
Time allotted for reading proof: 2-3 weeks

CONTRACT PROVISIONS

Copyright: Negotiable
Royalty provisions: Varies

PUBLICATION AND DISTRIBUTION INFORMATION

Forms of publication: Cloth, paper, electronic media
Titles published each year: 9
Print run: 1,500
Number of review copies: 100
Distribution area: Worldwide
Time in print: 6 years

(68)
COLUMBIA UNIVERSITY PRESS

562 West 113th St.
New York, NY 10025

Contact: Jennifer Crewe, Publisher for the Humanities (literary criticism, cultural studies, film)
Established: 1893
Telephone: 212 666-1000, ext. 7145
Fax: 212 316-3100
E-mail: jc373@columbia.edu

SCOPE

Publishing interests: English literature (nineteenth- and twentieth-century); American literature (nineteenth- and twentieth-century); feminist criticism; cultural criticism; Renaissance literature; African American literature; translations of French and German cultural criticism; psychoanalytic criticism; translations of Asian literature; gay criticism; lesbian criticism; new historicist criticism; film
Considers all literary and linguistic topics: No

Types of works not published: Unrevised dissertations; bibliographies; critical editions; Festschriften
Languages published: English
Series title(s): Gender and Culture; European Perspectives; Social Foundations of Aesthetic Forms; Translations from the Asian Classics; Between Men / Between Women; Psychoanalysis and Culture

SUBMISSION REQUIREMENTS

Initial contact: Letter, prospectus, and curriculum vitae
Considers simultaneous submissions: Yes, if informed
Will issue contract on the basis of proposal, prospectus, and/or sample chapter: Yes
Style: Chicago; house
Special requirements: Length: 400 pages maximum; does not accept dot-matrix printout; prefers electronic manuscripts; provides guidelines for manuscript preparation
Subvention: Only for specialized books with low projected sales

EDITORIAL INFORMATION

Manuscripts or proposals submitted each year: 400 (estimate)
Manuscripts sent to readers each year: 50 (estimate)
Manuscripts accepted each year: 12-16
Number of outside readers: 2
Author-anonymous submission: No
Time between submission and publication decision: 3 months
Time between decision and return of copyedited manuscript: 2 months
Time between decision and publication: 10-12 months
Time allotted for reading proof: 3-4 weeks

CONTRACT PROVISIONS

Copyright: Publisher
Royalty provisions: 0-10%

PUBLICATION AND DISTRIBUTION INFORMATION

Forms of publication: Cloth, paper, electronic media
Titles published each year: 17
Print run: 1,000-2,500 cloth or 250 cloth and 2,500 paper
Number of review copies: 75
Distribution area: Worldwide
Time in print: 5-6 years minimum

(69)
CONCEPT PUBLISHING CO.

A/15-16, Commercial Block
Mohan Garden
New Delhi 110059, India

Imprint(s) and subsidiary firm(s): Logos Press
Contact: Ashok Kumar Mittal
Established: 1975
Telephone: (011) 5504042; (011) 3272187
Fax: (011) 5598898

SCOPE

Publishing interests: Jainism; Vedic studies; Hindi literature; Moslem studies; English literature
Considers all literary and linguistic topics: Yes
Languages published: Hindi; English
Series title(s): Ayurveda

SUBMISSION REQUIREMENTS

Initial contact: Letter of inquiry
Style: Chicago
Subvention: Yes

EDITORIAL INFORMATION

Manuscripts or proposals submitted each year: 25
Manuscripts sent to readers each year: 10
Manuscripts accepted each year: 15
Number of outside readers: 0
Time between submission and publication decision: 1 month
Time between decision and return of copy-edited manuscript: 1 month
Time between decision and publication: 6 months

CONTRACT PROVISIONS

Copyright: Negotiable

PUBLICATION AND DISTRIBUTION INFORMATION

Forms of publication: Cloth, paper
Titles published each year: 10
Print run: 500
Number of review copies: 50
Distribution area: Worldwide
Time in print: 3 years

**(70)
CONTINUUM PUBLISHING COMPANY**

370 Lexington Ave.
New York, NY 10017-6503

Imprint(s) and subsidiary firm(s): Continuum
Contact: Evander Lomke, Managing Editor (reference, literary criticism, film and literature); Justus George Lawler, Senior Editor (literary criticism, women's studies, religion and literature, literature and social thought)
Established: 1980
Telephone: 212 953-5858

Fax: 212 953-5944

SCOPE

Publishing interests: American literature (especially twentieth-century); British literature (especially twentieth-century); German literature (especially twentieth-century); film and literature; arts and literature; women's studies
Considers all literary and linguistic topics: Yes (literature); no (linguistics)
Not interested in proposals on: Linguistic studies
Types of works not published: Bibliographies; collections of letters; biographies; textbooks; collections of essays by different authors; Festschriften; encyclopedias
Prizes and competitions: Continuum Book Award ($10,000 advance against royalties)
Languages published: English
Series title(s): German Library

SUBMISSION REQUIREMENTS

Initial contact: Letter, outline, sample chapter, and SASE
Considers simultaneous submissions: No
Will issue contract on the basis of proposal, prospectus, and/or sample chapter: Yes
Style: Chicago
Special requirements: Requires electronic manuscript
Subvention: No

EDITORIAL INFORMATION

Manuscripts accepted each year: 5-10
Time between submission and publication decision: 6-8 weeks
Time between decision and publication: 8 months
Time allotted for reading proof: 2 weeks

CONTRACT PROVISIONS

Copyright: Author

PUBLICATION AND DISTRIBUTION INFORMATION

Forms of publication: Cloth, paper
Titles published each year: 25
Number of review copies: 50-200

(71)
CORK UNIVERSITY PRESS

University College
Cork, Ireland

Contact: Sara Wilbourne, Publisher
Established: 1928
Telephone: (021) 276871, ext. 2163
Fax: (021) 273553

SCOPE

Publishing interests: Celtic literature; Irish literature; literary criticism; cultural studies
Considers all literary and linguistic topics: Yes
Types of works not published: Dissertations; bibliographies; critical editions; collections of letters; readers; literary reference works; Festschriften
Languages published: English

SUBMISSION REQUIREMENTS

Initial contact: Letter and outline
Considers simultaneous submissions: Yes
Style: Cambridge; Oxford
Special requirements: Length: prefers 60,000-120,000 words; does not accept camera-ready copy
Subvention: No (exceptions made)

EDITORIAL INFORMATION

Manuscripts or proposals submitted each year: 100
Manuscripts sent to readers each year: 20 (estimate)
Manuscripts accepted each year: 20-25
Number of outside readers: 2
Author-anonymous submission: No
Time between submission and publication decision: 2-3 months
Time between decision and return of copy-edited manuscript: 3 months
Time between decision and publication: 6-7 months
Time allotted for reading proof: 1 month

CONTRACT PROVISIONS

Copyright: Author
Royalty provisions: Varies

PUBLICATION AND DISTRIBUTION INFORMATION

Forms of publication: Cloth, paper
Titles published each year: 16
Print run: Varies
Number of review copies: 20-25
Distribution area: Ireland; United Kingdom; Europe; United States
Time in print: Varies

(72)
CORNELL UNIVERSITY PRESS

Box 250
Sage House
512 East State St.
Ithaca, NY 14851-0250

Contact: Bernhard Kendler, Executive Editor
Established: 1869
Telephone: 607 277-2338
Fax: 607 277-2374

SCOPE

Publishing interests: Literary theory;
feminist criticism; gender studies;
medieval studies; Renaissance studies;
American literature; English literature;
European literature; genre studies;
literary movements; comparative
literature; art and literature; history and
literature; politics and literature; religion
and literature; philosophy and literature;
classical literature; science and
literature; drama (theory and history);
film theory; Latin American literature;
West Indian literature; African
American literature; Asian literature;
travel literature; linguistics (as related to
literary theory); Slavic studies; cultural
studies
*Considers all literary and linguistic
topics:* Yes (literature); no (linguistics)
Not interested in proposals on: Single-
author or specialized studies in Latin
American, African, Asian, or West
Indian literatures
Types of works not published:
Festschriften; bibliographies; readers;
literary handbooks; literary encyclopedias; collections of previously
published unrevised essays; most
critical editions; most collections of
letters
Languages published: English
Series title(s): Reading Women Writing;
Myth and Poetics; Cornell Concor-
dances; Rhetoric and Society

SUBMISSION REQUIREMENTS

Initial contact: Letter of inquiry or letter
and prospectus
Considers simultaneous submissions:
Depends on topic
*Will issue contract on the basis of
proposal, prospectus, and/or sample
chapter:* Sometimes

Style: Chicago; house
Special requirements: Requests electronic
manuscript; does not accept dot-matrix
printout; provides guidelines for manuscript preparation
Subvention: Occasionally requests
subsidy for highly specialized works or
those with high production costs

EDITORIAL INFORMATION

*Manuscripts or proposals submitted each
year:* 500 (estimate)
Manuscripts sent to readers each year:
175 (estimate)
Manuscripts accepted each year: 40
(estimate)
Number of outside readers: 1-2
Author-anonymous submission: No
*Time between submission and publication
decision:* 3 months
*Time between decision and return of copy-
edited manuscript:* 3 months
Time between decision and publication:
1 year
Time allotted for reading proof: 1 month

CONTRACT PROVISIONS

Copyright: Publisher
Royalty provisions: 0-10% of net (cloth);
5-10% of net (paper)

PUBLICATION AND DISTRIBUTION INFORMATION

Forms of publication: Cloth, paper
Titles published each year: 35 (estimate)
Print run: 900-1,000 cloth or 400 cloth
and 1,500-2,000 paper
Number of review copies: 30-60
Distribution area: Worldwide
Time in print: 8-10 years minimum

(73)
LIBRAIRIE JOSE CORTI

11, rue de Médicis
75006 Paris, France

Contact: Bertrand Fillaudeau, Manager
Established: 1938
Telephone: (43) 266300
Fax: (40) 468924

SCOPE

Publishing interests: French literature
  (seventeenth- through twentieth-
  century); French translations of
  Romantic authors; literary theory
*Considers all literary and linguistic
  topics:* Eventually will consider other
  literary topics
Types of works not published: Disser-
  tations; bibliographies; biographies;
  literary encyclopedias
Languages published: French
Series title(s): Collection romantique;
  Collection ibérique; Les essais;
  Collection en lisant en écrivain;
  Littérature française

SUBMISSION REQUIREMENTS

Initial contact: Letter of inquiry
Considers simultaneous submissions: No
*Will issue contract on the basis of
  proposal, prospectus, and/or sample
  chapter:* No
Style: House
Subvention: Sometimes

EDITORIAL INFORMATION

*Manuscripts or proposals submitted each
  year:* 600 (estimate)
Manuscripts sent to readers each year:
  120 (estimate)
Manuscripts accepted each year: 30
Number of outside readers: 2

Author-anonymous submission: No
*Time between submission and publication
  decision:* 1-2 months
*Time between decision and return of copy-
  edited manuscript:* 6 months
Time between decision and publication:
  6-12 months
Time allotted for reading proof: 1 month

CONTRACT PROVISIONS

Copyright: Publisher
Royalty provisions: Royalties paid only
  for translations

PUBLICATION AND DISTRIBUTION
INFORMATION

Forms of publication: Cloth
Titles published each year: 48
Print run: 2,000
Number of review copies: 50-100
Distribution area: Worldwide
Time in print: Indefinitely

(74)
PRESSES UNIVERSITAIRES DE
COTE D'IVOIRE

BP V34
Abidjan, Ivory Coast

Contact: Alain Poiri, Director
Telephone: 448248

SCOPE

Publishing interests: Ethnolinguistics;
  drama
*Considers all literary and linguistic
  topics:* Yes
Types of works not published: Collections
  of letters; bibliographies
Languages published: French
Series title(s): Annales de l'Université
  d'Abidjan, série D: Lettres, arts et

sciences humaines; Annales de l'Université d'Abidjan, série H: Linguistique

SUBMISSION REQUIREMENTS

Initial contact: Letter, outline, and sample chapters
Considers simultaneous submissions: No
Will issue contract on the basis of proposal, prospectus, and/or sample chapter: No
Special requirements: Length restrictions
Subvention: Yes

EDITORIAL INFORMATION

Manuscripts or proposals submitted each year: 10
Manuscripts sent to readers each year: 5
Manuscripts accepted each year: 2-3
Number of outside readers: 2
Author-anonymous submission: Yes
Time between submission and publication decision: 1-2 years
Time between decision and publication: 2 years
Time allotted for reading proof: 3 months

CONTRACT PROVISIONS

Copyright: Publisher
Royalty provisions: 10%

PUBLICATION AND DISTRIBUTION INFORMATION

Forms of publication: Paper
Titles published each year: 10
Number of review copies: 100
Distribution area: Worldwide
Time in print: 10 years

(75)
CURRENCY PRESS

PO Box 451
Paddington, NSW 2021, Australia

Contact: Katharine Brisbane, publisher; Sandra Gorman, publishing director
Established: 1971
Telephone: (61) 2 3321300
Fax: (61) 2 3323848

SCOPE

Publishing interests: Australian drama; Australian theater; Australian film
Considers all literary and linguistic topics: No
Languages published: English

SUBMISSION REQUIREMENTS

Initial contact: Letter and outline
Considers simultaneous submissions: No
Will issue contract on the basis of proposal, prospectus, and/or sample chapter: Yes
Style: Australian Government Publishing Service
Subvention: No

EDITORIAL INFORMATION

Manuscripts or proposals submitted each year: 30-40
Manuscripts sent to readers each year: 20
Manuscripts accepted each year: 10
Number of outside readers: 2
Author-anonymous submission: No
Time between submission and publication decision: 6-12 months

CONTRACT PROVISIONS

Copyright: Author
Royalty provisions: 10% (paper); 12.5% (cloth)

PUBLICATION AND DISTRIBUTION INFORMATION

Forms of publication: Cloth, paper
Titles published each year: 30
Print run: 2,000-3,000

Number of review copies: 50
Distribution area: Worldwide
Time in print: 20 years

(76)
WALTER DE GRUYTER

Genthiner Strasse 13
10785 Berlin, Germany

Imprint(s) and subsidiary firm(s): Mouton
de Gruyter
Contact: Brigitte Schoening (language
and literature); Anke Beck (linguistics,
English language)
Established: 1919
Telephone: (030) 260050
Fax: (030) 26005251
E-mail: 10044.2657@compuserve.com

SCOPE

Publishing interests: German literature;
German language; dictionaries; literary
criticism; semiotics; minority
languages; cognitive linguistics
*Considers all literary and linguistic
topics:* No
Types of works not published: Disser-
tations; Festschriften
Languages published: English; German
Series title(s): Trends in Linguistics:
State-of-the-Art Reports; Research in
Text Theory; Contributions to the
Sociology of Language; Studia
Linguistica Germanica; Approaches to
Semiotics; Quellen und Forschungen
zur Literatur- und Kulturgeschichte

SUBMISSION REQUIREMENTS

Initial contact: Letter, outline, and sample
chapter

Considers simultaneous submissions: Yes
*Will issue contract on the basis of
proposal, prospectus, and/or sample
chapter:* No
Style: Chicago
Special requirements: Length: 250-500
pages; requires camera-ready copy
Subvention: Sometimes

EDITORIAL INFORMATION

*Manuscripts or proposals submitted each
year:* 250 (estimate)
Manuscripts sent to readers each year:
120 (estimate)
Manuscripts accepted each year: 75
(estimate)
Number of outside readers: 2-3
Author-anonymous submission: No
*Time between submission and publication
decision:* 3 months maximum
*Time between decision and return of copy-
edited manuscript:* 1-2 months
Time between decision and publication: 9
months
Time allotted for reading proof: 1 month

CONTRACT PROVISIONS

Copyright: Publisher
Royalty provisions: Varies (10% for
textbooks; none for monographs)

PUBLICATION AND DISTRIBUTION
INFORMATION

Forms of publication: Cloth, paper, elec-
tronic media
Titles published each year: 75 (estimate)
Print run: 1,000
Number of review copies: 20
Distribution area: Worldwide
Time in print: 25 years

(77)
UNIVERSITY OF DELAWARE
PRESS

326 Hullihen Hall
Newark, DE 19716

Contact: Jay L. Halio, Director
Established: 1975
Telephone: 302 831-1149
Fax: 302 831-6549
E-mail: ebr@brahms.udel.edu

SCOPE

Publishing interests: William Shakespeare; Renaissance literature; English literature (Renaissance and eighteenth-century); American literature (eighteenth-century); general literature
Considers all literary and linguistic topics: Yes
Types of works not published: Unrevised dissertations; readers; literary encyclopedias; collections of previously published essays
Prizes and competitions: Prize for best manuscript in Shakespeare studies and in eighteenth-century studies
Languages published: English
Series title(s): International Studies in Shakespeare and His Contemporaries

SUBMISSION REQUIREMENTS

Initial contact: Letter and prospectus
Considers simultaneous submissions: No
Will issue contract on the basis of proposal, prospectus, and/or sample chapter: No
Style: Chicago
Special requirements: Length: 60,000 words minimum and preferably not more than 500 pages; requires electronic manuscript in *WordPerfect* (5.0 or higher); does not accept dot-matrix printout

Subvention: No

EDITORIAL INFORMATION

Manuscripts or proposals submitted each year: 105 (estimate)
Manuscripts sent to readers each year: 40 (estimate)
Manuscripts accepted each year: 15 (estimate)
Number of outside readers: 1-2
Author-anonymous submission: No
Time between submission and publication decision: 3 months
Time between decision and return of copy-edited manuscript: 3 months
Time between decision and publication: 2 years maximum
Time allotted for reading proof: 3-4 weeks

CONTRACT PROVISIONS

Copyright: Publisher
Royalty provisions: 10% after first 800 copies

PUBLICATION AND DISTRIBUTION
INFORMATION

Forms of publication: Cloth
Titles published each year: 15
Print run: 1,000
Number of review copies: 50
Distribution area: Worldwide
Time in print: Varies

(78)
DOVEHOUSE EDITIONS

1890 Fairmeadow Crescent
Ottawa, ON K1H 7B9, Canada

Contact: D. A. Beecher
Established: 1984
Telephone: 613 731-7601

SCOPE

Publishing interests: English-language translations of Renaissance plays; Spanish literature (especially studies and editions of golden age theater); English Renaissance prose fiction
Considers all literary and linguistic topics: No
Languages published: English; Spanish; Italian; French
Series title(s): University of Toronto Italian Studies; Carleton Renaissance Plays in Translation; Ottawa Hispanic Studies; Publications of the Barnabe Riche Society

SUBMISSION REQUIREMENTS

Initial contact: Letter and prospectus
Special requirements: Prefers electronic manuscripts
Subvention: No; however, non-Canadian authors, since they are ineligible for funding by the Canadian Federation for the Humanities (which subsidizes Dovehouse's publication of Canadian scholars), are asked to seek publication grants.

EDITORIAL INFORMATION

Manuscripts or proposals submitted each year: 30 (estimate)
Manuscripts sent to readers each year: 15 (estimate)
Manuscripts accepted each year: 6 (estimate)
Number of outside readers: 2
Time between submission and publication decision: 3 months
Time between decision and return of copy-edited manuscript: 6 months
Time between decision and publication: 1 year

CONTRACT PROVISIONS

Copyright: Publisher
Royalty provisions: Royalty paid only after recovery of all production costs

PUBLICATION AND DISTRIBUTION INFORMATION

Forms of publication: Paper
Titles published each year: 5
Print run: 1,000
Number of review copies: 10-20
Distribution area: Worldwide
Time in print: 10 years minimum

Each series has its own editors and editorial board responsible for building, editing, and maintaining the quality of the series.

(79)
LIBRAIRIE DROZ

11, rue Massot
1211 Geneva, Switzerland

Established: 1924
Telephone: (022) 466666
Fax: (022) 472391

SCOPE

Publishing interests: French literature; French language; humanism; Renaissance literature
Languages published: French; English
Series title(s): Textes littéraires français; Publications romanes et françaises; Travaux d'humanisme et Renaissance; Histoire des idées et critique littéraire; Etudes de philologie et littérature

SUBMISSION REQUIREMENTS

Initial contact: Letter and prospectus
Subvention: Sometimes

EDITORIAL INFORMATION

Manuscripts or proposals submitted each year: 100 (estimate)
Manuscripts accepted each year: 50 (estimate)
Number of outside readers: Varies
Time between submission and publication decision: 3 months

PUBLICATION AND DISTRIBUTION INFORMATION

Forms of publication: Paper
Titles published each year: 60

(80)
DUCKWORTH

The Old Piano Factory
48 Hoxton Square
London N1 6PB, England

Imprint(s) and subsidiary firm(s): Bristol Classical Press
Contact: Colin Haycraft
Established: 1898
Telephone: (44) 71 7295986
Fax: (44) 71 7290015

SCOPE

Considers all literary and linguistic topics: Yes
Types of works not published: Dissertations; bibliographies; literary encyclopedias
Languages published: English
Series title(s): Criticism in Focus Series; Critical Studies in Russian Literature

SUBMISSION REQUIREMENTS

Initial contact: Letter, brief synopsis, and sample chapter
Considers simultaneous submissions: No

Will issue contract on the basis of proposal, prospectus, and/or sample chapter: No
Style: House
Special requirements: Requires electronic copy
Subvention: No

EDITORIAL INFORMATION

Manuscripts or proposals submitted each year: 400
Manuscripts sent to readers each year: 200
Manuscripts accepted each year: 70
Number of outside readers: 1
Author-anonymous submission: No
Time between submission and publication decision: 3 months
Time between decision and publication: 1 year
Time allotted for reading proof: 2 weeks

CONTRACT PROVISIONS

Copyright: Author
Royalty provisions: 10%

PUBLICATION AND DISTRIBUTION INFORMATION

Forms of publication: Cloth, paper
Titles published each year: 50
Print run: 4,000
Number of review copies: 30
Distribution area: United Kingdom
Time in print: 8 years

(81)
DUFOUR EDITIONS

PO Box 7
Chester Springs, PA 19425

Contact: Christopher May

Established: 1948
Telephone: 610 458-5005
Fax: 610 458-7103

SCOPE

Publishing interests: Irish literature;
  Welsh literature; Scottish literature;
  Celtic literature; English literature;
  Scandinavian literature; German
  literature; Slavic literature; poetry;
  fiction; drama; hermeneutics; critical
  theory
*Considers all literary and linguistic
  topics:* Yes
Languages published: English

SUBMISSION REQUIREMENTS

Initial contact: Letter, outline, and sample
  chapter
Considers simultaneous submissions: Yes
*Will issue contract on the basis of
  proposal, prospectus, and/or sample
  chapter:* No
Style: House
Special requirements: Prefers electronic
  manuscripts
Subvention: No

EDITORIAL INFORMATION

*Manuscripts or proposals submitted each
  year:* 50 (estimate)
Manuscripts sent to readers each year:
  0-2
Manuscripts accepted each year: 5
  (estimate)
Number of outside readers: 0-2
*Time between submission and publication
  decision:* 6 months
*Time between decision and return of copy-
  edited manuscript:* 6 months
Time between decision and publication:
  1 year
Time allotted for reading proof: 1 month

CONTRACT PROVISIONS

Copyright: Author

PUBLICATION AND DISTRIBUTION INFORMATION

Forms of publication: Cloth, paper
Titles published each year: 5
Print run: 500
Number of review copies: 50
Distribution area: Worldwide
Time in print: Varies

(82)
DUKE UNIVERSITY PRESS

PO Box 90660
Durham, NC 27708-0660

Contact: J. Reynolds Smith, Executive
  Editor; Ken Wissoker, Editor
Established: 1921
Telephone: 919 687-3637 (Smith); 919
  687-3648 (Wissoker)
Fax: 919 688-4574
E-mail: jrs3@acpub.duke.edu (Smith);
  kwiss@acpub.duke.edu (Wissoker)

SCOPE

Publishing interests: American literature;
  Hispanic literature; English literature;
  French literature; German literature;
  Italian literature; Japanese literature;
  Chinese literature; Russian literature;
  Third World literature; literary theory;
  film studies; ethnic studies; women's
  studies; African American studies;
  Chicano studies; mass culture; psychoanalytic criticism; discourse analysis;
  feminist studies; television studies;
  linguistic theory; lesbian and gay
  studies; postcolonial theory
*Considers all literary and linguistic
  topics:* Yes

Types of works not published: Bibliographies; Festschriften
Languages published: English
Series title(s): Post-contemporary Interventions; Sound and Meaning: The Roman Jakobson Series in Linguistics and Poetics; Duke Monographs in Medieval and Renaissance Studies; New Americanists; Series Q

SUBMISSION REQUIREMENTS

Initial contact: Letter and prospectus
Considers simultaneous submissions: Yes
Will issue contract on the basis of proposal, prospectus, and/or sample chapter: Yes
Subvention: No

EDITORIAL INFORMATION

Manuscripts accepted each year: 25 (estimate)
Number of outside readers: 2 minimum
Author-anonymous submission: No
Time between submission and publication decision: 3-4 months
Time between decision and return of copyedited manuscript: 6 weeks
Time between decision and publication: 9 months

CONTRACT PROVISIONS

Copyright: Negotiable

PUBLICATION AND DISTRIBUTION INFORMATION

Forms of publication: Cloth, paper, electronic media
Titles published each year: 24
Number of review copies: 60-100
Distribution area: Worldwide
Time in print: 10 years

(83)
DUQUESNE UNIVERSITY PRESS

600 Forbes Ave.
Pittsburgh, PA 15282-0101

Contact: Albert C. Labriola, Editor, Duquesne Studies: Language and Literature Series, Department of English, Duquesne University, Pittsburgh, PA 15282
Established: 1927
Telephone: 412 396-6610
Fax: 412 396-5780

SCOPE

Publishing interests: English literature (late medieval, Renaissance, and seventeenth-century); Edmund Spenser; John Milton; Ben Jonson
Considers all literary and linguistic topics: No
Types of works not published: Unrevised dissertations; readers; literary handbooks; literary encyclopedias
Languages published: English
Series title(s): Duquesne Studies: Language and Literature Series

SUBMISSION REQUIREMENTS

Initial contact: Letter and prospectus
Considers simultaneous submissions: Yes, if informed
Will issue contract on the basis of proposal, prospectus, and/or sample chapter: No
Style: Chicago
Special requirements: 2 printed copies and electronic manuscripts
Subvention: No

EDITORIAL INFORMATION

Manuscripts or proposals submitted each year: 30-40

Manuscripts sent to readers each year:
  5-8
Manuscripts accepted each year: 2-3
Number of outside readers: 2
Author-anonymous submission: No
*Time between submission and publication
  decision:* 6 months
*Time between decision and return of copy-
  edited manuscript:* 6 months
Time between decision and publication:
  1 year
Time allotted for reading proof: 2-3
  weeks

CONTRACT PROVISIONS

Copyright: Publisher
Royalty provisions: 10% of net

**PUBLICATION AND DISTRIBUTION
INFORMATION**

Forms of publication: Cloth
Titles published each year: 3
Print run: 500-1,000
Number of review copies: 20-35
Distribution area: Worldwide
Time in print: 5 years

**(84)
EARLY ENGLISH TEXT SOCIETY**

Exeter College
Oxford OX1 3DP, England

Contact: H. L. Spencer, Editorial
  Secretary
Established: 1864

SCOPE

Publishing interests: Critical editions of
  medieval English texts
*Considers all literary and linguistic
  topics:* No
Languages published: English

Series title(s): Early English Text Society

SUBMISSION REQUIREMENTS

Initial contact: Letter
Style: House
Special requirements: Provides guidelines
  for editors
Subvention: No

EDITORIAL INFORMATION

*Manuscripts or proposals submitted each
  year:* 5
Manuscripts sent to readers each year: 3
Manuscripts accepted each year: 2

CONTRACT PROVISIONS

Copyright: Publisher
Royalty provisions: No royalties

**PUBLICATION AND DISTRIBUTION
INFORMATION**

Forms of publication: Cloth
Titles published each year: 3
Print run: 1,700
Number of review copies: 20
Distribution area: Worldwide
Time in print: Indefinitely

Publishes only critical editions

**(85)
ECW PRESS**

2120 Queen St. East
Toronto, ON M4E 1E2, Canada

Contact: Jack David, President
Established: 1979
Telephone: 416 694-3348
Fax: 416 698-9906

SCOPE

Publishing interests: Canadian literature;
  bibliography (especially of Canadian
  literature and history); Canadian-
  American literary relations
*Considers all literary and linguistic
  topics:* Yes (but preference given to
  Canadian topics)
Languages published: English
Series title(s): Canadian Writers and
  Their Works; Annotated Bibliography
  of Canada's Major Authors; Canadian
  Fiction Studies

SUBMISSION REQUIREMENTS

Initial contact: Letter, outline, and sample
  chapter
Considers simultaneous submissions: Yes
*Will issue contract on the basis of
  proposal, prospectus, and/or sample
  chapter:* Yes
Style: MLA
Subvention: Sometimes

EDITORIAL INFORMATION

*Manuscripts or proposals submitted each
  year:* 75 (estimate)
Manuscripts sent to readers each year: 20
Manuscripts accepted each year: 10
Number of outside readers: 1-2
Author-anonymous submission: Yes
*Time between submission and publication
  decision:* 1 month
*Time between decision and return of copy-
  edited manuscript:* 2-3 months
Time between decision and publication:
  1 year maximum
Time allotted for reading proof: 1 week

CONTRACT PROVISIONS

Copyright: Author
Royalty provisions: 10% of gross

PUBLICATION AND DISTRIBUTION INFORMATION

Forms of publication: Cloth, paper
Titles published each year: 15
Print run: 1,000-1,500
Number of review copies: 30-40
Distribution area: Worldwide
Time in print: 5-10 years

ECW offers three free books to anyone
who spots a factual error in any of its
publications.

(86)
EDINBURGH UNIVERSITY PRESS

22 George Square
Edinburgh EH8 9LF, Scotland

Contact: V. C. Bone, Senior Editor
Established: 1946
Telephone: (031) 6504218
Fax: (031) 6620053

SCOPE

Publishing interests: Scottish literature;
  English literature (major writers);
  literary theory; linguistics
*Considers all literary and linguistic
  topics:* No
Types of works not published: Dissertations; bibliographies; Festschriften;
  literary reference works
Languages published: English

SUBMISSION REQUIREMENTS

Initial contact: Letter and outline
Style: House
Special requirements: Length: 120,000
  words maximum; accepts photocopies
  and dot-matrix printout; prefers electronic manuscripts

Subvention: No

EDITORIAL INFORMATION

*Manuscripts or proposals submitted each
year:* 65 (estimate)
Manuscripts sent to readers each year: 25
(estimate)
Manuscripts accepted each year: 5
(estimate)
Number of outside readers: 2
*Time between submission and publication
decision:* 3 months
*Time between decision and return of copy-
edited manuscript:* 3 months
Time between decision and publication:
9-12 months

CONTRACT PROVISIONS

Copyright: Author
Royalty provisions: 10% of net

**PUBLICATION AND DISTRIBUTION
INFORMATION**

Forms of publication: Cloth, paper
Titles published each year: 9
Print run: 1,000
Number of review copies: 30
Distribution area: Worldwide
Time in print: 3-20 years

**(87)
WM. B. EERDMANS PUBLISHING
CO.**

255 Jefferson Ave., SE
Grand Rapids, MI 49503

Contact: Jon Pott, Vice President and
Editor in Chief
Established: 1911
Telephone: 616 459-4591
Fax: 616 459-6540

SCOPE

Publishing interests: English literature;
American literature; religion and
literature
*Considers all literary and linguistic
topics:* No
Types of works not published: Bibli-
ographies
Languages published: English; Spanish

SUBMISSION REQUIREMENTS

Initial contact: Letter, outline, and sample
chapter(s)
Considers simultaneous submissions:
Yes, if informed
*Will issue contract on the basis of
proposal, prospectus, and/or sample
chapter:* No
Style: Chicago
Subvention: No

EDITORIAL INFORMATION

*Manuscripts or proposals submitted each
year:* 25
Manuscripts sent to readers each year: 6-
10
Manuscripts accepted each year: 6
Number of outside readers: 1
Author-anonymous submission: No
*Time between submission and publication
decision:* 4-8 months
Time between decision and publication:
12-18 months
Time allotted for reading proof: 3 weeks

CONTRACT PROVISIONS

Copyright: Publisher (unless author
requests otherwise)

**PUBLICATION AND DISTRIBUTION
INFORMATION**

Forms of publication: Cloth, paper, electronic media

Titles published each year: 12
Print run: 4,000-6,000
Number of review copies: 75-100
Distribution area: Worldwide
Time in print: 3-4 years

(88)
ELLUG (EDITIONS LITTERAIRES ET LINGUISTIQUES DE L'UNIVERSITE DE GRENOBLE)

Université Stendhal
B.P. 25
38040 Grenoble Cedex 9, France

Contact: Denise Pierrot, Director
Established: 1978
Telephone: (76) 824372
Fax: (76) 824112
E-mail: pierrot@stendhal.greneb.fr

SCOPE

Publishing interests: French literature; literary criticism; myth; European culture; communication; linguistics; phonetics; dialectology
Considers all literary and linguistic topics: No
Languages published: French

SUBMISSION REQUIREMENTS

Initial contact: Letter, outline, and sample chapter
Considers simultaneous submissions: Yes
Will issue contract on the basis of proposal, prospectus, and/or sample chapter: No
Style: House
Special requirements: Requires electronic manuscript
Subvention: No

EDITORIAL INFORMATION

Manuscripts accepted each year: 6
Number of outside readers: 2
Author-anonymous submission: No
Time between submission and publication decision: 6 months
Time between decision and publication: 6 months
Time allotted for reading proof: 1 month

CONTRACT PROVISIONS

Copyright: Publisher
Royalty provisions: 0

PUBLICATION AND DISTRIBUTION INFORMATION

Forms of publication: Paper
Titles published each year: 4
Print run: 500-2,000
Number of review copies: 100
Distribution area: France
Time in print: 10 years

(89)
ELSEVIER SCIENCE PUBLISHERS

PO Box 1991
1000 BZ Amsterdam, Netherlands

Imprint(s) and subsidiary firm(s): North-Holland
Contact: K. Michielsen
Established: 1947
Telephone: (020) 4852458
Fax: (020) 4852616
E-mail: k.michielsen@elsevier.nl

SCOPE

Publishing interests: Linguistics; general linguistics; applied linguistics; comparative linguistics; semantics; phonetics; sociolinguistics; psycholin-guistics; computational linguistics;

neurolinguistics; pragmatics; philosophy of language; language acquisition; language processing; language and cognition; literary theory; poetics
Considers all literary and linguistic topics: Yes
Not interested in proposals on: Prefers linguistic topics
Types of works not published: Collections of letters; biographies; readers; Festschriften
Languages published: English
Series title(s): North-Holland Linguistic Series

SUBMISSION REQUIREMENTS

Initial contact: Letter and manuscript; letter, outline, and sample chapters; or letter and prospectus
Considers simultaneous submissions: Yes, if informed
Will issue contract on the basis of proposal, prospectus, and/or sample chapter: Possibly
Style: House
Special requirements: Length: 120,000 words minimum; generally requires camera-ready copy; occasionally accepts electronic manuscripts; provides guidelines for manuscript preparation
Subvention: Rarely

EDITORIAL INFORMATION

Manuscripts or proposals submitted each year: 15 (estimate)
Manuscripts sent to readers each year: 8 (estimate)
Manuscripts accepted each year: 5 (estimate)
Number of outside readers: 1-2
Author-anonymous submission: Sometimes
Time between submission and publication decision: 6 weeks

Time between decision and publication: 5 months

CONTRACT PROVISIONS

Copyright: Publisher
Royalty provisions: 8-14% of net

PUBLICATION AND DISTRIBUTION INFORMATION

Forms of publication: Cloth, paper, some electronic media
Titles published each year: 5
Print run: 1,000-1,500
Number of review copies: 10-15
Distribution area: Worldwide
Time in print: 8 years

(90) ELT PRESS

English Dept.
University of North Carolina
Greensboro, NC 27412-5001

Contact: Robert Langenfeld, Editor
Established: 1988
Telephone: 910 334-5446
Fax: 910 334-3281
E-mail: langen@fagan.uncg.edu

SCOPE

Publishing interests: British literature, 1880-1920 (including editions and critical, biographical, and biblio-graphical studies); will consider colonial literature and other national literatures related to turn-of-the-century Great Britain
Considers all literary and linguistic topics: No
Types of works not published: Textbooks, literary handbooks
Prizes and competitions: No

Languages published: English
Series title(s): 1880-1920 British Authors
Series

SUBMISSION REQUIREMENTS

Restrictions on authors: No
Initial contact: Letter of inquiry
Considers simultaneous submissions: Yes
*Will issue contract on the basis of
proposal, prospectus, and/or sample
chapter:* No
Style: Chicago
Special requirements: Prefers electronic
copy
Subvention: No

EDITORIAL INFORMATION

*Manuscripts or proposals submitted each
year:* 50
Manuscripts sent to readers each year: 20
Manuscripts accepted each year: 2
Number of outside readers: 2
Author-anonymous submission: No
*Time between submission and publication
decision:* 3-5 months
Time between decision and publication:
12-16 months
Time allotted for reading proof: Varies;
author sees 3 sets of proof

CONTRACT PROVISIONS

Copyright: Publisher (but negotiable)
Royalty provisions: Typically no royalty

PUBLICATION AND DISTRIBUTION INFORMATION

Forms of publication: Cloth, paper
Titles published each year: 2
Print run: 500-800
Number of review copies: 20-35
Distribution area: North America and
Asia; Europe (by Colin Smythe)
Time in print: 10 years

(91) LAWRENCE ERLBAUM ASSOCIATES

365 Broadway
Hillsdale, NJ 07642

Contact: Judith Amsel, Vice President,
Editorial
Established: 1974
Telephone: 201 666-4110, ext. 136
Fax: 201 666-2394
E-mail:
jgamsel@leahq.mhs.compuserve.com

SCOPE

Publishing interests: Psycholinguistics;
language processing; language learning
(including second-language learning);
language disorders; language and
thought; natural language processing
*Considers all literary and linguistic
topics:* No
Types of works not published: Unrevised
dissertations; collections of letters;
biographies
Languages published: English
Series title(s): Crosslinguistic Studies of
Language Acquisition; Carnegie-Mellon
Symposia on Cognition; Neuropsy-
chology and Neurolinguistics

SUBMISSION REQUIREMENTS

Initial contact: Letter, prospectus or
outline, and sample chapters; provides
guidelines for preparation of prospectus
Style: American Psychological Association
Special requirements: Accepts camera-
ready copy and electronic manuscripts;
provides guidelines for manuscript
preparation
Subvention: No

EDITORIAL INFORMATION

Manuscripts or proposals submitted each year: 15 (estimate)
Manuscripts sent to readers each year: 9 (estimate)
Manuscripts accepted each year: 6 (estimate)
Number of outside readers: 2-3
Time between submission and publication decision: 2-4 months
Time between decision and return of copyedited manuscript: 2 months
Time between decision and publication: 9 months
Time allotted for reading proof: 1 month

CONTRACT PROVISIONS

Copyright: Publisher
Royalty provisions: 10% of net on first 2,000 copies, 12% on next 2,000, 15% thereafter

PUBLICATION AND DISTRIBUTION INFORMATION

Forms of publication: Cloth, paper, electronic media
Titles published each year: 15
Print run: 600 cloth; 1,000 paper
Number of review copies: 25 minimum
Distribution area: Worldwide
Time in print: 8 years minimum

(92)
EUROPA VERLAG

Altmannsdorferstr. 154-156
1231 Vienna, Austria

Contact: Gisela Anna Stümpel, Publisher
Established: 1933
Telephone: (667) 28200
Fax: (667) 282019

SCOPE

Publishing interests: Fiction (contemporary); biographies
Considers all literary and linguistic topics: No
Types of works not published: Dissertations; critical editions; collections of letters; textbooks; collections of essays; Festschriften; literary reference works
Languages published: German

SUBMISSION REQUIREMENTS

Initial contact: Letter, outline, and sample chapter
Subvention: Not necessarily

EDITORIAL INFORMATION

Manuscripts or proposals submitted each year: 120 (estimate)
Manuscripts sent to readers each year: 10 (estimate)
Manuscripts accepted each year: 2
Number of outside readers: 1-2
Time between submission and publication decision: 2-8 weeks
Time between decision and return of copyedited manuscript: 4-10 months
Time between decision and publication: 12-18 months

CONTRACT PROVISIONS

Copyright: Publisher
Royalty provisions: 10%

PUBLICATION AND DISTRIBUTION INFORMATION

Forms of publication: Cloth, paper
Titles published each year: 10
Print run: 2,000-5,000
Number of review copies: 100-200
Distribution area: Austria, Germany, and Switzerland
Time in print: Varies

(93)
FACTS ON FILE

11 Penn Plaza
New York, NY 10001

Contact: Lincoln Paine, Senior Editor
   (academic reference)
Established: 1941
Telephone: 212 683-2244
Fax: 212 213-4578

SCOPE

Publishing interests: Literary reference
   books for public, high school, and
   academic libraries
*Considers all literary and linguistic
   topics:* No
Types of works not published: Dissertations; critical editions; collections of
   letters; biographies; readers; collections
   of essays; Festschriften; textbooks
Languages published: English

SUBMISSION REQUIREMENTS

Initial contact: Letter, prospectus, and
   sample chapter
*Will issue contract on the basis of
   proposal, prospectus, and/or sample
   chapter:* Yes
Style: House
Special requirements: Provides guidelines
   for preparation of proposal and manuscript
Subvention: No

EDITORIAL INFORMATION

*Manuscripts or proposals submitted each
   year:* 100 (estimate)
Manuscripts accepted each year: 10
Number of outside readers: 0
Author-anonymous submission: No
*Time between submission and publication
   decision:* 1 month

*Time between decision and return of copy-
   edited manuscript:* 3 months
Time between decision and publication:
   10 months
Time allotted for reading proof: 2-3
   weeks

CONTRACT PROVISIONS

Copyright: Author
Royalty provisions: 10% of list

PUBLICATION AND DISTRIBUTION
INFORMATION

Forms of publication: Cloth, paper, elec-
   tronic media
Titles published each year: 8 (estimate)
Print run: 3,000-5,000
Number of review copies: 200
Distribution area: Worldwide
Time in print: 5 years

Publishes only books addressed to a
general audience and appropriate for
public, high school, and academic libraries

(94)
FAIRLEIGH DICKINSON
UNIVERSITY PRESS

285 Madison Ave.
Madison, NJ 07940

Contact: Harry Keyishian, Director
Established: 1967
Telephone: 201 593-8564; 201 593-8565
Fax: 201 593-8564
E-mail: harry@sun490.fdu.edu

SCOPE

Publishing interests: General literature;
   literary theory; film; Judaica; biography;
   theater; drama

Considers all literary and linguistic topics: Yes
Languages published: English

SUBMISSION REQUIREMENTS

Initial contact: Letter, prospectus, and curriculum vitae
Considers simultaneous submissions: No
Will issue contract on the basis of proposal, prospectus, and/or sample chapter: No
Style: Chicago (14th ed.)
Special requirements: Accepts photocopies; does not expect electronic manuscript or camera-ready copy; prefers not to receive dot-matrix printout
Subvention: No

EDITORIAL INFORMATION

Manuscripts or proposals submitted each year: 150 (estimate)
Manuscripts sent to readers each year: 70 (estimate)
Manuscripts accepted each year: 20 (estimate)
Number of outside readers: 1-3
Author-anonymous submission: No
Time between submission and publication decision: 2-5 months
Time between decision and return of copyedited manuscript: 4-6 months
Time between decision and publication: 12-15 months

CONTRACT PROVISIONS

Copyright: Negotiable
Royalty provisions: 10% of list

PUBLICATION AND DISTRIBUTION INFORMATION

Forms of publication: Cloth
Titles published each year: 15 (estimate)
Print run: 800-1,200

Number of review copies: 20-50
Distribution area: Worldwide
Time in print: Indefinitely

(95)
THE FEMINIST PRESS AT THE CITY UNIVERSITY OF NEW YORK

311 East 94th St.
New York, NY 10128

Contact: Florence Howe, Director; Susannah Driver, Senior Editor
Established: 1970
Telephone: 212 360-5790; 212 360-5791
Fax: 212 348-1241

SCOPE

Publishing interests: Women's studies; African American studies (especially women writers); black studies; Asian studies; American literature; critical editions; reference works in women's studies; working-class women; women and music; women, war, and peace; women writers; autobiography
Types of works not published: Unrevised dissertations; bibliographies; literary reference works; textbooks
Languages published: English
Series title(s): Cross-Cultural Memoir Series

SUBMISSION REQUIREMENTS

Initial contact: Letter, outline, table of contents, sample chapter, SASE, and curriculum vitae
Considers simultaneous submissions: Prefers single submission
Style: Chicago
Special requirements: Accepts photocopies and dot-matrix printout; prefers electronic manuscripts
Subvention: No

EDITORIAL INFORMATION

Manuscripts or proposals submitted each year: 500 (estimate)

Manuscripts sent to readers each year: 30 (estimate)

Manuscripts accepted each year: 5 (estimate)

Number of outside readers: 1-3

Author-anonymous submission: Yes, when possible

Time between decision and publication: 9 months

Time allotted for reading proof: 2 weeks

CONTRACT PROVISIONS

Copyright: Author

Royalty provisions: 10% of net

PUBLICATION AND DISTRIBUTION INFORMATION

Forms of publication: Cloth, paper

Titles published each year: 9

Print run: 500-800 (cloth); 4,000 (paper)

Number of review copies: 200

Distribution area: Worldwide

Time in print: Indefinitely

Especially interested in publishing editions of primary works that would significantly change the teaching of literature, history, and the social sciences; that would be useful also in women's studies, African American studies, and Asian studies; and that would appeal to a general audience

(96)
UNIVERSITY PRESS OF FLORIDA

15 Northwest 15th St.
Gainesville, FL 32611

Contact: Walda Metcalf, Associate Director and Editor in Chief

Established: 1945

Telephone: 904 392-1351

Fax: 904 392-7302

SCOPE

Publishing interests: Literary theory; contemporary literature; Latin American literature; modernism; medieval literature; Renaissance literature; James Joyce; British literature (1600-1900); French literature (1600-1900)

Considers all literary and linguistic topics: No

Types of works not published: Dissertations; bibliographies; critical editions; Festschriften; literary reference works

Prizes and competitions: SAMLA Book Award

Languages published: English

Series title(s): Florida James Joyce Series

SUBMISSION REQUIREMENTS

Initial contact: Letter and brief (2-page) prospectus

Considers simultaneous submissions: Yes

Will issue contract on the basis of proposal, prospectus, and/or sample chapter: No

Style: Chicago; MLA

Special requirements: Length: 200-350 pages in manuscript; requires electronic manuscript; does not accept dot-matrix printout; provides guidelines for manuscript preparation

Subvention: No

EDITORIAL INFORMATION

Manuscripts or proposals submitted each year: 300

Manuscripts sent to readers each year: 80-90

Manuscripts accepted each year: 20-25
Number of outside readers: 2-3
Author-anonymous submission: No
*Time between submission and publication
  decision:* 2-6 months
Time between decision and publication:
  1 year
Time allotted for reading proof: 2-3
  weeks

CONTRACT PROVISIONS

Copyright: Negotiable
Royalty provisions: 0-10% of net

**PUBLICATION AND DISTRIBUTION
INFORMATION**

Forms of publication: Cloth, paper
Titles published each year: 22
Print run: 700-2,000
Number of review copies: 80-200
Distribution area: Worldwide
Time in print: 10-12 years

**(97)
FORDHAM UNIVERSITY PRESS**

Box L
Bronx, NY 10458-5172

Imprint(s) and subsidiary firm(s): Rose
  Hill Books
Contact: Saverio Procario, Director
Established: 1907
Telephone: 718 817-4780
Fax: 718 817-4785
E-mail: procario@murray.fordham.edu

SCOPE

Publishing interests: American literature
  (nineteenth- and twentieth-century);
  New York City literature; Hudson
  Valley literature

*Considers all literary and linguistic
  topics:* Yes
Languages published: English

SUBMISSION REQUIREMENTS

Initial contact: Letter, prospectus, and
  introductory chapter
Style: MLA; Chicago
Special requirements: Prefers photocopy
Subvention: No

EDITORIAL INFORMATION

*Manuscripts or proposals submitted each
  year:* 10 (estimate)
Manuscripts sent to readers each year: 5
  (estimate)
Manuscripts accepted each year: 2
Number of outside readers: 2
Author-anonymous submission: No
*Time between submission and publication
  decision:* 5 months
*Time between decision and return of copy-
  edited manuscript:* 2 months
Time between decision and publication: 8
  months

CONTRACT PROVISIONS

Copyright: Publisher
Royalty provisions: 10% of net on first
  2,500 copies, 12.5% on next 2,500, and
  15% thereafter

**PUBLICATION AND DISTRIBUTION
INFORMATION**

Forms of publication: Cloth, paper, elec-
  tronic media
Titles published each year: 3
Print run: 1,000-2,000
Number of review copies: 75
Distribution area: Worldwide
Time in print: Indefinitely

(98)
*SAMUEL FRENCH

45 West 25th St.
New York, NY 10010

Contact: Editorial Department
Established: 1830
Telephone: 212 206-8990
Fax: 212 206-1429

SCOPE

Publishing interests: Theater
Considers all literary and linguistic topics: No
Types of works not published: Dissertations; bibliographies; critical editions; collections of letters; biographies; readers; collections of essays; Festschriften; literary reference works
Languages published: English

SUBMISSION REQUIREMENTS

Initial contact: Full manuscript
Style: House
Subvention: No

EDITORIAL INFORMATION

Number of outside readers: 1
Time between submission and publication decision: 2-8 months
Time between decision and return of copyedited manuscript: 3 months
Time between decision and publication: 5 months

CONTRACT PROVISIONS

Copyright: Author
Royalty provisions: 10%

PUBLICATION AND DISTRIBUTION INFORMATION

Print run: 1,000

Number of review copies: 15
Distribution area: Worldwide
Time in print: Indefinitely

(99)
FRENCH FORUM PUBLISHERS

PO Box 130
Nicholasville, KY 40340

Contact: Raymond C. La Charité, Editor; Virginia A. La Charité, Editor
Established: 1976
Telephone: 606 885-1446
E-mail: rcl@ukcc.uky.edu

SCOPE

Publishing interests: French literature
Considers all literary and linguistic topics: No
Types of works not published: Unrevised dissertations; bibliographies; critical editions; collections of letters; biographies; readers; literary reference works
Languages published: English; French
Series title(s): French Forum Monographs; Edward C. Armstrong Monographs on Medieval Literature

SUBMISSION REQUIREMENTS

Initial contact: Letter and prospectus
Considers simultaneous submissions: No
Will issue contract on the basis of proposal, prospectus, and/or sample chapter: No
Style: MLA
Special requirements: Length: 250 pages maximum; requires electronic manuscript
Subvention: Yes

EDITORIAL INFORMATION

Manuscripts or proposals submitted each year: 30 +
Manuscripts sent to readers each year: 12 +
Manuscripts accepted each year: 2-3
Number of outside readers: 2
Author-anonymous submission: Yes
Time between submission and publication decision: 3 months
Time between decision and return of copy-edited manuscript: 4-6 months
Time between decision and publication: 6-9 months
Time allotted for reading proof: 1 month (maximum)

CONTRACT PROVISIONS

Copyright: Publisher
Royalty provisions: No royalties

PUBLICATION AND DISTRIBUTION INFORMATION

Forms of publication: Paper
Titles published each year: 4
Print run: 500
Number of review copies: 20-25
Distribution area: Worldwide
Time in print: Indefinitely

(100)
GALE RESEARCH

835 Penobscot Bldg.
Detroit, MI 48226

Imprint(s) and subsidiary firm(s): St. James Press
Contact: Christine Nasso, Director, New Publication Development
Established: 1954
Telephone: 313 961-2242
Fax: 313 961-6241

SCOPE

Publishing interests: Biographies of literary authors; literary reference works; American literature; British literature; African American literature; Hispanic literature; Native American literature; Asian literature; children's literature; literary criticism; science fiction; western American literature; mystery; romance fiction; fantasy fiction; horror fiction; folklore
Considers all literary and linguistic topics: Yes (literature); no (linguistics)
Types of works not published: Dissertations; bibliographies; critical editions; collections of letters; readers; Festschriften
Languages published: English

SUBMISSION REQUIREMENTS

Initial contact: Letter or letter and prospectus
Considers simultaneous submissions: Yes, if notified
Will issue contract on the basis of proposal, prospectus, and/or sample chapter: Yes
Style: Chicago
Special requirements: Typically requests electronic manuscript
Subvention: No

EDITORIAL INFORMATION

Number of outside readers: 3-6
Author-anonymous submission: Yes
Time between submission and publication decision: 3-4 months
Time between decision and return of copy-edited manuscript: 2-3 months
Time between decision and publication: 5-6 months
Time allotted for reading proof: 2-8 weeks

CONTRACT PROVISIONS

Copyright: Author (royalty contract); publisher (work for hire contract)
Royalty provisions: 10% for royalty contract

PUBLICATION AND DISTRIBUTION INFORMATION

Forms of publication: Cloth, paper, electronic media
Titles published each year: 50 (estimate)
Print run: Varies
Number of review copies: 50-100
Distribution area: Worldwide
Time in print: Indefinitely

Publishes reference books for public, school, and academic libraries and is interested primarily in titles for these markets; also interested in identifying qualified individuals to write or edit literary reference titles developed in-house

(101)
GARLAND PUBLISHING

717 Fifth Ave.
New York, NY 10022

Contact: Gary Kuris
Established: 1969
Telephone: 212 751-7447
Fax: 212 308-9399

SCOPE

Publishing interests: Native American studies; women's studies; medieval literature; Renaissance literature; African American literature; English literature; American literature; folklore
Considers all literary and linguistic topics: No

Types of works not published: Dissertations; bibliographies; Festschriften; concordances
Languages published: English
Series title(s): Garland Reference Library of the Humanities; Gender and Genre in Literature; Theorists of Myth; Origins of Modernism: Garland Studies in British Literature; Casebooks on Modern Dramatists; Garland Studies in Nineteenth-Century American Literature; Shakespeare Criticism; Garland Shakespeare Bibliographies; Garland Medieval Casebooks; Studies in Modern Drama; Latin American Studies; Wellesley Studies in Critical Theory, Literary History, and Culture; Literature and Society in Victorian Britain; Critical Studies in Black Life and Culture

SUBMISSION REQUIREMENTS

Initial contact: Letter and prospectus
Considers simultaneous submissions: No
Will issue contract on the basis of proposal, prospectus, and/or sample chapter: Sometimes
Style: Chicago
Special requirements: Usually requires camera-ready copy
Subvention: No

EDITORIAL INFORMATION

Manuscripts or proposals submitted each year: 300 (estimate)
Manuscripts sent to readers each year: 50
Manuscripts accepted each year: 100 (estimate)
Number of outside readers: 1-2
Author-anonymous submission: No
Time between submission and publication decision: 1-3 months
Time between decision and publication: 9-18 months

CONTRACT PROVISIONS

Copyright: Author
Royalty provisions: 10%

PUBLICATION AND DISTRIBUTION INFORMATION

Forms of publication: Cloth, paper
Titles published each year: 100
Print run: 500
Number of review copies: 5-10
Distribution area: Worldwide
Time in print: 3 years

(102)
GASLIGHT PUBLICATIONS

2809 Wilmington Way
Las Vegas, NV 89102-5989

Imprint(s) and subsidiary firm(s):
  McGuffin Books
Contact: Jack W. Tracy, Publisher
Established: 1979
Telephone: 702 221-8495
Fax: 702 221-8297

SCOPE

Publishing interests: Sherlock Holmes;
  Arthur Conan Doyle; mystery fiction
*Considers all literary and linguistic
  topics:* No
Types of works not published: Readers;
  collections of essays
Languages published: English

SUBMISSION REQUIREMENTS

Initial contact: Accepts outline and
  sample chapters; prefers complete
  manuscript
Considers simultaneous submissions: Yes
*Will issue contract on the basis of
  proposal, prospectus, and/or sample
  chapter:* Yes

Style: Chicago
Special requirements: Length: 12,000
  words minimum; does not accept dot-
  matrix printout or electronic manuscripts
Subvention: No

EDITORIAL INFORMATION

*Manuscripts or proposals submitted each
  year:* 15 (estimate)
Manuscripts sent to readers each year:
  10
Manuscripts accepted each year: 6
Number of outside readers: 0-4
Author-anonymous submission: No
*Time between submission and publication
  decision:* 1 month
*Time between decision and return of copy-
  edited manuscript:* 2-3 months
Time between decision and publication:
  1-2 years
Time allotted for reading proof: 1 month

CONTRACT PROVISIONS

Copyright: Author
Royalty provisions: 10% of net

PUBLICATION AND DISTRIBUTION INFORMATION

Forms of publication: Cloth, paper
Titles published each year: 3
Print run: 3,000-5,000
Number of review copies: 20-40
Distribution area: Worldwide
Time in print: 2-5 years

(103)
GEORGETOWN UNIVERSITY PRESS

3619 O St., NW
Washington, DC 20007

Contact: John Samples, Director
Established: 1966
Telephone: 202 687-5912
Fax: 202 687-6340
E-mail: samplesj@gusun.georgetown.edu

SCOPE

Publishing interests: Linguistics;
  Romance linguistics
*Considers all literary and linguistic
  topics:* No
Types of works not published: Bibliographies; biographies; collections of
  letters; Festschriften
Languages published: English; Romance
  languages; Arabic; Russian; Japanese
Series title(s): Georgetown Round Table
  on Languages and Linguistics

SUBMISSION REQUIREMENTS

Initial contact: Full manuscript or letter,
  outline, and sample chapters
Considers simultaneous submissions:
  Yes, if informed
*Will issue contract on the basis of
  proposal, prospectus, and/or sample
  chapter:* No
Style: MLA
Special requirements: Prefers not to
  receive dot-matrix printout
Subvention: No

EDITORIAL INFORMATION

Number of outside readers: 1-3
Author-anonymous submission: No
*Time between submission and publication
  decision:* 1-4 months
Time between decision and publication:
  1 year

CONTRACT PROVISIONS

Copyright: Negotiable
Royalty provisions: 10%

PUBLICATION AND DISTRIBUTION INFORMATION

Forms of publication: Cloth, paper
Titles published each year: 5
Print run: 500-2,000
Number of review copies: 15-25
Distribution area: Worldwide
Time in print: 5 years minimum

(104)
UNIVERSITY OF GEORGIA PRESS

330 Research Dr.
Athens, GA 30602-4901

Contact: Karen Orchard, Executive
  Editor; Nancy Grayson Holmes, Editor
Established: 1938
Telephone: 706 369-6130
Fax: 706 369-6131
E-mail: ugapress@uga.cc.uga.edu

SCOPE

Publishing interests: African American
  literature; folklore (especially American
  and southern American); American
  literature; southern American literature;
  multicultural studies; eighteenth-century
  studies (English and American); English
  literature; world literature; literary
  theory; medieval studies; Renaissance
  studies; American studies
*Considers all literary and linguistic
  topics:* Yes (literature); rarely
  (linguistics)
Types of works not published: Bibliographies; readers; Festschriften
Languages published: English
Series title(s): Chaucer Library

SUBMISSION REQUIREMENTS

Initial contact: Letter and prospectus
Considers simultaneous submissions: No

*Will issue contract on the basis of
proposal, prospectus, and/or sample
chapter:* Rarely
Style: Chicago
Special requirements: Does not accept
dot-matrix printout; prefers electronic
manuscripts
Subvention: Yes, for lengthy or complex
books

EDITORIAL INFORMATION

Manuscripts accepted each year: 25
Number of outside readers: 2
Author-anonymous submission: No
*Time between submission and publication
decision:* 4-6 months
*Time between decision and return of copy-
edited manuscript:* 2-3 months
Time between decision and publication:
12-14 months

CONTRACT PROVISIONS

Copyright: Negotiable

**PUBLICATION AND DISTRIBUTION
INFORMATION**

Forms of publication: Cloth, paper
Titles published each year: 38
Print run: 800-1,500
Distribution area: Worldwide
Time in print: 10 years

**(105)
GILL & MACMILLAN**

Goldenbridge
Inchicore
Dublin 8, Ireland

Contact: Fergal Tobin, General and
Academic Editor
Established: 1968
Telephone: (01) 4531005

Fax: (01) 4549813

SCOPE

Publishing interests: Irish literature; Irish
folklore; James Joyce; Samuel Beckett;
W. B. Yeats
*Considers all literary and linguistic
topics:* No
Types of works not published: Bibli-
ographies; critical editions; collections
of letters; readers; collections of essays;
Festschriften; literary handbooks;
literary encyclopedias
Languages published: English
Series title(s): Gill's Studies in Irish
Literature

SUBMISSION REQUIREMENTS

Initial contact: Letter, outline, and sample
chapter
Considers simultaneous submissions: Yes
*Will issue contract on the basis of
proposal, prospectus, and/or sample
chapter:* Yes
Style: House
Special requirements: Length: 110,000
words maximum; accepts photocopies,
camera-ready copy, dot-matrix printout,
and electronic manuscripts; provides
guidelines for manuscript preparation
Subvention: Usually not

EDITORIAL INFORMATION

*Manuscripts or proposals submitted each
year:* 40 (estimate)
Manuscripts sent to readers each year: 6
(estimate)
Manuscripts accepted each year: 10
Number of outside readers: 1
Author-anonymous submission: No
*Time between submission and publication
decision:* 2 months
*Time between decision and return of copy-
edited manuscript:* 30 months

Time between decision and publication:
  1 year
Time allotted for reading proof: 3-4
  weeks

CONTRACT PROVISIONS

Copyright: Author
Royalty provisions: 8% of list on first
  impression, 10% thereafter (cloth); 15%
  of net (paper)

**PUBLICATION AND DISTRIBUTION
INFORMATION**

Forms of publication: Cloth, paper
Titles published each year: 3
Print run: 1,000
Number of review copies: 50
Distribution area: Worldwide (except for
  North America)
Time in print: 3 years

Literary criticism is a small but growing
part of the publisher's list.

**(106)
UNIVERSITY OF GLASGOW
FRENCH AND GERMAN
PUBLICATIONS**

Modern Languages Bldg.
University Gardens
Glasgow G12 8QL, Scotland

Contact: Geoff Woollen (French); Mark
  Ward (German)
Established: 1988
Telephone: (041) 339-8855, ext. 6343
  (French); (041) 339-8855, ext. 4599
  (German)
Fax: (041) 330-4234

SCOPE

Publishing interests: French literature;
  German literature (including
  Festschriften and conference
  proceedings)
*Considers all literary and linguistic
  topics:* Yes
Types of works not published: Bibli-
  ographies; literary encyclopedias
Languages published: English; French
Series title(s): Glasgow Introductory
  Guides to French Literature; Glasgow
  Introductory Guides to German
  Literature

SUBMISSION REQUIREMENTS

Restrictions on authors: Prefers native
  English speakers
Initial contact: Letter, outline, and sample
  chapter
Considers simultaneous submissions: No
*Will issue contract on the basis of
  proposal, prospectus, and/or sample
  chapter:* No
Style: Modern Humanities Research
  Association
Special requirements: Expects electronic
  manuscript or camera-ready copy
Subvention: Yes (repaid from sales)

EDITORIAL INFORMATION

*Manuscripts or proposals submitted each
  year:* 6 (estimate)
Manuscripts sent to readers each year: 4
Manuscripts accepted each year: 4
Number of outside readers: 1
Author-anonymous submission: No
*Time between submission and publication
  decision:* 1 month
*Time between decision and return of copy-
  edited manuscript:* 6 months
Time between decision and publication:
  1 year
Time allotted for reading proof: 1 month

CONTRACT PROVISIONS

Copyright: Publisher
Royalty provisions: No royalties

PUBLICATION AND DISTRIBUTION INFORMATION

Forms of publication: Paper
Titles published each year: 8
Print run: 200
Number of review copies: 6
Distribution area: Worldwide
Time in print: 5 years

Volumes in both Introductory Guides series are commissioned.

(107) GOLDSMITH PRESS

Newbridge, Ireland

Contact: Bernadette Smyth
Established: 1972
Telephone: (045) 33613
Fax: (045) 32283

SCOPE

Publishing interests: Irish literature
Considers all literary and linguistic topics: Yes (literary topics)
Languages published: English

SUBMISSION REQUIREMENTS

Initial contact: Letter of inquiry
Will issue contract on the basis of proposal, prospectus, and/or sample chapter: No
Style: House
Special requirements: Prefers camera-ready copy or electronic manuscripts
Subvention: No

EDITORIAL INFORMATION

Manuscripts or proposals submitted each year: 45 (estimate)
Manuscripts sent to readers each year: 20 (estimate)
Manuscripts accepted each year: 10
Number of outside readers: 1-2
Author-anonymous submission: No
Time between submission and publication decision: 1 month
Time between decision and return of copy-edited manuscript: 6 months
Time between decision and publication: 9 months
Time allotted for reading proof: 2 weeks

CONTRACT PROVISIONS

Copyright: Author
Royalty provisions: 10%

PUBLICATION AND DISTRIBUTION INFORMATION

Forms of publication: Cloth, paper
Titles published each year: 10
Print run: 1,000-2,000
Number of review copies: 40
Distribution area: Worldwide
Time in print: Indefinitely

(108) GRAMMALEA

Calle Eusebio Gonzalez Suarez, 36, 2-20
47014 Valladolid, Spain

Contact: Anselmo Rosales, Editor
Established: 1993
Telephone: (83) 401391
E-mail: blasco@cpd.uva.es

SCOPE

Publishing interests: Literary theory; Spanish literature; comparative

literature; cultural criticism; critical editions; bibliographies; literary reference works; conference proceedings; genre studies
Considers all literary and linguistic topics: Yes
Types of works not published: Unrevised dissertations
Languages published: Spanish; English

SUBMISSION REQUIREMENTS

Initial contact: Letter, table of contents, and summary
Considers simultaneous submissions: Yes, if notified
Will issue contract on the basis of proposal, prospectus, and/or sample chapter: No
Style: MLA; house
Subvention: No

EDITORIAL INFORMATION

Manuscripts or proposals submitted each year: 75
Manuscripts sent to readers each year: 25
Manuscripts accepted each year: 1
Number of outside readers: 2
Author-anonymous submission: Yes
Time between submission and publication decision: 4 months
Time between decision and publication: 1 year
Time allotted for reading proof: 1 month

CONTRACT PROVISIONS

Copyright: Author and publisher
Royalty provisions: Negotiable

PUBLICATION AND DISTRIBUTION INFORMATION

Forms of publication: Cloth, paper, electronic media
Titles published each year: 6
Print run: 1,000

Number of review copies: 25
Distribution area: Worldwide
Time in print: 5 years

Grammalea is especially interested in serving as a bridge between conventional means of publication and the new possibilities offered by electronic media.

(109)
*EDITORIAL GREDOS

Sánchez Pacheco, 81
28002 Madrid, Spain

Contact: Julio Calonge Ruiz; Pilar García Mouton
Established: 1944
Telephone: (91) 4157408
Fax: (91) 5192033

SCOPE

Publishing interests: Spanish literature; Spanish language; linguistics; classical studies; lexicography
Types of works not published: Collections of letters; biographies
Languages published: Spanish
Series title(s): Biblioteca románica hispánica; Biblioteca clásica Gredos

SUBMISSION REQUIREMENTS

Initial contact: Letter or letter and table of contents
Special requirements: Accepts electronic manuscripts (IBM-compatible)
Subvention: No

EDITORIAL INFORMATION

Manuscripts or proposals submitted each year: 50 (estimate)
Manuscripts sent to readers each year: 40 (estimate)

Manuscripts accepted each year: 31
Number of outside readers: 2
Time between submission and publication decision: 2-3 months
Time between decision and return of copy-edited manuscript: 8-12 months
Time between decision and publication: 12-18 months

CONTRACT PROVISIONS

Copyright: Author and publisher
Royalty provisions: 10%

PUBLICATION AND DISTRIBUTION INFORMATION

Forms of publication: Paper
Titles published each year: 18 (estimate)
Number of review copies: 50
Distribution area: Worldwide

(110)
GREENWOOD PUBLISHING GROUP

88 Post Road West
PO Box 5007
Westport, CT 06881-9990

Imprint(s) and subsidiary firm(s):
  Greenwood Press; Praeger Publishers
Contact: George Butler, Associate Editor (literature, drama, reference books); Nina Pearlstein, Editor (humanities)
Established: Greenwood (1967), Praeger (1950)
Telephone: 203 226-3571
Fax: 203 222-1502

SCOPE

Publishing interests: General literature; women's studies; children's literature; popular literature; periodicals; drama; theater; multicultural studies; gay and lesbian studies; critical theory. Especially interested in reference books and in broad approaches to national literatures, periods, movements, genres, regional and ethnic literatures.
Considers all literary and linguistic topics: Yes
Types of works not published: Festschriften; collections of previously published essays
Languages published: English
Series title(s): Contributions to the Study of World Literature; Contributions to the Study of Science Fiction and Fantasy; Bibliographies and Indexes in American Literature; Bibliographies and Indexes in World Literature; Bibliographies and Indexes in Afro-American and African Studies; Critical Responses in Arts and Letters; Landmarks of American Jewish Thought and Letters; Contributions in American Studies; Contributions in Afro-American and African Studies (including a subseries, Contemporary Black Poets); Contributions in Women's Studies; Contributions to the Study of Popular Culture; Movements in the Arts; Contributions in Drama and Theatre Studies (including a subseries, Lives of the Theatre); Contributions in Ethnic Studies; Modern Dramatists Research and Production Source Books; Historical Guides to the World's Periodicals and Newspapers; Bio-bibliographies in the Performing Arts; Bio-bibliographies in American Literature; Bio-bibliographies in World Literature

SUBMISSION REQUIREMENTS

Initial contact: Letter and prospectus or letter, outline, and sample chapter; provides guidelines for preparing a prospectus for a reference book
Style: MLA; Chicago

Special requirements: Length: prefers
60,000-100,000 words for monographs,
150,000-210,000 words for reference
books depending on topic; accepts electronic manuscripts; requires camera-
ready copy for bibliographies, highly
specialized studies, or lengthy manuscripts; provides guidelines for camera-
ready manuscript preparation
Subvention: No

EDITORIAL INFORMATION

*Manuscripts or proposals submitted each
year:* 125 (estimate)
Manuscripts sent to readers each year: 60
(estimate)
Manuscripts accepted each year: 40
(estimate)
Number of outside readers: 1-2
*Time between submission and publication
decision:* 1-3 months
*Time between decision and return of copy-
edited manuscript:* 3 months
Time between decision and publication:
6-12 months

CONTRACT PROVISIONS

Copyright: Author

**PUBLICATION AND DISTRIBUTION
INFORMATION**

Forms of publication: Cloth, paper
Titles published each year: 55 (estimate)
Number of review copies: 30-50
Distribution area: Worldwide
Time in print: Indefinitely

**(111)
JULIUS GROOS VERLAG**

Postfach 102423
69044 Heidelberg, Germany

Contact: D. Wolff
Established: 1804
Telephone: (06221) 303621
Fax: (06221) 301993
E-mail: http://www.geist.spacenet.de

SCOPE

Publishing interests: Languages;
descriptive linguistics
*Considers all literary and linguistic
topics:* No
Types of works not published: Bibliographies; collections of letters;
biographies; collections of essays;
literary handbooks; literary encyclopedias
Series title(s): Studies in Descriptive
Linguistics; Deutsch im Kontrast;
Beihefte zur Zeitschrift
Hörgeschädigtenpädagogik; Sinolin-
guistica; Beihefte zu TextconText;
Deutsch und Japanisch im Kontrast;
Sammlung Groos; Studienbiblio-
graphien Sprachwissenschaft

SUBMISSION REQUIREMENTS

Initial contact: Letter and full manuscript
Considers simultaneous submissions: No
*Will issue contract on the basis of
proposal, prospectus, and/or sample
chapter:* No
Style: MLA
Special requirements: Requires camera-
ready copy and electronic manuscripts
Subvention: Yes

EDITORIAL INFORMATION

*Manuscripts or proposals submitted each
year:* 45 (estimate)
Manuscripts sent to readers each year: 25
(estimate)
Manuscripts accepted each year: 16
Number of outside readers: 2
Author-anonymous submission: No

Time between submission and publication decision: 2 months
Time between decision and return of copy-edited manuscript: 3 months
Time between decision and publication: 6 months
Time allotted for reading proof: 2-4 weeks

CONTRACT PROVISIONS

Copyright: Publisher
Royalty provisions: 5-7% of list

PUBLICATION AND DISTRIBUTION INFORMATION

Forms of publication: Cloth, paper, electronic media
Titles published each year: 20
Print run: 300-10,000
Number of review copies: 100
Distribution area: Worldwide
Time in print: 10-15 years

**(112)
GUILFORD PRESS**

72 Spring St.
New York, NY 10012

Contact: Peter Wissoker, Acquisitions Editor
Established: 1978
Telephone: 212 431-9800
Fax: 212 966-6708

SCOPE

Publishing interests: Cultural studies; postcolonial studies; colonial studies; communication; rhetoric
Considers all literary and linguistic topics: No
Types of works not published: Bibliographies; Festschriften

Languages published: English

SUBMISSION REQUIREMENTS

Initial contact: Letter, prospectus, sample chapter(s), and curriculum vitae
Considers simultaneous submissions: Yes
Will issue contract on the basis of proposal, prospectus, and/or sample chapter: Yes
Style: American Psychological Association
Special requirements: Requires electronic copy
Subvention: No

EDITORIAL INFORMATION

Manuscripts or proposals submitted each year: 10
Manuscripts sent to readers each year: 3
Manuscripts accepted each year: 2
Number of outside readers: 2-3
Author-anonymous submission: No
Time between submission and publication decision: 3 months
Time between decision and publication: 7 months
Time allotted for reading proof: 2 weeks

CONTRACT PROVISIONS

Copyright: Publisher (typically)
Royalty provisions: Varies

PUBLICATION AND DISTRIBUTION INFORMATION

Forms of publication: Cloth, paper
Titles published each year: 2
Print run: 2,000-3,000
Number of review copies: 75
Distribution area: Worldwide
Time in print: Indefinitely

(113)
*G. K. HALL

866 Third Ave.
New York, NY 10022

Contact: Catherine E. Carter
Telephone: 212 702-9852
Fax: 212 605-9368

PUBLICATION AND DISTRIBUTION
INFORMATION

Not acquiring new projects at this time.

(114)
*EDITIONS L'HARMATTAN

7, rue de l'Ecole Polytechnique
75005 Paris, France

Contact: Denis Pryen, Gérant; Alix
Willaert, Secrétaire d'Edition
Established: 1975
Telephone: (1) 43547910
Fax: (1) 43258203

SCOPE

Publishing interests: African literature
(both black African and Arabic
literatures); Middle Eastern literature;
Latin American literature; Caribbean
literature; Asian literature
Languages published: French
Series title(s): Collection critiques
littéraires

SUBMISSION REQUIREMENTS

Initial contact: Letter, outline, and manuscript
Subvention: No

EDITORIAL INFORMATION

*Manuscripts or proposals submitted each
year:* 750
Manuscripts accepted each year: 75
Number of outside readers: 3
*Time between submission and publication
decision:* 6-8 weeks
*Time between decision and return of copy-
edited manuscript:* 2 months
Time between decision and publication: 6
months

CONTRACT PROVISIONS

Copyright: Publisher
Royalty provisions: No royalties for first
1,000 copies, 7% on next 2,000, 10%
thereafter

PUBLICATION AND DISTRIBUTION
INFORMATION

Forms of publication: Paper
Titles published each year: 75
Number of review copies: 40
Distribution area: Europe; Africa;
Canada
Time in print: Indefinitely

(115)
HARRASSOWITZ VERLAG

Postfach 2929
65019 Wiesbaden, Germany

Contact: Michael Langfeld
Established: 1872
Telephone: (0611) 5300
Fax: (0611) 530570

SCOPE

Publishing interests: Oriental studies;
linguistics; publishing; book trade;
Slavic studies

*Considers all literary and linguistic
topics:* No
Types of works not published: Unrevised
dissertations; collections of letters;
biographies
Languages published: German; English;
French
Series title(s): Asiatische Forschungen;
Semitica Viva; Slavistische Studien-
bücher; Opera Slavica; Beiträge zum
Buch- und Bibliothekswesen; Turco-
logica; Göttinger Orientforschungen;
Khoj: A Series of Modern South Asian
Studies; Porta Linguarum Orientalium;
Wolfenbütteler Schriften zur Geschichte
des Buchwesens; Wolfenbütteler
Forschungen; Wolfenbütteler Arbeiten
zur Barockforschung; Mediterranean
Language and Culture Monograph
Series; Beiträge zum Büchereiwesen;
Wolfenbütteler Abhandlungen zur
Renaissanceforschung; Wolfenbütteler
Mittelalter-Studien

SUBMISSION REQUIREMENTS

Initial contact: Letter of inquiry
Considers simultaneous submissions: No
*Will issue contract on the basis of
proposal, prospectus, and/or sample
chapter:* No
Subvention: Generally

EDITORIAL INFORMATION

*Manuscripts or proposals submitted each
year:* 30 (estimate)
Manuscripts accepted each year: 10
(estimate)
Number of outside readers: 0
*Time between submission and publication
decision:* 1-6 weeks
*Time between decision and return of copy-
edited manuscript:* 3-10 months
Time between decision and publication:
3-10 months

CONTRACT PROVISIONS

Copyright: Publisher
Royalty provisions: Usually does not pay
royalties

PUBLICATION AND DISTRIBUTION INFORMATION

Forms of publication: Paper
Titles published each year: 40-50
(estimate)
Print run: 300
Number of review copies: 15
Distribution area: Worldwide
Time in print: Indefinitely

(116)
HARVARD UNIVERSITY PRESS

Editorial Department
79 Garden St.
Cambridge, MA 02138-1499

Imprint(s) and subsidiary firm(s):
Belknap Press
Contact: Lindsay Waters, Executive
Editor for the Humanities (literary
criticism, cultural studies, philosophy)
Established: 1913
Telephone: 617 495-2611
Fax: 617 496-4677
E-mail: lwaters@harvarda.harvard.edu

SCOPE

Publishing interests: General literature;
critical movements; biography;
women's studies; cultural studies;
philosophy of language; linguistics;
African American studies; ethnic
studies; gay and lesbian studies
*Considers all literary and linguistic
topics:* Yes
Types of works not published: Unrevised
dissertations; Festschriften;

bibliographies; collections of essays by different authors

Prizes and competitions: Thomas J. Wilson Prize (best first book of a young author)
Languages published: English
Series title(s): Harvard English Studies

SUBMISSION REQUIREMENTS

Initial contact: Letter, outline, sample chapter, and curriculum vitae
Considers simultaneous submissions: Yes
Will issue contract on the basis of proposal, prospectus, and/or sample chapter: No
Style: Chicago; house
Special requirements: Length: prefers 400 pages (including notes) maximum; requires electronic manuscript; does not accept dot-matrix printout; provides guidelines for manuscript preparation
Subvention: No

EDITORIAL INFORMATION

Manuscripts or proposals submitted each year: 200 (estimate)
Manuscripts sent to readers each year: 20
Manuscripts accepted each year: 15 (estimate)
Number of outside readers: 2
Author-anonymous submission: No
Time between submission and publication decision: 6-12 weeks
Time between decision and return of copy-edited manuscript: 2-3 months
Time between decision and publication: 10-14 months
Time allotted for reading proof: 3 weeks

CONTRACT PROVISIONS

Copyright: Publisher (usually)
Royalty provisions: 10% of net on first 5,000, 12.5% on next 10,000, 15% thereafter (cloth); 10% of net (paper)

PUBLICATION AND DISTRIBUTION INFORMATION

Forms of publication: Cloth, paper, electronic media
Titles published each year: 18
Print run: 1,500-3,000
Number of review copies: 40-100
Distribution area: Worldwide
Time in print: 5-20 years

(117)
UNIVERSITY OF HAWAII PRESS

2840 Kolowalu St.
Honolulu, HI 96822

Imprint(s) and subsidiary firm(s): Kolowalu Books
Contact: Iris Wiley, Executive Editor (children's literature, mythology, Hawaiiana); Sharon F. Yamamoto, Editor (literature in translation, literary theory, biography, comparative literature, and East Asian literatures); Pamela Kelley, Editor (Pacific and Southeast Asian studies)
Established: 1947
Telephone: 808 956-8694
Fax: 808 988-6052

SCOPE

Publishing interests: Asian literature; Pacific-area literature; Asian American studies; comparative literature
Considers all literary and linguistic topics: No
Types of works not published: Unrevised dissertations; Festschriften; readers; literary encyclopedias; literary handbooks; critical editions
Languages published: English
Series title(s): Biography Monographs; Culture Learning Institute Monographs; Institute for Polynesian Studies

Monographs; Literary Studies: East and West; Oceanic Linguistics Special Publications; Pali Language Texts; Pacific Poetry Series; Talanoa: Contemporary Pacific Literature

SUBMISSION REQUIREMENTS

Initial contact: Letter and prospectus
Style: Chicago
Special requirements: Prefers electronic manuscripts; provides guidelines for manuscript preparation
Subvention: Only for exceptionally long or extensively illustrated manuscripts

EDITORIAL INFORMATION

Manuscripts or proposals submitted each year: 120 (estimate)
Manuscripts sent to readers each year: 40 (estimate)
Manuscripts accepted each year: 13
Number of outside readers: 2 minimum
Author-anonymous submission: No
Time between submission and publication decision: 6 months
Time between decision and return of copyedited manuscript: 4 months
Time between decision and publication: 1 year

CONTRACT PROVISIONS

Copyright: Publisher
Royalty provisions: No royalties for first 1,500 copies, 10% on next 8,500, 12.5% on next 10,000, and 15% thereafter

PUBLICATION AND DISTRIBUTION INFORMATION

Forms of publication: Cloth, paper
Titles published each year: 13
Print run: 2,000
Number of review copies: 25
Distribution area: Worldwide

Time in print: 8 years minimum

(118)
HEMINGWAY WESTERN STUDIES SERIES

Hemingway Western Studies Center
Boise State University
Boise, ID 83725

Contact: Tom Trusky, Editor
Established: 1986
Telephone: 208 385-1999
Fax: 208 385-4373
E-mail: rentrusk@idbsu.idbsu.edu

SCOPE

Publishing interests: Issues of interest to Rocky Mountain readership (including environment, gender, race, and religion)
Considers all literary and linguistic topics: No
Prizes and competitions: National Artists/Eccentrics Book Competition
Languages published: English; considers Spanish, Basque, and Native American languages

SUBMISSION REQUIREMENTS

Initial contact: Request guidelines from editor
Considers simultaneous submissions: Yes
Will issue contract on the basis of proposal, prospectus, and/or sample chapter: No
Special requirements: Request guidelines from editor
Subvention: No

EDITORIAL INFORMATION

Manuscripts or proposals submitted each year: 50
Manuscripts sent to readers each year: 50

Manuscripts accepted each year: 1
Number of outside readers: 8
Author-anonymous submission: No
*Time between submission and publication
decision:* 8 months
*Time between decision and return of copy-
edited manuscript:* 3 months
Time between decision and publication:
9-18 months
Time allotted for reading proof: 1 month

CONTRACT PROVISIONS

Copyright: Author
Royalty provisions: 12%

**PUBLICATION AND DISTRIBUTION
INFORMATION**

Forms of publication: Cloth, paper, elec-
tronic media
Titles published each year: 1
Print run: 1,000
Distribution area: United States
Time in print: Indefinitely

**(119)
HERMAGORAS PRESS**

PO Box 1555
Davis, CA 95617

Contact: James J. Murphy, Publisher
Established: 1983
Telephone: 916 753-1222
Fax: 916 756-0227

SCOPE

Publishing interests: Rhetoric; composition; rhetorical criticism; history of
rhetoric; language use; oratory
*Considers all literary and linguistic
topics:* Yes, if related to language use

Types of works not published: Collections
of letters; biographies; Festschriften;
textbooks
Languages published: English
Series title(s): Landmark Essays

SUBMISSION REQUIREMENTS

Initial contact: Letter with preface and
outline
Considers simultaneous submissions: No
*Will issue contract on the basis of
proposal, prospectus, and/or sample
chapter:* Yes
Style: Chicago
Subvention: No

EDITORIAL INFORMATION

*Manuscripts or proposals submitted each
year:* 8
Manuscripts sent to readers each year: 3
Manuscripts accepted each year: 3
Number of outside readers: 1-3
Author-anonymous submission: Yes
*Time between submission and publication
decision:* 3 months
*Time between decision and return of copy-
edited manuscript:* 6 months
Time between decision and publication: 8
months
Time allotted for reading proof: 2 weeks

CONTRACT PROVISIONS

Copyright: Publisher
Royalty provisions: 5% of net

**PUBLICATION AND DISTRIBUTION
INFORMATION**

Forms of publication: Cloth, paper
Titles published each year: 9
Print run: 400 cloth; 2,000 paper
Number of review copies: 25
Distribution area: United States; Canada
Time in print: Indefinitely

(120)
HOLLAND UNIVERSITY PRESS

Postbus 122
3600 AC Maarssen, Netherlands

Established: 1972
Telephone: (31) 30 436166

SCOPE

Publishing interests: Historical
  linguistics; literary history; oriental
  languages
*Considers all literary and linguistic
  topics:* No
Languages published: Western European
  languages

SUBMISSION REQUIREMENTS

Initial contact: Letter of inquiry
Considers simultaneous submissions: No
*Will issue contract on the basis of
  proposal, prospectus, and/or sample
  chapter:* No
Style: House
Subvention: Yes

EDITORIAL INFORMATION

Author-anonymous submission: No
*Time between submission and publication
  decision:* 6 months
Time between decision and publication:
  1 year
Time allotted for reading proof: 1 month

CONTRACT PROVISIONS

Copyright: Publisher
Royalty provisions: None on first edition

PUBLICATION AND DISTRIBUTION
INFORMATION

Forms of publication: Cloth, paper
Titles published each year: 4

Number of review copies: 25
Distribution area: Worldwide
Time in print: Indefinitely

(121)
HOLMES AND MEIER PUBLISHERS

160 Broadway
New York, NY 10038

Imprint(s) and subsidiary firm(s):
  Africana Publishing Co.
Contact: Miriam Holmes, Managing
  Director
Established: 1969
Telephone: 212 374-0100
Fax: 212 374-1313

SCOPE

Publishing interests: European literature;
  women's studies; gender studies;
  African literature; Latin American
  literature; Judaism; Holocaust studies;
  ethnic literature; society and literature;
  politics and literature; critical editions;
  film studies; biography (literary); bibli-
  ographies
*Considers all literary and linguistic
  topics:* No
Types of works not published: Disser-
  tations
Languages published: English
Series title(s): Women and Literature
  Series; Writers and Politics Series; Latin
  America in Its Literature Series;
  Contexts of English Literature Series;
  Stratford-upon-Avon Studies; Modern
  German Voices; French Expressions;
  New Perspectives: Jewish Life and
  Thought

SUBMISSION REQUIREMENTS

Initial contact: Letter, prospectus or
  outline, and curriculum vitae

Considers simultaneous submissions:
  Prefers single submission
Will issue contract on the basis of
  proposal, prospectus, and/or sample
  chapter: Rarely
Style: Chicago
Subvention: Not always

EDITORIAL INFORMATION

Manuscripts or proposals submitted each
  year: 55 (estimate)
Manuscripts sent to readers each year: 5
  (estimate)
Manuscripts accepted each year: 3
Number of outside readers: 1-2
Author-anonymous submission: No
Time between submission and publication
  decision: 2-6 months
Time between decision and publication:
  6-18 months
Time allotted for reading proof: 2-5
  weeks

CONTRACT PROVISIONS

Copyright: Publisher

PUBLICATION AND DISTRIBUTION
INFORMATION

Forms of publication: Cloth, paper
Titles published each year: 2
Print run: Varies
Number of review copies: 10-100
Distribution area: Worldwide
Time in print: 3-10 years

Generally more interested in literary
history than in literary criticism

(122)
UNIVERSITY OF HULL PRESS

The University of Hull
Cottingham Rd.
Hull HU6 7RX, England

Contact: J. M. Smith, Assistant Registrar
Established: 1970
Telephone: (01482) 465322
Fax: (01482) 465936

SCOPE

Publishing interests: General literature;
  modern languages
Considers all literary and linguistic
  topics: Yes
Types of works not published: Disser-
  tations; bibliographies; critical editions;
  literary reference works
Languages published: English
Series title(s): Monographs in Modern
  Languages

SUBMISSION REQUIREMENTS

Initial contact: No preference
Style: House
Special requirements: Prefers electronic
  manuscripts
Subvention: If possible

EDITORIAL INFORMATION

Manuscripts or proposals submitted each
  year: 5 (estimate)
Manuscripts sent to readers each year: 3
  (estimate)
Manuscripts accepted each year: 2
Number of outside readers: 1
Author-anonymous submission: No
Time between submission and publication
  decision: 3 months
Time between decision and return of copy-
  edited manuscript: 3 months

Time between decision and publication:
  10 months

CONTRACT PROVISIONS

Copyright: Publisher

PUBLICATION AND DISTRIBUTION
INFORMATION

Forms of publication: Cloth, paper
Titles published each year: 2
Print run: 750
Number of review copies: 15
Distribution area: Worldwide
Time in print: 5 years

(123)
HUMANITIES PRESS
INTERNATIONAL

165 First Ave.
Atlantic Highlands, NJ 07716

Contact: Keith M. Ashfield, Publisher
Established: 1952
Telephone: 201 872-1441
Fax: 201 872-0717

SCOPE

Publishing interests: Literary theory
  (modern period to present); philosophy
  and literary theory
*Considers all literary and linguistic
  topics:* No
Types of works not published: Disser-
  tations; bibliographies; critical editions;
  collections of letters; biographies;
  Festschriften; literary handbooks;
  literary encyclopedias
Languages published: English
Series title(s): Philosophy and Literary
  Theory; Contemporary Studies in
  Philosophy and the Human Sciences

SUBMISSION REQUIREMENTS

Initial contact: Letter, prospectus, intro-
  ductory chapter, and curriculum vitae
Considers simultaneous submissions: No
*Will issue contract on the basis of
  proposal, prospectus, and/or sample
  chapter:* Rarely
Style: Chicago
Special requirements: Length restrictions;
  requires electronic manuscript
Subvention: No

EDITORIAL INFORMATION

*Manuscripts or proposals submitted each
  year:* 150 (estimate)
Manuscripts sent to readers each year: 20
  (estimate)
Manuscripts accepted each year: 10
  (estimate)
Number of outside readers: 2-3
Author-anonymous submission: Yes
*Time between submission and publication
  decision:* 3 months
*Time between decision and return of copy-
  edited manuscript:* 6 weeks
Time between decision and publication:
  1 year
Time allotted for reading proof: 1 month

CONTRACT PROVISIONS

Copyright: Author
Royalty provisions: 8-10% (cloth); 6-
  7.5% (paper)

PUBLICATION AND DISTRIBUTION
INFORMATION

Forms of publication: Cloth, paper
Titles published each year: 15 (estimate)
Print run: 1,000
Number of review copies: 50
Distribution area: Worldwide
Time in print: 5-7 years

(124)
HUNTINGTON LIBRARY PRESS

1151 Oxford Rd.
San Marino, CA 91108

Contact: Peggy Park Bernal, Publications
Director
Established: 1929
Telephone: 818 405-2038
Fax: 818 405-0225
E-mail: hlq@hss.caltech.uds

SCOPE

Publishing interests: American literature
(sixteenth-, seventeenth-, and eighteenth-century); English literature
(sixteenth-, seventeenth-, and eighteenth-century); western American
literature; topics related to the library's
collections
*Considers all literary and linguistic
topics:* No
Types of works not published: Readers;
literary handbooks
Languages published: English

SUBMISSION REQUIREMENTS

Initial contact: Letter of inquiry,
prospectus, outline, and sample chapter;
welcomes appointments from scholars
working at the Huntington Library
Considers simultaneous submissions:
Yes, if informed
*Will issue contract on the basis of
proposal, prospectus, and/or sample
chapter:* No
Style: Chicago
Special requirements: Expects electronic
manuscript
Subvention: No

EDITORIAL INFORMATION

*Manuscripts or proposals submitted each
year:* 8 (estimate)
Manuscripts sent to readers each year: 5
(estimate)
Manuscripts accepted each year: 3
(estimate)
Number of outside readers: 2
Author-anonymous submission: Yes
*Time between submission and publication
decision:* 6 months
*Time between decision and return of copy-
edited manuscript:* 1 year
Time between decision and publication:
18 months
Time allotted for reading proof: 6 weeks

CONTRACT PROVISIONS

Copyright: Publisher
Royalty provisions: No royalties

PUBLICATION AND DISTRIBUTION
INFORMATION

Forms of publication: Cloth, paper
Titles published each year: 4
Print run: 1,000
Number of review copies: 25
Distribution area: Worldwide
Time in print: Indefinitely

Essentially publishes only works based on
research in the library's collections

(125)
UNIVERSITY OF IDAHO PRESS

16 Brink Hall
University of Idaho
Moscow, ID 83844-1107

Contact: Peggy Pace, Director
Established: 1972
Telephone: 800 847-7377

Fax: 208 885-9059
E-mail: uipress@uidaho.edu

SCOPE

Publishing interests: Western American
literature; western American folklore;
Native American literature; Native
American languages; linguistics (Native
American); Vardis Fisher; H. L. Davis;
Ernest Hemingway; David Lavender
*Considers all literary and linguistic
topics:* No
Types of works not published: Unrevised
dissertations; Festschriften
Languages published: English
Series title(s): Idaho Yesterdays and
Northwest Folklife Series

SUBMISSION REQUIREMENTS

Initial contact: Letter, prospectus, and
curriculum vitae or letter, outline,
sample chapter, and curriculum vitae
Considers simultaneous submissions: Yes
*Will issue contract on the basis of
proposal, prospectus, and/or sample
chapter:* Yes
Style: Chicago
Special requirements: Requires electronic
manuscript; provides guidelines for
manuscript preparation
Subvention: No

EDITORIAL INFORMATION

*Manuscripts or proposals submitted each
year:* 20 (estimate)
Manuscripts sent to readers each year: 3
(estimate)
Manuscripts accepted each year: 1
(estimate)
Number of outside readers: 1-3
Author-anonymous submission: No
*Time between submission and publication
decision:* 6-8 months

*Time between decision and return of copy-
edited manuscript:* 3 months
Time between decision and publication:
18 months
Time allotted for reading proof: 3-4
weeks

CONTRACT PROVISIONS

Copyright: Publisher (unless author
requests)
Royalty provisions: 7-10% of net

PUBLICATION AND DISTRIBUTION
INFORMATION

Forms of publication: Cloth, paper
Titles published each year: 2
Print run: 750
Number of review copies: 20
Distribution area: United States; Europe
Time in print: 5 years

(126)
UNIVERSITY OF ILLINOIS PRESS

1325 South Oak
Champaign, IL 61820-6993

Contact: Ann Lowry, Senior Editor
Established: 1918
Telephone: 217 244-6856
Fax: 217 244-8082
E-mail: alowry@ux1.cso.uiuc.edu

SCOPE

Publishing interests: Literary theory;
critical theory; cultural studies; feminist
studies in literature; American literature
(modern and contemporary); English
literature (modern and contemporary);
African American literature; psychoanalysis and literature; critical theory
and pedagogy; Renaissance literature;

English as an international language;
film studies
*Considers all literary and linguistic
topics:* Depends on topic
Types of works not published:
Festschriften
Prizes and competitions: Illinois-NWSA
Book Award (for a book in women's
studies)
Languages published: English
Series title(s): English in the Global
Context

SUBMISSION REQUIREMENTS

Initial contact: Letter and prospectus
Style: Chicago; MLA
Subvention: Sometimes

EDITORIAL INFORMATION

*Manuscripts or proposals submitted each
year:* Several hundred (estimate)
Manuscripts sent to readers each year:
100 (estimate)
Manuscripts accepted each year: 25
(estimate)
Number of outside readers: 1 minimum
Author-anonymous submission: No
*Time between submission and publication
decision:* 3 months
Time between decision and publication:
1 year
Time allotted for reading proof: 3 weeks

CONTRACT PROVISIONS

Copyright: Publisher
Royalty provisions: Varies (cloth); 7.5%
of net (paper)

**PUBLICATION AND DISTRIBUTION
INFORMATION**

Forms of publication: Cloth, paper
Titles published each year: 20
Number of review copies: 50
Distribution area: Worldwide

Time in print: 3-5 years minimum

**(127)
INDIANA UNIVERSITY PRESS**

610 North Morton St.
Bloomington, IN 47404-3797

Contact: Joan Catapano, Senior Spon-
soring Editor (women's studies, cultural
criticism)
Established: 1950
Telephone: 812 855-4203
Fax: 812 855-7931
E-mail: jcatapan@indiana.edu

SCOPE

Publishing interests: Literary theory;
semiotics of literature; feminist studies;
cultural criticism; Russian literature;
Chinese literature; Middle Eastern
literature; general literature; American
literature; film and literature; folklore
and literature
*Considers all literary and linguistic
topics:* Yes
Types of works not published:
Festschriften
Languages published: English
Series title(s): Advances in Semiotics;
Chinese Literature in Translation;
Everywoman: Studies in History,
Literature, and Culture; Folklore Studies
in Translation; Indiana Studies in
Biblical Literature; Jewish Literature
and Culture; Peirce Studies; Studies in
Chinese Literature and Society; Women
of Letters; Theories of Representation
and Difference; Unnatural Acts

SUBMISSION REQUIREMENTS

Initial contact: Letter of inquiry
Style: Chicago; MLA

Special requirements: Accepts electronic manuscripts; does not accept dot-matrix printout; provides guidelines for manuscript preparation
Subvention: No

EDITORIAL INFORMATION

Manuscripts or proposals submitted each year: 300 (estimate)
Manuscripts sent to readers each year: 40-50 (estimate)
Manuscripts accepted each year: 45 (estimate)
Number of outside readers: 1-3
Author-anonymous submission: Yes
Time between submission and publication decision: 2 months minimum
Time between decision and return of copyedited manuscript: 1-2 months
Time between decision and publication: 1 year

CONTRACT PROVISIONS

Copyright: Author
Royalty provisions: Negotiable

PUBLICATION AND DISTRIBUTION INFORMATION

Forms of publication: Cloth, paper
Titles published each year: 44
Print run: 1,500 cloth or 400 cloth and 2,500 paper
Number of review copies: 80-100
Distribution area: Worldwide
Time in print: 5-10 years

**(128)
INSTITUT FÜR ANGLISTIK UND AMERIKANISTIK**

Universität Salzburg
Akademiestr. 24
5020 Salzburg, Austria

Contact: James Hogg
Established: 1970
Telephone: (662) 80444424
Fax: (662) 8044613

SCOPE

Publishing interests: English literature; American literature; Middle English literature (especially religious literature); Elizabethan literature; Jacobean literature; Romantic literature (especially poetry); Victorian literature (especially poetry); drama
Considers all literary and linguistic topics: Yes
Types of works not published: Textbooks; literary handbooks and encyclopedias
Languages published: English; German; French; Italian
Series title(s): Salzburg Studies in English Literature; Salzburg English and American Studies; Analecta Carthusiana

SUBMISSION REQUIREMENTS

Initial contact: Letter and outline
Considers simultaneous submissions: No
Will issue contract on the basis of proposal, prospectus, and/or sample chapter: Yes
Style: Varies
Special requirements: Requires camera-ready copy and electronic manuscripts
Subvention: No

EDITORIAL INFORMATION

Manuscripts or proposals submitted each year: 150
Manuscripts sent to readers each year: 60-70
Manuscripts accepted each year: 40-50
Number of outside readers: Generally 0
Author-anonymous submission: No

Time between submission and publication decision: 2 months
Time between decision and publication: 6 months
Time allotted for reading proof: 1 month

CONTRACT PROVISIONS

Copyright: Publisher
Royalty provisions: 0

PUBLICATION AND DISTRIBUTION INFORMATION

Forms of publication: Cloth, paper
Titles published each year: 35
Print run: 200-500
Number of review copies: 20
Distribution area: Worldwide
Time in print: Indefinitely

(129)
INTERNATIONAL SCHOLARS PUBLICATIONS

PO Box 2590
San Francisco, CA 94126

7831 Woodmont Ave., Suite 345
Bethesda, MD 20814

Imprint(s) and subsidiary firm(s):
Catholic Scholars Press; Christian Universities Press; Jewish Scholars Press
Contact: Robert West (literary topics, language studies, biographies, bibliographies); Andrew Woznicki (philosophy, linguistics, Catholicism)
Established: 1992
Telephone: 415 397-9525
Fax: 415 981-6313

SCOPE

Publishing interests: Central European literatures; central European languages; Irish literature; Irish language; Catholicism and literature (nineteenth- and twentieth-century American and European literature); Jewish literature (central and eastern Europe); Arabic poetry (modern); Iberian literatures
Considers all literary and linguistic topics: Yes
Not interested in proposals on: Neo-Marxist, feminist, and gender studies
Languages published: English; Spanish; German
Series title(s): Iberian Studies in History, Literature, and Culture

SUBMISSION REQUIREMENTS

Initial contact: Letter, prospectus, 2 sample chapters, and curriculum vitae; provides guide for prospective authors
Considers simultaneous submissions: Yes
Will issue contract on the basis of proposal, prospectus, and/or sample chapter: Yes
Style: Chicago; MLA
Special requirements: Requires camera-ready copy
Subvention: Generally not

EDITORIAL INFORMATION

Manuscripts or proposals submitted each year: 30
Manuscripts sent to readers each year: 21
Manuscripts accepted each year: 12-14
Number of outside readers: 1
Author-anonymous submission: Yes
Time between submission and publication decision: 3-4 months
Time between decision and publication: 6-8 months
Time allotted for reading proof: 2 weeks

CONTRACT PROVISIONS

Copyright: Author
Royalty provisions: 8% of net

PUBLICATION AND DISTRIBUTION INFORMATION

Forms of publication: Cloth, paper
Titles published each year: 8 (1993); 12-14 (1994)
Print run: 500
Number of review copies: 75
Distribution area: Worldwide
Time in print: Indefinitely

Has strong commitment to publishing first-rate revised dissertations

**(130)
UNIVERSITY OF IOWA PRESS**

The Kuhl House
119 West Park Rd.
Iowa City, IA 52242

Contact: Paul Zimmer, Director
Established: 1969
Telephone: 319 335-2000
Fax: 319 335-2055

SCOPE

Publishing interests: American literature; British literature (especially Elizabethan, Victorian, and contemporary); African American literature; major contemporary writers
Considers all literary and linguistic topics: Yes
Types of works not published: Unrevised dissertations; readers; Festschriften
Languages published: English
Series title(s): American Land and Life Series; Singular Lives: The Iowa Series in North American Autobiography

SUBMISSION REQUIREMENTS

Initial contact: Letter and prospectus or letter, prospectus, and sample chapter
Style: Chicago
Special requirements: Accepts photocopies (if author guarantees that no other publisher is considering manuscript) and electronic manuscripts; prefers not to receive dot-matrix printout; provides guidelines for manuscript preparation
Subvention: No

EDITORIAL INFORMATION

Manuscripts or proposals submitted each year: 200 (estimate)
Manuscripts sent to readers each year: 70 (estimate)
Manuscripts accepted each year: 20 (estimate)
Number of outside readers: 2
Author-anonymous submission: No
Time between submission and publication decision: 2-3 months
Time between decision and return of copyedited manuscript: 2-3 months
Time between decision and publication: 9-10 months
Time allotted for reading proof: 1 month

CONTRACT PROVISIONS

Copyright: Negotiable
Royalty provisions: 10% of net (cloth); 7% (paper); sometimes withholds royalty until initial sales quota is met

PUBLICATION AND DISTRIBUTION INFORMATION

Forms of publication: Cloth, paper
Titles published each year: 18 (estimate)
Print run: 1,000-3,000
Number of review copies: 70-100
Distribution area: Worldwide
Time in print: 3-5 years minimum

(131)
IOWA STATE UNIVERSITY PRESS

2121 South State Ave.
Ames, IA 50014-8300

Contact: Linda E. Speth, Director
Established: 1934
Telephone: 515 292-0140
Fax: 515 292-3348

SCOPE

Publishing interests: African American studies; American theater history; journalism history
Considers all literary and linguistic topics: No
Types of works not published: Dissertations; Festschriften
Languages published: English

SUBMISSION REQUIREMENTS

Initial contact: Letter, outline, and sample chapters
Considers simultaneous submissions: Yes
Will issue contract on the basis of proposal, prospectus, and/or sample chapter: No
Style: Chicago
Special requirements: Accepts photocopies and dot-matrix printout; prefers electronic manuscripts
Subvention: Occasionally

EDITORIAL INFORMATION

Manuscripts or proposals submitted each year: 100 (estimate)
Manuscripts sent to readers each year: 10 (estimate)
Manuscripts accepted each year: 10
Number of outside readers: 2 minimum
Author-anonymous submission: No
Time between submission and publication decision: 3 months

Time between decision and return of copy-edited manuscript: 3 months
Time between decision and publication: 9-15 months

CONTRACT PROVISIONS

Copyright: Negotiable
Royalty provisions: 0-15% of net

PUBLICATION AND DISTRIBUTION INFORMATION

Forms of publication: Cloth, paper
Titles published each year: 10
Print run: 1,500
Distribution area: Worldwide
Time in print: 3-5 years

(132)
IRANBOOKS, INC.

8014 Old Georgetown Rd.
Bethesda, MD 20814

Contact: Farhad Shirzad
Established: 1979
Telephone: 301 718-8188
Fax: 301 907-8707

SCOPE

Publishing interests: Iran; Persian language; Middle East
Considers all literary and linguistic topics: Yes
Languages published: English; Persian
Series title(s): Classics of Persian Literature

SUBMISSION REQUIREMENTS

Restrictions on authors: No
Initial contact: Letter and prospectus
Considers simultaneous submissions: Yes

*Will issue contract on the basis of
proposal, prospectus, and/or sample
chapter:* No
Special requirements: Prefers electronic
copy
Subvention: Sometimes

EDITORIAL INFORMATION

Number of outside readers: 2-3
Author-anonymous submission: No
*Time between submission and publication
decision:* 2-3 months
Time between decision and publication: 6
months

CONTRACT PROVISIONS

Copyright: Author or publisher

**PUBLICATION AND DISTRIBUTION
INFORMATION**

Forms of publication: Cloth, paper
Titles published each year: 8
Print run: 1,500
Number of review copies: 50-100
Distribution area: Worldwide

**(133)
IRISH ACADEMIC PRESS**

Kill Lane
Blackrock
Co. Dublin, Ireland

Contact: Michael Adams, Managing
Director
Established: 1974
Telephone: 2892922
Fax: 2893072

SCOPE

Publishing interests: Irish literature;
Italian literature

*Considers all literary and linguistic
topics:* No
Types of works not published: Critical
editions; literary reference works
Languages published: English
Series title(s): Italian Studies Series

SUBMISSION REQUIREMENTS

Initial contact: Letter, outline, and sample
chapter; provides questionnaire for
authors
Considers simultaneous submissions: No
*Will issue contract on the basis of
proposal, prospectus, and/or sample
chapter:* Possibly
Style: Chicago
Special requirements: Expects electronic
manuscript
Subvention: Sometimes (for highly
specialized topics)

EDITORIAL INFORMATION

*Manuscripts or proposals submitted each
year:* 10 (estimate)
Manuscripts sent to readers each year: 2
Manuscripts accepted each year: 2
Number of outside readers: 1
Author-anonymous submission: No
*Time between submission and publication
decision:* 3 months
*Time between decision and return of copy-
edited manuscript:* 3 months
Time between decision and publication:
9-12 months
Time allotted for reading proof: 4 weeks

CONTRACT PROVISIONS

Copyright: Author
Royalty provisions: 0-10%

**PUBLICATION AND DISTRIBUTION
INFORMATION**

Forms of publication: Cloth
Titles published each year: 2

Print run: 750-1,000
Number of review copies: 30-40
Distribution area: Worldwide
Time in print: 8 years

(134)
ITALICA PRESS

595 Main St.
Suite 605
New York, NY 10044

Contact: Ronald G. Musto, Publisher;
Eileen Gardiner, Publisher
Established: 1985
Telephone: 212 935-4230
Fax: 212 838-7812
E-mail: italica@aol.com

SCOPE

Publishing interests: English-language
translations of Latin literature (medieval
and Renaissance) and Italian literature
(medieval, Renaissance, and twentieth-
century [especially novels])
*Considers all literary and linguistic
topics:* No
Languages published: English

SUBMISSION REQUIREMENTS

Initial contact: Letter of inquiry
Considers simultaneous submissions: Yes
(if informed)
*Will issue contract on the basis of
proposal, prospectus, and/or sample
chapter:* No
Style: Chicago
Subvention: No

EDITORIAL INFORMATION

*Manuscripts or proposals submitted each
year:* 50 (estimate)

Manuscripts sent to readers each year:
10 (estimate)
Manuscripts accepted each year: 5
(estimate)
Number of outside readers: 1-3
Author-anonymous submission: Yes
*Time between submission and publication
decision:* 3 months
*Time between decision and return of copy-
edited manuscript:* 6-9 months
Time between decision and publication:
1 year
Time allotted for reading proof: 6 weeks

CONTRACT PROVISIONS

Copyright: Author
Royalty provisions: 7-10% on first 1,000
copies

PUBLICATION AND DISTRIBUTION INFORMATION

Forms of publication: Paper
Titles published each year: 5
Print run: 1,500
Number of review copies: 50
Distribution area: Worldwide
Time in print: Indefinitely

(135)
JAIN PUBLISHING CO.

PO Box 3523
Fremont, CA 94539

Imprint(s) and subsidiary firm(s): Asian
Humanities Press
Contact: M. K. Jain, Editor in Chief
Established: 1986
Telephone: 510 659-8272
Fax: 510 659-0501

SCOPE

Publishing interests: Asian languages;
   Asian literature; translations
*Considers all literary and linguistic
   topics:* No
Types of works not published: Disser-
   tations; bibliographies; critical editions;
   collections of letters
Languages published: English

SUBMISSION REQUIREMENTS

Initial contact: Letter and prospectus
   (including SASE); provides guidelines
   for submitting a proposal
Considers simultaneous submissions: No
*Will issue contract on the basis of
   proposal, prospectus, and/or sample
   chapter:* No
Style: Chicago
Special requirements: Length: 400 pages
   maximum; prefers camera-ready copy
Subvention: No

EDITORIAL INFORMATION

*Manuscripts or proposals submitted each
   year:* 20 (estimate)
Manuscripts sent to readers each year: 5
Manuscripts accepted each year: 3
Number of outside readers: 2
Author-anonymous submission: No
*Time between submission and publication
   decision:* 6 months
*Time between decision and return of copy-
   edited manuscript:* 3 months
Time between decision and publication:
   9-12 months
Time allotted for reading proof: 1 month

CONTRACT PROVISIONS

Copyright: Negotiable
Royalty provisions: 8% of net for first
   5,000 copies, 10% thereafter

PUBLICATION AND DISTRIBUTION INFORMATION

Forms of publication: Cloth, paper
Titles published each year: 2
Print run: 1,000-2,000
Number of review copies: 25
Distribution area: Worldwide
Time in print: 5 years

(136) JOHNS HOPKINS UNIVERSITY PRESS

2175 North Charles St.
Baltimore, MD 21218-4319

Contact: Eric Halpern, Editor in Chief
Established: 1878
Telephone: 410 338-6903
Fax: 410 338-6998
E-mail: acquire@jhuvms.hcf.jhu.edu

SCOPE

Publishing interests: Literary theory;
   literary history; comparative literature;
   American literature; American studies;
   cultural studies; cultural criticism;
   English literature (Renaissance to
   present); French literature; German
   literature; Italian literature; genre
   studies; biography
*Considers all literary and linguistic
   topics:* Yes
Types of works not published:
   Festschriften; conference proceedings;
   unrevised dissertations
Languages published: English
Series title(s): Parallax: Re-Visions of
   Culture and Society; Psychiatry and the
   Humanities; Johns Hopkins Jewish
   Studies

SUBMISSION REQUIREMENTS

Initial contact: Letter of inquiry;
completion of questionnaire used in
preliminary evaluation of manuscript
Considers simultaneous submissions:
Prefers single submission
*Will issue contract on the basis of
proposal, prospectus, and/or sample
chapter:* Occasionally
Style: Chicago
Special requirements: Accepts photocopies and electronic manuscripts;
rarely accepts dot-matrix printout;
provides guidelines for manuscript
preparation
Subvention: No

EDITORIAL INFORMATION

*Manuscripts or proposals submitted each
year:* 300-500 (estimate)
Manuscripts sent to readers each year:
120 (estimate)
Manuscripts accepted each year: 33
Number of outside readers: 1 minimum
Author-anonymous submission: No
*Time between submission and publication
decision:* 3 months maximum
*Time between decision and return of copy-
edited manuscript:* 2 months
Time between decision and publication:
1 year

CONTRACT PROVISIONS

Copyright: Publisher
Royalty provisions: 10% of net (cloth);
6% of list (paper)

PUBLICATION AND DISTRIBUTION
INFORMATION

Forms of publication: Cloth, paper
Titles published each year: 35
Print run: 1,200 (cloth)
Number of review copies: 50
Distribution area: Worldwide

Time in print: 3-10 years

(137)
UNIVERSITY PRESS OF KANSAS

2501 West 15th St.
Lawrence, KS 66049-3904

Contact: Cynthia Miller, Editor in Chief
Established: 1946
Telephone: 913 864-4154
Fax: 913 864-4586
E-mail: upkansas@kuhub.cc.ukans.edu

SCOPE

Publishing interests: American studies;
women's studies; American literature
(nineteenth-century)
*Considers all literary and linguistic
topics:* No
Not interested in proposals on: American
literature (colonial period); literatures
outside the United States; literary theory
Types of works not published: Bibliographies; critical editions; textbooks;
Festschriften; literary handbooks and
encyclopedias
Languages published: English

SUBMISSION REQUIREMENTS

Initial contact: Letter of inquiry and
prospectus
Considers simultaneous submissions:
Prefers single submission
*Will issue contract on the basis of
proposal, prospectus, and/or sample
chapter:* Yes
Style: Chicago
Special requirements: Prefers electronic
manuscripts
Subvention: No

EDITORIAL INFORMATION

Manuscripts or proposals submitted each year: 30-50
Manuscripts sent to readers each year: 10-12
Manuscripts accepted each year: 4-6
Number of outside readers: 2
Author-anonymous submission: No
Time between submission and publication decision: 3-4 months
Time between decision and publication: 10-12 months
Time allotted for reading proof: 4-6 weeks

CONTRACT PROVISIONS

Copyright: Author or publisher
Royalty provisions: Negotiable

PUBLICATION AND DISTRIBUTION INFORMATION

Forms of publication: Cloth, paper
Titles published each year: 3
Print run: 1,000-1,200 (cloth); 1,500-2,000 (paper)
Number of review copies: 100-120
Distribution area: Worldwide
Time in print: 10 years

(138)
KENDALL/HUNT PUBLISHING CO.

4050 Westmark Dr.
Dubuque, IA 52004

Contact: A. C. Grisanti, Director of National Book Program
Established: 1944
Telephone: 319 588-1451
Fax: 319 589-1116

SCOPE

Publishing interests: Composition; rhetoric; textbooks
Considers all literary and linguistic topics: No
Types of works not published: Dissertations; bibliographies; critical editions; collections of letters; biographies; collections of essays; literary reference works
Languages published: English

SUBMISSION REQUIREMENTS

Initial contact: Letter and prospectus
Considers simultaneous submissions: Yes
Will issue contract on the basis of proposal, prospectus, and/or sample chapter: Yes
Style: Chicago
Special requirements: Prefers electronic manuscripts
Subvention: No

EDITORIAL INFORMATION

Manuscripts accepted each year: 50 (estimate)
Number of outside readers: 2-6
Author-anonymous submission: Yes
Time between submission and publication decision: 6 months
Time between decision and return of copy-edited manuscript: 2 months
Time between decision and publication: 1 year

CONTRACT PROVISIONS

Copyright: Publisher
Royalty provisions: 5-15%

PUBLICATION AND DISTRIBUTION INFORMATION

Forms of publication: Cloth, paper
Titles published each year: 200

Print run: 2,000
Number of review copies: 50-500
Distribution area: North America
Time in print: Varies

Primarily a textbook publisher

(139)
KENT STATE UNIVERSITY PRESS

PO Box 5190
Kent, OH 44242-0001

Imprint(s) and subsidiary firm(s): Black
Squirrel Books
Contact: Julia Morton, Senior Editor
Established: 1965
Telephone: 216 672-7913
Fax: 216 672-3104

SCOPE

Publishing interests: American literature
(eighteenth-, nineteenth-, and twentieth-
century); English literature; science
fiction studies; fantasy fiction;
collections of letters; Dorothy L. Sayers;
Inklings group; C. S. Lewis; Charles
Williams; J. R. R. Tolkien; popular
writers
*Considers all literary and linguistic
topics:* Yes
Types of works not published: Unrevised
dissertations; bibliographies;
Festschriften; literary reference works
Languages published: English
Series title(s): Translation Studies

SUBMISSION REQUIREMENTS

Initial contact: Letter, outline, and sample
chapter
Considers simultaneous submissions: No
*Will issue contract on the basis of
proposal, prospectus, and/or sample
chapter:* No

Style: MLA; Chicago
Special requirements: Prefers not to
receive dot-matrix printout; expects
electronic manuscript or camera-ready
copy; provides guidelines for manuscript preparation
Subvention: No

EDITORIAL INFORMATION

*Manuscripts or proposals submitted each
year:* 30 (estimate)
Manuscripts sent to readers each year: 7
(estimate)
Manuscripts accepted each year: 4
Number of outside readers: 2
Author-anonymous submission: No
*Time between submission and publication
decision:* 4-6 months
*Time between decision and return of copy-
edited manuscript:* 6-12 months
Time between decision and publication:
12-18 months
Time allotted for reading proof: 2-3
weeks

CONTRACT PROVISIONS

Copyright: Publisher
Royalty provisions: 10% of net after first
400 copies

PUBLICATION AND DISTRIBUTION
INFORMATION

Forms of publication: Cloth, paper
Titles published each year: 6
Print run: 1,200
Number of review copies: 100-125
Distribution area: Worldwide
Time in print: 8 years

(140)
UNIVERSITY PRESS OF
KENTUCKY

663 South Limestone St.
Lexington, KY 40508-4008

Contact: Nancy Grayson Holmes, Editor
in Chief (literature, women's studies);
Craig Gill, Acquisitions Editor
(folklore, film)
Established: 1943
Telephone: 606 257-2951
Fax: 606 257-2984
E-mail: nholmes@uklans.uky.edu;
kcherry@uklans.uky.edu

SCOPE

Publishing interests: English literature
(especially Renaissance and eighteenth-
century); American literature; women's
studies; African American literature;
southern American literature;
Appalachian literature; folklore; film
studies
*Considers all literary and linguistic
topics:* No
Types of works not published: Unrevised
dissertations; Festschriften; bibli-
ographies
Prizes and competitions: Appalachian
Studies Award
Languages published: English
Series title(s): Studies in the English
Renaissance; Eighteenth-Century
Novels by Women; Studies in Romance
Languages

SUBMISSION REQUIREMENTS

Initial contact: Letter and prospectus
Considers simultaneous submissions: No
*Will issue contract on the basis of
proposal, prospectus, and/or sample
chapter:* Occasionally
Style: Chicago; MLA

Special requirements: Accepts electronic
manuscripts; provides guidelines for
manuscript preparation
Subvention: Sometimes

EDITORIAL INFORMATION

*Manuscripts or proposals submitted each
year:* 300
Manuscripts sent to readers each year: 30
Manuscripts accepted each year: 15
Number of outside readers: 2
Author-anonymous submission: No
*Time between submission and publication
decision:* 2-4 months
*Time between decision and return of copy-
edited manuscript:* 3 months
Time between decision and publication:
1 year
Time allotted for reading proof: 3 weeks

CONTRACT PROVISIONS

Copyright: Publisher
Royalty provisions: 10% of net after a
certain number of copies

PUBLICATION AND DISTRIBUTION
INFORMATION

Forms of publication: Cloth, paper, CD-
ROM
Titles published each year: 11
Print run: 1,250
Number of review copies: 50
Distribution area: Worldwide
Time in print: 10 years

(141)
***KRAUS INTERNATIONAL**
PUBLICATIONS

Route 100
Millwood, NY 10546

Contact: Barry Katzen, Director

Established: 1974
Telephone: 914 946-3275; 800 223-8323
Fax: 914 946-1195

SCOPE

Publishing interests: American literature
(especially twentieth-century); English
literature; French literature; German
literature; expressionism; Russian
literature; reference works; bibliographies; indexes
*Considers all literary and linguistic
topics:* Yes
Types of works not published: Dissertations; Festschriften; critical editions
Languages published: English

SUBMISSION REQUIREMENTS

Initial contact: Letter, outline, and sample
chapter
Special requirements: Requires camera-
ready copy for brief works; accepts
electronic manuscripts
Subvention: No

EDITORIAL INFORMATION

*Manuscripts or proposals submitted each
year:* 10 (estimate)
Manuscripts sent to readers each year: 4
(estimate)
Manuscripts accepted each year: 2
Number of outside readers: 2-3
*Time between submission and publication
decision:* 3-4 months
*Time between decision and return of copy-
edited manuscript:* 3 months
Time between decision and publication:
9-24 months

CONTRACT PROVISIONS

Copyright: Author
Royalty provisions: 10-15% of net

PUBLICATION AND DISTRIBUTION
INFORMATION

Forms of publication: Cloth, paper, even-
tually electronic media
Titles published each year: 2 (estimate)
Print run: 1,500
Number of review copies: 5-10
Distribution area: Worldwide
Time in print: 7 years

**(142)
ALFRED KRÖNER VERLAG**

Postfach 10 28 62
70024 Stuttgart, Germany

Contact: Imma Klemm
Established: 1905
Telephone: (0711) 620221
Fax: (0711) 6159946

SCOPE

Publishing interests: German literature;
world literature; linguistics; reference
books
*Considers all literary and linguistic
topics:* Yes
Types of works not published: Dissertations; bibliographies; critical editions;
collections of letters; Festschriften
Languages published: German

SUBMISSION REQUIREMENTS

Initial contact: Letter and prospectus
Considers simultaneous submissions: No
*Will issue contract on the basis of
proposal, prospectus, and/or sample
chapter:* No
Style: House
Special requirements: Does not accept
photocopies
Subvention: No

EDITORIAL INFORMATION

*Manuscripts or proposals submitted each
   year:* 50 (estimate)
Manuscripts sent to readers each year:
   10 (estimate)
Manuscripts accepted each year: 3
Number of outside readers: Varies
*Time between submission and publication
   decision:* 2 months
Time between decision and publication: 6
   months

CONTRACT PROVISIONS

Copyright: Publisher

**PUBLICATION AND DISTRIBUTION
INFORMATION**

Forms of publication: Cloth
Titles published each year: 5
Number of review copies: 50-100
Distribution area: Worldwide
Time in print: 10-80 years

**(143)
KTAV PUBLISHING HOUSE**

900 Jefferson St.
Hoboken, NJ 07030

Imprint(s) and subsidiary firm(s): Yeshiva
   University Press
Contact: Yaakov Elman
Established: 1922
Telephone: 201 963-9524
Fax: 201 963-0102

SCOPE

Publishing interests: Judaic studies
*Considers all literary and linguistic
   topics:* No
Languages published: English; Hebrew

SUBMISSION REQUIREMENTS

Initial contact: Letter, outline, and sample
   chapter(s)
Style: Chicago
Subvention: Not necessarily

EDITORIAL INFORMATION

*Manuscripts or proposals submitted each
   year:* 75 (estimate)
Manuscripts sent to readers each year: 40
   (estimate)
Manuscripts accepted each year: 20
   (estimate)
Number of outside readers: 1-3
Author-anonymous submission: Yes
*Time between submission and publication
   decision:* 1-3 months
*Time between decision and return of copy-
   edited manuscript:* 1-2 months
Time between decision and publication:
   6-12 months

CONTRACT PROVISIONS

Copyright: Author
Royalty provisions: 10% of list

**PUBLICATION AND DISTRIBUTION
INFORMATION**

Forms of publication: Cloth, paper
Titles published each year: 25 (estimate)
Print run: 1,000-2,000
Number of review copies: 20 minimum
Distribution area: Worldwide
Time in print: 10 years

**(144)
PETER LANG PUBLISHING CO.**

62 West 45th St.
New York, NY 10036

Contact: Owen Lancer, Acquisitions
   Editor

Established: 1980
Telephone: 212 302-6740
Fax: 212 302-7374

SCOPE

Publishing interests: General literature;
  modern languages; linguistics; linguistic
  theory
*Considers all literary and linguistic
  topics:* Yes
Prizes and competitions: Northeast
  Modern Language Foreign Language
  Award ($1,000 and publication by
  Lang)
Languages published: All modern
  languages
Series title(s): American University
  Studies Series

SUBMISSION REQUIREMENTS

Initial contact: Letter and prospectus
Considers simultaneous submissions:
  Prefers single submission
*Will issue contract on the basis of
  proposal, prospectus, and/or sample
  chapter:* No
Style: Prefers MLA; accepts Chicago and
  American Psychological Association
Special requirements: Length: generally
  prefers 150-600 pages
Subvention: Occasionally (especially for
  revised dissertations)

EDITORIAL INFORMATION

*Manuscripts or proposals submitted each
  year:* 400 (estimate)
Manuscripts sent to readers each year:
  250 (estimate)
Manuscripts accepted each year: 200
  (estimate)
Number of outside readers: 2
Author-anonymous submission: No
*Time between submission and publication
  decision:* 3 months

*Time between decision and return of copy-
  edited manuscript:* 6 months
Time between decision and publication:
  9-12 months

CONTRACT PROVISIONS

Copyright: Negotiable

**PUBLICATION AND DISTRIBUTION
INFORMATION**

Forms of publication: Cloth, paper
Titles published each year: 120 (estimate)
Print run: 500-1,000
Number of review copies: 20-50
Distribution area: Worldwide
Time in print: 7 years

**(145)
PRESSES DE L'UNIVERSITE LAVAL**

Edifice Jean-Durand
2336, chemin Sainte Foy, 2ᵉ étage
Sainte-Foy, PQ G1K 7P4, Canada

Contact: Denis Vaugeois, Directeur
  Général
Established: 1950
Telephone: 418 656-3001
Fax: 418 656-3305

SCOPE

Publishing interests: Linguistics; bilingualism; Amerindian languages; French
  language in Quebec; Quebecois
  literature; psycholinguistics; Gustave
  Guillaume
*Considers all literary and linguistic
  topics:* Yes
Types of works not published: Dissertations; collections of letters;
  biographies
Languages published: French

Series title(s): Travaux du Centre International de Recherche sur le Bilinguisme; Vie des lettres québecoises; Leçons de linguistique de Gustave Guillaume; Cahiers de psychomécanique du langage; Langue française au Québec

SUBMISSION REQUIREMENTS

Restrictions on authors: Must be Canadian residents because of subvention requirements
Initial contact: Letter, prospectus, and sample chapter
Special requirements: Accepts electronic manuscripts
Subvention: Yes

EDITORIAL INFORMATION

Manuscripts or proposals submitted each year: 25 (estimate)
Manuscripts sent to readers each year: 10 (estimate)
Manuscripts accepted each year: 6
Number of outside readers: 2
Time between submission and publication decision: 4-6 months
Time between decision and return of copy-edited manuscript: 3-6 months
Time between decision and publication: 6-12 months

CONTRACT PROVISIONS

Copyright: Publisher
Royalty provisions: 10% of list

PUBLICATION AND DISTRIBUTION INFORMATION

Forms of publication: Cloth, paper
Titles published each year: 6
Print run: 1,000
Number of review copies: 25-50
Distribution area: Worldwide
Time in print: 10 years minimum

(146)
LEHIGH UNIVERSITY PRESS

302 Linderman Library
30 Library Dr.
Bethlehem, PA 18018-3067

Contact: Philip A. Metzger, Director
Established: 1985
Telephone: 610 758-3933
Fax: 610 758-3079
E-mail: inlup@lehigh.edu

SCOPE

Publishing interests: Eighteenth-century studies; biography; film; theater; bibliographies
Considers all literary and linguistic topics: Yes
Types of works not published: Unrevised dissertations; textbooks
Languages published: English

SUBMISSION REQUIREMENTS

Initial contact: Letter, prospectus, table of contents, and sample chapters or full manuscript
Considers simultaneous submissions: Prefers single submission
Will issue contract on the basis of proposal, prospectus, and/or sample chapter: No
Style: Chicago
Special requirements: Length: prefers 200 pages minimum
Subvention: No

EDITORIAL INFORMATION

Manuscripts or proposals submitted each year: 5
Manuscripts sent to readers each year: 2
Manuscripts accepted each year: 2
Number of outside readers: 1-2
Author-anonymous submission: Yes

Time between submission and publication decision: 3 months
Time between decision and return of copy-edited manuscript: 3-4 months
Time between decision and publication: 15 months
Time allotted for reading proof: 10-30 days

CONTRACT PROVISIONS

Copyright: Publisher
Royalty provisions: 10% after production costs have been met

PUBLICATION AND DISTRIBUTION INFORMATION

Forms of publication: Cloth
Titles published each year: 3
Print run: Varies
Number of review copies: 20-25
Distribution area: Worldwide
Time in print: Varies

(147)
*LEICESTER UNIVERSITY PRESS

Fielding Johnson Bldg.
University of Leicester
Leicester LE1 7RH, England

Contact: Alec McAulay
Established: 1952
Telephone: (0533) 523333
Fax: (0533) 522200

SCOPE

Publishing interests: English literature (Old English and eighteenth-, nine-teenth-, and twentieth-century); American literature; European literature and film; periodicals (especially eigh-teenth- and nineteenth-century); Victorian studies (including political

philosophy, scientific writing, and criticism)
Considers all literary and linguistic topics: No
Languages published: English; French; German; Italian
Series title(s): Modern German Poets; The Victorian Library

SUBMISSION REQUIREMENTS

Initial contact: Letter and prospectus
Style: Cambridge; house
Subvention: No

EDITORIAL INFORMATION

Manuscripts or proposals submitted each year: 40 (estimate)
Manuscripts sent to readers each year: 10 (estimate)
Manuscripts accepted each year: 6 (estimate)
Number of outside readers: 1 minimum
Time between submission and publication decision: 3 months
Time between decision and return of copy-edited manuscript: 1 month
Time between decision and publication: 10 months

CONTRACT PROVISIONS

Copyright: Author
Royalty provisions: 10% of net (cloth); 7.5% (paper)

PUBLICATION AND DISTRIBUTION INFORMATION

Forms of publication: Cloth, paper, elec-tronic media
Titles published each year: 6
Print run: 1,250 (cloth)
Number of review copies: 40
Distribution area: Worldwide
Time in print: 8 years

Leicester University Press is a division of Pinter Publishers.

(148)
LIBRARY ASSOCIATION PUBLISHING

7 Ridgmount St.
London WC1E 7AE, England

Contact: Helen Carley
Established: 1980
Telephone: (071) 6367543
Fax: (071) 6363627
E-mail: lapublishing@la-hq.org.uk

SCOPE

Publishing interests: Literary reference works; bibliographies; information science
Considers all literary and linguistic topics: No
Types of works not published: Critical editions; collections of letters; biographies; collections of essays; Festschriften; literary handbooks; literary encyclopedias
Languages published: English

SUBMISSION REQUIREMENTS

Initial contact: Letter and outline
Will issue contract on the basis of proposal, prospectus, and/or sample chapter: Yes
Style: House
Special requirements: Accepts photocopies, dot-matrix printout, and electronic manuscripts; provides guidelines for manuscript preparation
Subvention: Occasionally

EDITORIAL INFORMATION

Number of outside readers: 1

Time between submission and publication decision: 2 months
Time between decision and return of copy-edited manuscript: 7 months
Time between decision and publication: 5 months
Time allotted for reading proof: 2 weeks

CONTRACT PROVISIONS

Copyright: Publisher

PUBLICATION AND DISTRIBUTION INFORMATION

Forms of publication: Cloth, paper, electronic media
Distribution area: Worldwide
Time in print: Varies

Publishes few titles in language and literature

(149)
PRESSES UNIVERSITAIRES DE LILLE

rue du Barreau
B.P. 199
59654 Villeneuve d'Ascq Cédex, France

Contact: P. Leconte, Directeur
Telephone: (20) 916535
Fax: (20) 910395

SCOPE

Publishing interests: Linguistics; psycholinguistics; French literature; German literature; English literature; Irish literature; Spanish literature; Scandinavian literature; Netherlandic literature; Slavic literature; philology
Types of works not published: Literary encyclopedias
Languages published: French

SUBMISSION REQUIREMENTS

Subvention: Yes

EDITORIAL INFORMATION

Manuscripts or proposals submitted each year: 60 (estimate)
Manuscripts accepted each year: 30
Number of outside readers: 2
Time between submission and publication decision: 6 months
Time between decision and return of copy-edited manuscript: 12-18 months
Time between decision and publication: 12-18 months

CONTRACT PROVISIONS

Copyright: Publisher

PUBLICATION AND DISTRIBUTION INFORMATION

Forms of publication: Paper
Titles published each year: 30
Distribution area: Worldwide
Time in print: 3 years

(150)
LOCUST HILL PRESS

PO Box 260
West Cornwall, CT 06796

Contact: Thomas C. Bechtle, Publisher
Established: 1984
Telephone: 203 672-0060
Fax: 203 672-4968

SCOPE

Publishing interests: English literature; American literature; English-language literatures; Romance-language literatures; general literature

Considers all literary and linguistic topics: Yes
Languages published: English
Series title(s): Locust Hill Literary Studies

SUBMISSION REQUIREMENTS

Initial contact: Letter and prospectus
Considers simultaneous submissions: Yes
Will issue contract on the basis of proposal, prospectus, and/or sample chapter: No
Special requirements: Requires electronic manuscript
Subvention: No

EDITORIAL INFORMATION

Manuscripts or proposals submitted each year: 60 (estimate)
Manuscripts sent to readers each year: 10 (estimate)
Manuscripts accepted each year: 12 (estimate)
Number of outside readers: 1
Author-anonymous submission: Yes
Time between submission and publication decision: 6 weeks
Time between decision and return of copy-edited manuscript: 2 months
Time between decision and publication: 5 months

CONTRACT PROVISIONS

Copyright: Author
Royalty provisions: 12%

PUBLICATION AND DISTRIBUTION INFORMATION

Forms of publication: Cloth
Titles published each year: 12 (estimate)
Print run: 500
Number of review copies: 25
Distribution area: Worldwide
Time in print: Indefinitely

(151)
LONGMAN GROUP LTD.

Academic Department
Longman Higher Education Division
Longman House
Burnt Mill
Harlow, Essex CM20 2JE, England

Contact: Elizabeth Mann, Literature
  Publisher
Established: 1724
Telephone: (0279) 426721
Fax: (0279) 431059

SCOPE

Publishing interests: English literature;
  linguistics (theoretical and applied);
  European literature; cultural studies;
  critical editions of major works; literary
  theory; drama; genres (all of the
  preceding designed for an international
  university-level student audience and
  appropriate for publication in paper)
*Considers all literary and linguistic
  topics:* No
Types of works not published:
  Festschriften; most collections of letters
Languages published: English
Series title(s): Studies in Eighteenth- and
  Nineteenth-Century Literature;
  Longman Twentieth-Century Literature;
  Modern Literatures in Perspective;
  Longman Literature in English Series;
  Longman Critical Readers; Longman
  Medieval and Renaissance Library;
  Longman Annotated English Poets;
  Longman Annotated Texts; Longman
  Linguistics Library; English Language
  Series; Studies in Language and
  Linguistics; Language in Social Life;
  Applied Linguistics and Language
  Study

SUBMISSION REQUIREMENTS

Initial contact: Letter and prospectus
  (with outline and discussion of market
  and competition)
Considers simultaneous submissions: Yes
Subvention: Rarely

EDITORIAL INFORMATION

*Manuscripts or proposals submitted each
  year:* 80 (estimate)
Manuscripts sent to readers each year: 48
Manuscripts accepted each year: 48
Number of outside readers: 1
*Time between submission and publication
  decision:* 1-2 months
*Time between decision and return of copy-
  edited manuscript:* 6 weeks
Time between decision and publication:
  1 year

CONTRACT PROVISIONS

Copyright: Publisher

PUBLICATION AND DISTRIBUTION
INFORMATION

Forms of publication: Cloth, paper
Titles published each year: 12
Number of review copies: 150-300
Distribution area: Worldwide
Time in print: 5 years minimum

(152)
ANGELO LONGO EDITORE

Via Paolo Costa, 33
48100 Ravenna, Italy

Contact: Alfio Longo, Publishing
  Director
Established: 1965
Telephone: (0544) 217026
Fax: (0544) 217554

SCOPE

Publishing interests: Italian literature;
Dante; Giovanni Boccaccio; Petrarch;
Ludovico Ariosto; Torquato Tasso;
Niccolò Machiavelli; Ruzzante (Angelo
Beolco); Baldassare Castiglione;
Vittorio Alfieri; Carlo Goldoni;
Vincenzo Monti; Giuseppe Parini; Ugo
Foscolo; Giacomo Leopardi; Alessandro
Manzoni; Ippolito Nievo; Giovanni
Verga; Antonio Fogazzaro; Luigi
Pirandello; Italo Svevo; Vasco Pratolini;
Guido Gozzano; Giorgio Bassani;
Beppe Fenoglio; Cesare Pavese;
Eugenio Montale; Elsa Morante; Dino
Buzzati; Leonardo Sciascia; Italo
Calvino; English literature; Irish
literature; Jane Austen; Samuel Beckett;
William Blake; George Gordon, Lord
Byron; Joseph Conrad; Geoffrey
Chaucer; Oliver Goldsmith; James
Joyce; Gerard Manley Hopkins; John
Keats; D. H. Lawrence; Harold Pinter;
Alexander Pope; William Shakespeare;
Percy Shelley; Robert Louis Stevenson;
Tom Stoppard; Dylan Thomas; Virginia
Woolf; Thomas Wyatt; French
literature; Honoré de Balzac; Charles
Baudelaire; Simone de Beauvoir; André
Breton; Albert Camus; Pierre-Eugène
Drieu La Rochelle; Gustave Flaubert;
André Gide; Louise Labé; Clément
Marot; Marcel Proust; Arthur Rimbaud;
Jean-Jacques Rousseau; Charles-
Augustin Saint-Beuve; Jean-Paul Sartre;
Madeleine de Scudéry; Stendhal; Emile
Zola; American literature; T. S. Eliot;
Herman Melville; Edgar Allan Poe;
ethnic literatures; Spanish literature;
Lazarillo de Tormes; Lope Félix de
Vega Carpio; Antonio Machado y Ruiz;
Francisco Gómez de Quevedo y
Villegas; Federico García Lorca;
linguistics; semiotics; comparative
literature; dialectology; women's studies

*Considers all literary and linguistic
topics:* Yes
Types of works not published: Literary
encyclopedias
Languages published: English; French;
Italian; Spanish; German
Series title(s): Classici italiani minori; Il
portico; L'interprete; Speculum Artium;
Testi e studi umanistici; Pleiadi; Teatro;
Studi danteschi; Linguistica e dialetti;
Bibliografia e storia della critica;
Biblioteche italiane e strumenti bibli-
ografici; Musica, cinema, immagine,
teatro

SUBMISSION REQUIREMENTS

Initial contact: Letter and outline
Considers simultaneous submissions: Yes
*Will issue contract on the basis of
proposal, prospectus, and/or sample
chapter:* No
Style: MLA; Chicago
Special requirements: Expects electronic
copy
Subvention: Sometimes

EDITORIAL INFORMATION

*Manuscripts or proposals submitted each
year:* 112
Manuscripts sent to readers each year: 64
Manuscripts accepted each year: 36
Number of outside readers: 2
Author-anonymous submission: No
*Time between submission and publication
decision:* 5-6 months
Time between decision and publication:
6-7 months
Time allotted for reading proof: 1 month

CONTRACT PROVISIONS

Copyright: Publisher
Royalty provisions: 7-10%

PUBLICATION AND DISTRIBUTION INFORMATION

Forms of publication: Cloth, paper
Titles published each year: 29
Print run: 700-2,000
Number of review copies: 30-40
Distribution area: Worldwide
Time in print: 15-20 years

(153)
LOUISIANA STATE UNIVERSITY PRESS

PO Box 25053
Baton Rouge, LA 70894-5053

Established: 1935
Telephone: 504 388-6618
Fax: 504 388-6461

SCOPE

Publishing interests: Southern American literature; American literature (nineteenth- and twentieth-century); French literature (nineteenth- and twentieth-century); literary theory; African American literature; linguistics (involving Louisiana ethnic groups)
Considers all literary and linguistic topics: Yes
Types of works not published: Bibliographies; readers; Festschriften; literary handbooks
Languages published: English
Series title(s): Southern Literary Studies; Library of Southern Civilization; Modernist Studies

SUBMISSION REQUIREMENTS

Initial contact: Letter and prospectus or letter, outline, and sample chapter
Considers simultaneous submissions: Prefers single submission

Will issue contract on the basis of proposal, prospectus, and/or sample chapter: Rarely
Style: Chicago; house
Special requirements: Accepts photocopies and dot-matrix printout; prefers electronic manuscripts; provides guidelines for manuscript preparation
Subvention: No

EDITORIAL INFORMATION

Manuscripts or proposals submitted each year: 500 (estimate)
Manuscripts sent to readers each year: 200 (estimate)
Manuscripts accepted each year: 40 (estimate)
Number of outside readers: 2
Author-anonymous submission: No
Time between submission and publication decision: 2-6 months
Time between decision and publication: 10-12 months
Time allotted for reading proof: 2 weeks

CONTRACT PROVISIONS

Copyright: Negotiable
Royalty provisions: Negotiable

PUBLICATION AND DISTRIBUTION INFORMATION

Forms of publication: Cloth, paper
Titles published each year: 20 (estimate)
Print run: 1,250-1,500
Number of review copies: 60-75
Distribution area: Worldwide
Time in print: 5-10 years

(154)
EDIÇOES LOYOLA

Rua 1822, no. 347
04216 São Paulo, Brazil

Contact: Roberto Girola, Editor
Established: 1965
Telephone: (011) 9141922
Fax: (011) 634275

SCOPE

Publishing interests: Brazilian literature;
Portuguese literature; literary theory;
children's literature; general literature
*Considers all literary and linguistic
topics:* No
Types of works not published: Disser-
tations; bibliographies; critical editions;
Festschriften; collections of letters
Languages published: Portuguese

SUBMISSION REQUIREMENTS

Initial contact: Letter, outline, and sample
chapter
Considers simultaneous submissions: Yes
*Will issue contract on the basis of
proposal, prospectus, and/or sample
chapter:* No
Special requirements: Accepts electronic
manuscripts
Subvention: Sometimes

EDITORIAL INFORMATION

*Manuscripts or proposals submitted each
year:* 4 (estimate)
Manuscripts sent to readers each year: 2
Manuscripts accepted each year: 2
Number of outside readers: 1
Author-anonymous submission: No
*Time between submission and publication
decision:* 2 months
*Time between decision and return of copy-
edited manuscript:* 10 months
Time between decision and publication:
1 year
Time allotted for reading proof: 3 months

CONTRACT PROVISIONS

Copyright: Publisher

Royalty provisions: 7% on first edition,
9% thereafter

**PUBLICATION AND DISTRIBUTION
INFORMATION**

Forms of publication: Paper
Titles published each year: 2
Print run: 2,500
Number of review copies: 20
Distribution area: Brazil; Portugal;
Germany; Italy
Time in print: 8 years

**(155)
LOYOLA UNIVERSITY PRESS**

3441 North Ashland Ave.
Chicago, IL 60657

Imprint(s) and subsidiary firm(s):
Campion Books
Contact: Joseph P. Downey, S.J.,
Editorial Director
Established: 1912
Telephone: 312 281-1818
Fax: 312 281-0885

SCOPE

Publishing interests: Jesuit studies;
Ignatius Loyola; theology and literature;
religion and literature
*Considers all literary and linguistic
topics:* No
Types of works not published: Unrevised
dissertations; critical editions;
collections of letters; textbooks;
collections of essays; Festschriften;
literary encyclopedias
Languages published: English

SUBMISSION REQUIREMENTS

Initial contact: Letter and prospectus
Considers simultaneous submissions: Yes

*Will issue contract on the basis of
proposal, prospectus, and/or sample
chapter:* No
Style: Chicago
Special requirements: Accepts photocopies; prefers electronic manuscripts
Subvention: No

EDITORIAL INFORMATION

*Manuscripts or proposals submitted each
year:* 10 (estimate)
Manuscripts sent to readers each year: 2
Manuscripts accepted each year: 2
Number of outside readers: 1-2
*Time between submission and publication
decision:* 1-2 months
*Time between decision and return of copy-
edited manuscript:* 6 months
Time between decision and publication:
1 year
Time allotted for reading proof: 3-4
weeks

CONTRACT PROVISIONS

Copyright: Author
Royalty provisions: 10%

**PUBLICATION AND DISTRIBUTION
INFORMATION**

Forms of publication: Cloth, paper
Titles published each year: 2
Print run: 2,500
Number of review copies: 50
Distribution area: Worldwide
Time in print: 15 years

**(156)
LUND UNIVERSITY PRESS**

Box 141
22100 Lund, Sweden

Contact: Karin Hogman, Marketing
Assistant
Established: 1986
Telephone: (4646) 312000
Fax: (4646) 305338
E-mail: karin.hogman@studli.se

SCOPE

Languages published: Swedish; English;
French
Series title(s): Lund Studies in English

SUBMISSION REQUIREMENTS

Restrictions on authors: Accepts
submissions only from scholars associated with Lund University

EDITORIAL INFORMATION

*Manuscripts or proposals submitted each
year:* 15
Manuscripts sent to readers each year:
15
Manuscripts accepted each year: 15
*Time between submission and publication
decision:* 8 weeks

CONTRACT PROVISIONS

Copyright: Author
Royalty provisions: 50%

**PUBLICATION AND DISTRIBUTION
INFORMATION**

Titles published each year: 15

**(157)
MACMILLAN PRESS**

Houndsmills
Basingstoke, Hants RG21 2XS, England

Contact: Charmian Hearne, Commissioning Editor (literature, cultural studies)
Established: 1843
Telephone: (01256) 29242
Fax: (01256) 479476

SCOPE

Publishing interests: W. B. Yeats; Thomas Hardy; nineteenth-century literature; Romanticism; William Shakespeare; English literature; American literature; European literatures; biography; collections of letters; literary theory; Anglo-Irish literature; eighteenth-century literature; early modern literature; postcolonial literature; cultural studies; contemporary literature
Considers all literary and linguistic topics: Yes
Types of works not published: Bibliographies; critical editions
Languages published: English
Series title(s): Macmillan Literary Lives; Insights; Studies in Literature and Religion; Macmillan Author Chronologies; Edinburgh Studies in Culture and Society; Language, Discourse, Society; Interviews and Recollections; Language and Literature; New Directions in Theatre; Women in Society: A Feminist List; Text and Performance; The Critics Debate; Early Modern Literature in History

SUBMISSION REQUIREMENTS

Initial contact: Letter and prospectus
Considers simultaneous submissions: Prefers single submission
Will issue contract on the basis of proposal, prospectus, and/or sample chapter: Yes
Style: House
Special requirements: Length: usually 80,000 words; accepts photocopies, dot-matrix printout, and electronic manuscripts; welcomes camera-ready copy; provides guidelines for manuscript preparation
Subvention: Very occasionally

EDITORIAL INFORMATION

Manuscripts or proposals submitted each year: 200 (estimate)
Manuscripts sent to readers each year: 40-50 (estimate)
Manuscripts accepted each year: 50-60 (estimate)
Number of outside readers: 1
Author-anonymous submission: No
Time between submission and publication decision: 6 weeks
Time between decision and publication: 10-12 months
Time allotted for reading proof: 3-4 weeks

CONTRACT PROVISIONS

Copyright: Author
Royalty provisions: 10% of net on first 1,000 copies, 12.5% thereafter (cloth); 7.5% of net on first 2,000 copies, 10% thereafter (paper)

PUBLICATION AND DISTRIBUTION INFORMATION

Forms of publication: Cloth, paper
Titles published each year: 55
Print run: 2,000
Number of review copies: 30-40
Distribution area: Worldwide
Time in print: 5 years minimum

(158)
*MACMILLAN PUBLISHING CO.

866 Third Ave.
New York, NY 10022

PUBLICATION AND DISTRIBUTION

INFORMATION

Does not accept unsolicited manuscripts

(159)
STOFNUN ARNA MAGNUSSONAR A ISLANDI

Arnagarður-Suðurgata
IS-101 Reykjavík, Iceland

Contact: Stefán Karlsson
Established: 1971
Telephone: (354) 5694010
E-mail: stefkarl@rhi.hi.is

SCOPE

Publishing interests: Icelandic literature;
Icelandic language; Icelandic folklore;
editions of Icelandic texts
*Considers all literary and linguistic
topics:* No
Types of works not published: Unrevised
dissertations; literary encyclopedias
Languages published: Icelandic; Scandi-
navian languages; English; German
Series title(s): Stofnun Arna
Magnússonar á Islandi Series; Gripla

SUBMISSION REQUIREMENTS

Initial contact: Letter, outline, and sample
chapters
Considers simultaneous submissions: No
*Will issue contract on the basis of
proposal, prospectus, and/or sample
chapter:* No
Style: House
Special requirements: Expects electronic
manuscript
Subvention: Yes, if available

EDITORIAL INFORMATION

*Manuscripts or proposals submitted each
year:* 3 (estimate)
Manuscripts sent to readers each year: 2
Manuscripts accepted each year: 1
Number of outside readers: 2-3
Author-anonymous submission: No
*Time between submission and publication
decision:* 6 months
*Time between decision and return of copy-
edited manuscript:* 2 years
Time between decision and publication:
4 years

CONTRACT PROVISIONS

Copyright: Author or author and
publisher
Royalty provisions: No royalties

PUBLICATION AND DISTRIBUTION
INFORMATION

Forms of publication: Cloth
Titles published each year: 3
Print run: 800
Number of review copies: 20
Distribution area: Worldwide
Time in print: 20 years minimum

(160)
MANCHESTER UNIVERSITY PRESS

Oxford Rd.
Manchester M13 9NR, England

Contact: Anita Roy, Literature, Cultural
Studies, and Languages Editor
Established: 1911
Telephone: (0161) 2735539
Fax: (0161) 2743346
E-mail: mup@man.ac.uk

SCOPE

Publishing interests: William Shakespeare; theater studies; cultural studies;
media studies; communication studies;
literary theory; literary criticism; French
literature (modern); Italian literature
(modern); German literature (modern);
Spanish literature (modern); post-
colonial discourse; feminist theory
*Considers all literary and linguistic
topics:* No
Types of works not published:
Festschriften; bibliographies
Languages published: English; Italian;
German; Spanish
Series title(s): Revels Plays; Shakespeare
in Performance; Revels Plays
Companion Library; Cultural Politics;
Manchester Medieval Classics; Old and
Middle English Texts; Theory and
History of Literature; Hispanic Texts;
German Texts; Italian Texts; Texts in
Culture; Music and Society

SUBMISSION REQUIREMENTS

Initial contact: Letter, outline, and sample
chapter
Considers simultaneous submissions: Yes
*Will issue contract on the basis of
proposal, prospectus, and/or sample
chapter:* Yes
Style: House
Special requirements: Length: prefers
100,000 words maximum; provides
guidelines for manuscript preparation
Subvention: No

EDITORIAL INFORMATION

*Manuscripts or proposals submitted each
year:* 200 (estimate)
Manuscripts sent to readers each year: 60
(estimate)
Manuscripts accepted each year: 40
(estimate)

Number of outside readers: 2-3
Author-anonymous submission: No
*Time between submission and publication
decision:* 1 month
*Time between decision and return of copy-
edited manuscript:* 3 months
Time between decision and publication:
10 months
Time allotted for reading proof: 2 weeks

CONTRACT PROVISIONS

Copyright: Author
Royalty provisions: 5-10% of net

PUBLICATION AND DISTRIBUTION
INFORMATION

Forms of publication: Cloth, paper
Titles published each year: 30
Print run: 600 (cloth); 3,500 (paper)
Number of review copies: 50-100
Distribution area: Worldwide
Time in print: 3 years

(161)
MANSELL PUBLISHING

Villiers House
41-47 Strand
London WC2N 5JE, England

Contact: Veronica Higgs, Commissioning
Editor
Established: 1966
Telephone: (0171) 8394900
Fax: (0171) 8391804

SCOPE

Publishing interests: Reference works;
bibliographies; indexes
*Considers all literary and linguistic
topics:* No
Types of works not published: Dissertations; critical editions; collections of

letters; biographies; textbooks;
collections of essays; Festschriften
Languages published: English

SUBMISSION REQUIREMENTS

Restrictions on authors: No
Initial contact: Letter, synopsis or outline,
and list of contents; provides author
questionnaire
Considers simultaneous submissions: Yes
*Will issue contract on the basis of
proposal, prospectus, and/or sample
chapter:* Yes
Style: Chicago; Cambridge
Special requirements: Provides guidelines
for authors
Subvention: No

EDITORIAL INFORMATION

*Manuscripts or proposals submitted each
year:* 10
Manuscripts sent to readers each year: 6
Manuscripts accepted each year: 4
Number of outside readers: 2
Author-anonymous submission: Yes
*Time between submission and publication
decision:* 3 months
Time between decision and publication: 9
months
Time allotted for reading proof: 3-6
weeks

CONTRACT PROVISIONS

Copyright: Author
Royalty provisions: 5-7.5% of net

PUBLICATION AND DISTRIBUTION
INFORMATION

Forms of publication: Varies
Titles published each year: 4
Print run: 600
Number of review copies: 30
Distribution area: Worldwide
Time in print: 3 years

(162)
**UNIVERSITY OF MASSACHUSETTS
PRESS**

PO Box 429
Amherst, MA 01004-0429

Contact: Clark Dougan, Senior Editor
Established: 1964
Telephone: 413 545-2217
Fax: 413 545-1226

SCOPE

Publishing interests: American literature;
British literature; European literature;
African literature; Asian literature;
Renaissance literature; modern
literature; contemporary literature;
literary criticism; literary history;
literary theory; literary biography;
Caribbean studies; African American
studies; women's studies; ethnic studies
*Considers all literary and linguistic
topics:* Yes
Types of works not published: Bibli-
ographies; readers; Festschriften;
literary reference works
Languages published: English
Series title(s): Massachusetts Studies in
Early Modern Culture

SUBMISSION REQUIREMENTS

Initial contact: Letter and prospectus or
letter, outline, and sample chapter
Considers simultaneous submissions:
Prefers single submission
*Will issue contract on the basis of
proposal, prospectus, and/or sample
chapter:* Occasionally
Style: Chicago
Special requirements: Length: prefers 400
pages maximum
Subvention: No

EDITORIAL INFORMATION

*Manuscripts or proposals submitted each
  year:* 200 (estimate)
Manuscripts sent to readers each year: 20
  (estimate)
Manuscripts accepted each year: 10
  (estimate)
Number of outside readers: 2 minimum
Author-anonymous submission: No
*Time between submission and publication
  decision:* 5 months
*Time between decision and return of copy-
  edited manuscript:* 2 months
Time between decision and publication:
  1 year
Time allotted for reading proof: 4 weeks

CONTRACT PROVISIONS

Copyright: Negotiable
Royalty provisions: Varies

**PUBLICATION AND DISTRIBUTION
INFORMATION**

Forms of publication: Cloth, paper
Titles published each year: 20 (estimate)
Print run: 1,000-3,000
Number of review copies: 100-150
Distribution area: Worldwide
Time in print: 20 years

**(163)
MCFARLAND AND CO.,
PUBLISHERS**

Box 611
Jefferson, NC 28640

Contact: Robert Franklin, President and
  Editor in Chief
Established: 1979
Telephone: 910 246-4460
Fax: 910 246-5018

SCOPE

Publishing interests: Theater; playwrights; American literature; Eugene
  O'Neill; modern literature (early-
  twentieth-century); African American
  writers; Hispanic American writers;
  women writers; Gertrude Stein; African
  literature in English; east European
  literature; Russian literature; Soviet
  literature; reference works in all fields
  of literature; reference works in
  language or linguistics; Greek literature
  (classical); Roman literature
*Considers all literary and linguistic
  topics:* Yes
Languages published: English; Spanish

SUBMISSION REQUIREMENTS

Initial contact: Letter, outline, and sample
  chapters
Considers simultaneous submissions: Yes
*Will issue contract on the basis of
  proposal, prospectus, and/or sample
  chapter:* Yes
Special requirements: Length: 225 pages
  minimum; accepts dot-matrix printout
  for sample but not for final manuscript
Subvention: No

EDITORIAL INFORMATION

*Manuscripts or proposals submitted each
  year:* 90 (estimate)
Manuscripts accepted each year: 15
  (estimate)
Number of outside readers: 0
*Time between submission and publication
  decision:* 5 days
Time between decision and publication:
  8-14 months

CONTRACT PROVISIONS

Copyright: Author
Royalty provisions: 10% of net on first
  1,000 copies, 12.5% thereafter

PUBLICATION AND DISTRIBUTION
INFORMATION

Forms of publication: Cloth, paper
Titles published each year: 14
Print run: 1,000
Number of review copies: 30-40
Distribution area: Worldwide
Time in print: 5-10 years

(164)
*MCGILL-QUEEN'S UNIVERSITY PRESS

3430 McTavish St.
Montreal, PQ H3A 1X9, Canada

Contact: Philip J. Cercone, Executive
Director and Editor; Peter B. Blaney,
Acquisitions Editor
Established: 1960
Telephone: 514 398-3750
Fax: 514 398-4333

SCOPE

Publishing interests: Literatures in
English (nineteenth- and twentieth-
century); Canadian literature (especially
Quebecois literature); English literature
(nineteenth- and twentieth-century);
comparative literature; critical theory;
linguistics; classical literature
*Considers all literary and linguistic
topics:* No
Types of works not published: Bibliographies; readers; literary handbooks;
literary encyclopedias; most
Festschriften
Languages published: English

SUBMISSION REQUIREMENTS

Restrictions on authors: Usually must be
Canadian residents because of funding
restrictions

Initial contact: Letter and prospectus
Style: House; Chicago
Special requirements: Accepts dot-matrix
printout; prefers electronic manuscripts;
provides guidelines for manuscript
preparation
Subvention: Yes (from institutional or
governmental sources)

EDITORIAL INFORMATION

*Manuscripts or proposals submitted each
year:* 15 (estimate)
Manuscripts sent to readers each year:
10 (estimate)
Manuscripts accepted each year: 8
Number of outside readers: 2-3
*Time between submission and publication
decision:* 2-3 months
*Time between decision and return of copy-
edited manuscript:* 3 months
Time between decision and publication:
11-12 months

CONTRACT PROVISIONS

Copyright: Publisher
Royalty provisions: 5% of net (paper); 5%
of first 2,000, 10% thereafter (cloth)

PUBLICATION AND DISTRIBUTION
INFORMATION

Forms of publication: Cloth, paper
Titles published each year: 9
Print run: 1,000
Number of review copies: 60-70
Distribution area: Worldwide
Time in print: 5 years

(165)
*CENTER FOR MEDIEVAL AND EARLY RENAISSANCE STUDIES

MRTS-LN G99
State University of New York
Binghamton, NY 13902-6000

Imprint(s) and subsidiary firm(s):
Medieval and Renaissance Texts and
Studies (MRTS); Pegasus Paperbooks
Contact: Mario A. DiCesare, Director
Established: 1978 (MRTS); 1989
(Pegasus)
Telephone: 607 777-6758
E-mail: mrts@bingvma

SCOPE

Publishing interests: (MRTS): medieval
studies; Renaissance studies; critical
editions of medieval and Renaissance
works; translations of medieval and
Renaissance works; bibliographies
(medieval and Renaissance topics);
literary reference works (medieval and
Renaissance studies); John Milton.
(Pegasus): Classroom-related materials
on all aspects of medieval and
Renaissance studies, with special
emphasis on minor authors and
reference works (e.g., selective
annotated bibliographies)
*Considers all literary and linguistic
topics:* Yes (if involving medieval or
Renaissance studies)
Types of works not published: Disser-
tatations; Festschriften
Languages published: English; will
consider other languages

SUBMISSION REQUIREMENTS

Initial contact: (MRTS): Letter and
manuscript or letter and prospectus;
(Pegasus): Letter and prospectus

Style: Chicago
Special requirements: Accepts electronic
manuscripts; provides guidelines for
manuscript preparation; length: prefers
300 pages maximum for Pegasus
Paperbooks
Subvention: No

EDITORIAL INFORMATION

*Manuscripts or proposals submitted each
year:* (MRTS) 60 (estimate); (Pegasus)
25 (estimate)
Manuscripts sent to readers each year:
(MRTS) 24 (estimate); (Pegasus) 11
Manuscripts accepted each year: (MRTS)
8; (Pegasus) 3
Number of outside readers: (MRTS) 2-3;
(Pegasus) 1-2
*Time between submission and publication
decision:* 6 months
*Time between decision and return of copy-
edited manuscript:* 2-4 months
Time between decision and publication:
1 year

CONTRACT PROVISIONS

Copyright: Publisher
Royalty provisions: (MRTS) No royalties;
(Pegasus) 10%

PUBLICATION AND DISTRIBUTION INFORMATION

Forms of publication: (MRTS) Cloth;
(Pegasus) Paper
Titles published each year: (MRTS) 7;
(Pegasus) 1
Print run: (MRTS) 800; (Pegasus) 1,500-
3,000
Number of review copies: 30
Distribution area: Worldwide
Time in print: Indefinitely

(166)
*MEDIEVAL INSTITUTE PUBLICATIONS

Western Michigan University
Kalamazoo, MI 49008-3851

Contact: Thomas H. Seiler, Managing
  Editor
Established: 1978
Telephone: 616 387-4154
Fax: 616 387-4150

SCOPE

Publishing interests: Medieval literature
  (A.D. 500-1500)
*Considers all literary and linguistic
  topics:* No
Types of works not published: Disser-
  tations
Languages published: English; French;
  German; Italian
Series title(s): Studies in Medieval
  Culture; Early Drama, Art, and Music

SUBMISSION REQUIREMENTS

Initial contact: Letter of inquiry or letter
  and prospectus
Style: Chicago
Special requirements: Discourages dot-
  matrix printout; accepts electronic
  manuscripts
Subvention: No

EDITORIAL INFORMATION

*Manuscripts or proposals submitted each
  year:* 9
Manuscripts sent to readers each year: 4
Manuscripts accepted each year: 2
Number of outside readers: 2
*Time between submission and publication
  decision:* 3-6 months
*Time between decision and return of copy-
  edited manuscript:* 6 months

Time between decision and publication:
  12-18 months

CONTRACT PROVISIONS

Copyright: Publisher
Royalty provisions: No royalties

**PUBLICATION AND DISTRIBUTION
INFORMATION**

Forms of publication: Cloth, paper
Titles published each year: 1
Print run: 1,000
Number of review copies: 15-20
Distribution area: Worldwide
Time in print: Indefinitely

(167)
MELBOURNE UNIVERSITY PRESS

PO Box 278
Carlton South 3053, Australia

Imprint(s) and subsidiary firm(s):
  Miegunyah Press
Contact: Brian Wilder (academic books);
  Diana O'Neil (general books); Andrew
  Watson (electronic publishing); John
  Currey (Miegunyah Press)
Established: 1922
Telephone: (03) 3473455
Fax: (03) 3492527

SCOPE

Publishing interests: Australian literature;
  biographies of Australians; Pacific and
  Southeast Asian studies emphasizing
  relations with Australia
*Considers all literary and linguistic
  topics:* Yes
Types of works not published: Unrevised
  dissertations; collections of essays;
  Festschriften
Languages published: English

Series title(s): Interpretations

SUBMISSION REQUIREMENTS

Initial contact: Letter, outline, and sample chapters
Considers simultaneous submissions: Yes
Will issue contract on the basis of proposal, prospectus, and/or sample chapter: Yes
Style: House; Australian Government Printing Service Style Manual
Special requirements: Accepts photocopies and dot-matrix printout; expects electronic manuscript; provides guidelines for manuscript preparation
Subvention: Prefers subvention

EDITORIAL INFORMATION

Manuscripts or proposals submitted each year: 80 (estimate)
Manuscripts sent to readers each year: 15 (estimate)
Manuscripts accepted each year: 15
Number of outside readers: 1-2
Author-anonymous submission: No
Time between submission and publication decision: 4 weeks
Time between decision and publication: 9-12 months
Time allotted for reading proof: 2-3 weeks

CONTRACT PROVISIONS

Copyright: Author
Royalty provisions: 10% of net

PUBLICATION AND DISTRIBUTION INFORMATION

Forms of publication: Cloth, paper, electronic media
Titles published each year: 10
Print run: 1,500
Number of review copies: 40-50
Distribution area: Worldwide

Time in print: Indefinitely

**(168)
EDWIN MELLEN PRESS**

PO Box 450
Lewiston, NY 14092-0450

Contact: John Rupnow, Acquisitions Editor
Established: 1974
Telephone: 716 754-2266
Fax: 716 754-4056

SCOPE

Publishing interests: Medieval literature; American literature; British literature; Celtic literature; Chinese literature; classical literature; comparative literature; film; historical novel; Renaissance literature; African literature; French literature; German literature; Spanish literature; Russian literature; Italian literature; Judaism; literature and religion; Native American literature; Scandinavian literature; theater; performing arts; women's studies; Welsh literature; Slavic literature; literary theory
Considers all literary and linguistic topics: Yes
Languages published: English; French; German; Spanish; Italian; Welsh
Series title(s): Hispanic Literature; Jewish Studies; Mediaeval Studies; Scandinavian Studies; Schlegel Translations; Slavic Studies; Studies in African Literature; Studies in American Literature; Studies in British Literature; Studies in Comparative Literature; Studies in Epic and Romance Literature; Studies in French Literature; Studies in German Literature; Welsh Studies; Studies in Slavic Languages and

Literature; Distinguished Dissertation
Series

SUBMISSION REQUIREMENTS

Initial contact: Letter, outline, and
curriculum vitae
Considers simultaneous submissions: Yes
*Will issue contract on the basis of
proposal, prospectus, and/or sample
chapter:* Yes
Special requirements: Requires camera-
ready copy in both print and electronic
copies
Subvention: Usually no

EDITORIAL INFORMATION

*Manuscripts or proposals submitted each
year:* 240
Manuscripts accepted each year: 60
Number of outside readers: 0
*Time between submission and publication
decision:* 2-3 months
Time between decision and publication:
1-2 years

CONTRACT PROVISIONS

Copyright: Author
Royalty provisions: No royalties

**PUBLICATION AND DISTRIBUTION
INFORMATION**

Forms of publication: Cloth
Titles published each year: 60
Print run: 200
Number of review copies: 7-12
Distribution area: Worldwide
Time in print: Indefinitely

**(169)
MERCER UNIVERSITY PRESS**

6316 Peake Rd.
Macon, GA 31210-3960

Contact: Scott Nash, Managing Editor
Established: 1979
Telephone: 912 752-2880
Fax: 912 752-2264

SCOPE

Publishing interests: Religion and
literature; southern American literature
(especially twentieth-century); Christian
authors of the United States; Greek
language; Coptic language; biblical
Hebrew language
*Considers all literary and linguistic
topics:* Usually no
Types of works not published: Unrevised
dissertations; readers; literary
handbooks
Languages published: English

SUBMISSION REQUIREMENTS

Initial contact: Letter, outline, and sample
chapters
Considers simultaneous submissions: Yes
*Will issue contract on the basis of
proposal, prospectus, and/or sample
chapter:* Yes
Style: Chicago
Special requirements: Requires electronic
manuscript
Subvention: From institutions

EDITORIAL INFORMATION

*Manuscripts or proposals submitted each
year:* 5 (estimate)
Manuscripts sent to readers each year: 3
Manuscripts accepted each year: 3
Number of outside readers: 1-2
Author-anonymous submission: Yes
*Time between submission and publication
decision:* 2-8 months
*Time between decision and return of copy-
edited manuscript:* 2 months
Time between decision and publication:
6-12 months

Time allotted for reading proof: 1 month

CONTRACT PROVISIONS

Copyright: Publisher
Royalty provisions: Nothing on first 1,500
copies, 10% of net thereafter

**PUBLICATION AND DISTRIBUTION
INFORMATION**

Forms of publication: Cloth, paper
Titles published each year: 1
Print run: 750-1,500
Number of review copies: 25
Distribution area: Worldwide
Time in print: Indefinitely

**(170)
*J. B. METZLER VERLAG**

Lektorat Literaturwissenschaft
PO Box 103241
7000 Stuttgart 1, Germany

Contact: Bernd Lutz; Uwe Schweikert;
Petra Wägenbaur
Established: 1682
Telephone: (0711) 2290243
Fax: (0711) 2290290

SCOPE

Publishing interests: Children's literature;
adolescent literature; expressionism;
feminist studies; literary reference
works; exile literature; literary histories;
German literature; linguistics
*Considers all literary and linguistic
topics:* Yes
Types of works not published: Disser-
tations (in languages other than
German); Festschriften
Languages published: German
Series title(s): Sammlung Metzler;
Germanistische Abhandlungen; Metzler

Studienausgabe; Manifeste und
Dokumente zur deutschen Literatur;
Romanistische Abhandlungen

SUBMISSION REQUIREMENTS

Initial contact: Letter and outline
Special requirements: Requires electronic
manuscript or camera-ready copy for
dissertations
Subvention: For dissertations

EDITORIAL INFORMATION

*Manuscripts or proposals submitted each
year:* 100-150 (estimate)
Manuscripts accepted each year: 30
(estimate)
Number of outside readers: 0-1
*Time between submission and publication
decision:* 2 months
Time between decision and publication: 6
months

CONTRACT PROVISIONS

Copyright: Publisher
Royalty provisions: 8% of net (less VAT)

**PUBLICATION AND DISTRIBUTION
INFORMATION**

Forms of publication: Cloth, paper
Titles published each year: 60 (estimate)
Distribution area: German-speaking
countries
Time in print: 6-8 years

**(171)
EL COLEGIO DE MEXICO**

Camino al Ajusco 20
Pedregal de Sta. Teresa
10740 Mexico D.F., Mexico

Contact: Maria Lilia Prieto, Head of the
Department of Publications

Established: 1940
Telephone: 645-5955, ext. 3080 or 3139
Fax: 645-0464

SCOPE

Publishing interests: Hispanic American
literature; ethnic languages of
Hispanoamerica; linguistics
(Hispanoamerican)
Languages published: Spanish

SUBMISSION REQUIREMENTS

Restrictions on authors: Mainly publishes
works by members of the institution
Subvention: No

CONTRACT PROVISIONS

Copyright: Publisher
Royalty provisions: 10% of net

**PUBLICATION AND DISTRIBUTION
INFORMATION**

Forms of publication: Paper
Titles published each year: 7
Print run: 1,000
Number of review copies: 50
Distribution area: Worldwide
Time in print: 5 years

**(172)
UNIVERSITY OF MICHIGAN PRESS**

839 Greene St.
Box 1104
Ann Arbor, MI 48106-1104

Contact: LeAnn Fields
Established: 1930
Telephone: 313 764-4388
Fax: 313 936-0456
E-mail: umpress@umich.edu

SCOPE

Publishing interests: Drama; literary
criticism; literature and other arts;
science and literature; medieval
literature; Renaissance literature;
baroque literature; Romanticism;
African American literature; ethnic
literature; women's studies in literature;
gay studies in literature; Old English
literature; Middle English literature;
Middle English language; English
literature (Renaissance, Victorian, late-
nineteenth-century, twentieth-century);
French literature; German literature;
composition (history and theory); interdisciplinary approaches to culture and
society; lexicography; Slavic poetics;
textual editing; editorial theory
*Considers all literary and linguistic
topics:* Yes
Prizes and competitions: University of
Michigan Press Book Award
Languages published: English
Series title(s): The Body, in Theory;
Critical Perspectives on Women and
Gender; Poets on Poetry; Studies in
medieval and Early Modern Civi-
lization; Theater: Theory/Text/
Performance; Under Discussion;
Women and Culture Series; Editorial
Theory and Literary Criticism

SUBMISSION REQUIREMENTS

Initial contact: Letter and prospectus or
letter, outline, and sample chapter
Considers simultaneous submissions:
Yes, with editor's consent
*Will issue contract on the basis of
proposal, prospectus, and/or sample
chapter:* Sometimes
Style: Chicago; MLA; house
Special requirements: Length: prefers 500
pages maximum; accepts photocopies,
camera-ready copy, and electronic

manuscripts; provides guidelines for
manuscript preparation
Subvention: Sometimes

EDITORIAL INFORMATION

*Manuscripts or proposals submitted each
year:* 400 (estimate)
Manuscripts sent to readers each year: 60
(estimate)
Manuscripts accepted each year: 35
(estimate)
Number of outside readers: 2-3
Author-anonymous submission: No
*Time between submission and publication
decision:* 3-6 months
*Time between decision and return of copy-
edited manuscript:* 1-3 months
Time between decision and publication:
8-14 months
Time allotted for reading proof: 1 month

CONTRACT PROVISIONS

Copyright: Publisher
Royalty provisions: Negotiable

**PUBLICATION AND DISTRIBUTION
INFORMATION**

Forms of publication: Cloth, paper
Titles published each year: 50
Print run: 1,000
Number of review copies: 50-100
Distribution area: Worldwide
Time in print: 10 years

**(173)
MICHIGAN STATE UNIVERSITY
PRESS**

1405 South Harrison Rd., Suite 25
East Lansing, MI 48823-5202

Contact: Julie Loehr, Editor in Chief
Established: 1947

Telephone: 517 355-9543
Fax: 517 432-2611
E-mail: msp03@msu.edu

SCOPE

Publishing interests: American literature;
African literatures; Canadian literature
*Considers all literary and linguistic
topics:* Yes
Types of works not published: Dissertations; bibliographies; Festschriften;
biographies; collections of letters;
literary handbooks; literary encyclopedias
Languages published: English

SUBMISSION REQUIREMENTS

Initial contact: Prospectus, sample
chapter, and curriculum vitae
Considers simultaneous submissions: Yes
*Will issue contract on the basis of
proposal, prospectus, and/or sample
chapter:* Sometimes
Style: Chicago
Special requirements: Requires electronic
manuscript
Subvention: No

EDITORIAL INFORMATION

*Manuscripts or proposals submitted each
year:* 200 (estimate)
Manuscripts sent to readers each year: 40
(estimate)
Manuscripts accepted each year: 10
(estimate)
Number of outside readers: 2-3
Author-anonymous submission: Yes
*Time between submission and publication
decision:* 3-5 months
*Time between decision and return of copy-
edited manuscript:* 4 months
Time between decision and publication:
6-12 months

Time allotted for reading proof: 2-3
  weeks

CONTRACT PROVISIONS

Copyright: Negotiable
Royalty provisions: 10% of net

**PUBLICATION AND DISTRIBUTION
INFORMATION**

Forms of publication: Cloth, paper
Titles published each year: 4 (estimate)
Print run: 1,000
Number of review copies: 20-30
Distribution area: United States; Canada;
  Europe
Time in print: 3-5 years

**(174)
CENTER FOR MIDDLE EASTERN
STUDIES**

F9400
University of Texas
Austin, TX 78712

Contact: Annes McCann-Baker
Established: 1976
Telephone: 512 471-3881
Fax: 512 471-7834
E-mail: annes@uts.cc.utexas.edu

SCOPE

Publishing interests: Middle Eastern
  literature; translations of Middle Eastern
  fiction
*Considers all literary and linguistic
  topics:* No
Languages published: English
Series title(s): Modern Middle Eastern
  Literatures in Translation Series

SUBMISSION REQUIREMENTS

Initial contact: Letter of inquiry and
  proposal
Considers simultaneous submissions:
  Prefers single submission
*Will issue contract on the basis of
  proposal, prospectus, and/or sample
  chapter:* No
Style: Chicago
Special requirements: Prefers electronic
  manuscripts
Subvention: Sometimes

EDITORIAL INFORMATION

*Manuscripts or proposals submitted each
  year:* 100 (estimate)
Manuscripts sent to readers each year:
  10 (estimate)
Manuscripts accepted each year: 10
  (estimate)
Number of outside readers: 2-4
Author-anonymous submission: No

CONTRACT PROVISIONS

Copyright: Publisher

**PUBLICATION AND DISTRIBUTION
INFORMATION**

Forms of publication: Cloth
Titles published each year: 2
Print run: 1,500-2,000
Number of review copies: 50
Time in print: 3-5 years

**(175)
MILKWEED EDITIONS**

430 First Ave. North, Suite 400
Minneapolis, MN 55401

Contact: Emile Buchwald, Publisher and
  Editor
Established: 1984

Telephone: 612 332-3192

SCOPE

Publishing interests: Nonacademic
literary nonfiction; gender issues;
education
*Considers all literary and linguistic
topics:* No
Not interested in proposals on: Literary
criticism; literary history
Types of works not published: Collections
of essays by different authors
Languages published: English

SUBMISSION REQUIREMENTS

Initial contact: Letter and sample
chapters
Considers simultaneous submissions: Yes
*Will issue contract on the basis of
proposal, prospectus, and/or sample
chapter:* No
Style: Chicago
Subvention: No

EDITORIAL INFORMATION

*Manuscripts or proposals submitted each
year:* 312
Manuscripts sent to readers each year:
150
Manuscripts accepted each year: 2
Number of outside readers: 1
Author-anonymous submission: No
*Time between submission and publication
decision:* 4-6 months
Time between decision and publication: 1
month

CONTRACT PROVISIONS

Copyright: Author

PUBLICATION AND DISTRIBUTION
INFORMATION

Forms of publication: Cloth, paper

Titles published each year: 2
Print run: 3,000-5,000
Number of review copies: 150
Distribution area: United States; Canada
Time in print: Varies

(176)
MINERVA ASSOCIATES

7-B Lake Place
Calcutta 700029, India

Contact: Sushil Mukherjea
Established: 1973
Telephone: 42-3783

SCOPE

Publishing interests: General literature;
Indian literature
*Considers all literary and linguistic
topics:* Yes
Types of works not published: Textbooks;
bibliographies; Festschriften; literary
encyclopedias
Languages published: English

SUBMISSION REQUIREMENTS

Initial contact: Letter and manuscript
Considers simultaneous submissions: No
*Will issue contract on the basis of
proposal, prospectus, and/or sample
chapter:* No
Style: House
Special requirements: Accepts photo-
copies, dot-matrix printout, and camera-
ready copy
Subvention: Yes

EDITORIAL INFORMATION

*Manuscripts or proposals submitted each
year:* 20
Manuscripts sent to readers each year:
12

Manuscripts accepted each year: 12
Number of outside readers: 6
Author-anonymous submission: Yes
*Time between submission and publication
   decision:* 2 months
*Time between decision and return of copy-
   edited manuscript:* 1 month
Time between decision and publication:
   4-6 months

CONTRACT PROVISIONS

Copyright: Author
Royalty provisions: 10%

**PUBLICATION AND DISTRIBUTION
INFORMATION**

Forms of publication: Cloth
Titles published each year: 12
Print run: 500-1,000
Number of review copies: 40
Distribution area: Worldwide
Time in print: 6 years

**(177)
UNIVERSITY OF MINNESOTA
PRESS**

111 Third Ave. South
Minneapolis, MN 55401

Contact: Lisa Freeman
Telephone: 612 627-1970
Fax: 612 627-1980
E-mail: ump@maroon.tc.unm.edu

SCOPE

Publishing interests: Literary theory
   (especially related to postmodern
   French philosophy); emergent literatures; technology and literature; media
   and literature; rhetoric; linguistics;
   semiotics; medieval studies; Hispanic

studies; cultural politics; postcolonial
discourse
*Considers all literary and linguistic
   topics:* Yes
Types of works not published: Bibli-
   ographies; collections of letters;
   textbooks; Festschriften; literary
   handbooks and encyclopedias
Languages published: English
Series title(s): Theory and History of
   Literature; Medieval Cultures; Theory
   Out of Bounds; Cultural Politics;
   Cultural Studies of the Americas

SUBMISSION REQUIREMENTS

Initial contact: Letter, prospectus, table of
   contents, and 2 sample chapters
Considers simultaneous submissions: Yes
*Will issue contract on the basis of
   proposal, prospectus, and/or sample
   chapter:* Yes
Style: Chicago
Special requirements: Accepts electronic
   manuscripts; provides guidelines for
   manuscript preparation
Subvention: No

EDITORIAL INFORMATION

*Manuscripts or proposals submitted each
   year:* 260 (estimate)
Manuscripts sent to readers each year: 60
   (estimate)
Manuscripts accepted each year: 40
   (estimate)
Number of outside readers: 2 minimum
Author-anonymous submission: No
*Time between submission and publication
   decision:* 2 months maximum
*Time between decision and return of copy-
   edited manuscript:* 5-6 months
Time between decision and publication:
   10 months
Time allotted for reading proof: 3 weeks

CONTRACT PROVISIONS

Copyright: Publisher
Royalty provisions: 5-10% of net

PUBLICATION AND DISTRIBUTION
INFORMATION

Forms of publication: Cloth, paper
Titles published each year: 40 (estimate)
Print run: 500-1,000 cloth; 2,000-5,000
  paper
Number of review copies: 100-300
Distribution area: Worldwide
Time in print: Depends on sales

(178)
UNIVERSITY PRESS OF
MISSISSIPPI

3825 Ridgewood Rd.
Jackson, MS 39211-6492

Imprint(s) and subsidiary firm(s): Banner
  Books; Muscadine Books
Contact: Richard M. Abel, Director and
  Publisher (American studies); Seetha A.
  Srinivasan, Associate Director and
  Editor in Chief (literary and ethnic
  studies); JoAnne Prichard, Executive
  Editor (folklore and performance
  studies)
Established: 1970
Telephone: 601 982-6205
Fax: 601 982-6610
E-mail: mpress@ihl.state.ms.us

SCOPE

Publishing interests: African American
  studies; American culture; American
  literature (nineteenth- and twentieth-
  century); southern American literature;
  American studies; Native American
  studies; literary reference works;
  biography; British literature; ethnic

studies; William Faulkner; fiction; film
studies; folklore; gender studies; interdisciplinary studies; literary criticism;
literary history; literary theory; modern
literature; novel; performance studies;
popular culture; theater; Eudora Welty;
women's studies
*Considers all literary and linguistic
  topics:* No
Types of works not published:
  Festschriften
Prizes and competitions: Eudora Welty
  Prize (annual prize for a work in
  women's studies, southern American
  studies, or modern letters)
Languages published: English
Series title(s): Literary Conversations
  Series; Author and Artist Series; Studies
  in Popular Culture Series; Faulkner and
  Yoknapatawpha; Folklife in the South
  Series; Center for the Study of Southern
  Culture Series; American Literature /
  American Studies; Performance Studies:
  Expressive Behavior in Culture; Folk
  Art and Artist

SUBMISSION REQUIREMENTS

Initial contact: Letter, prospectus, table of
  contents, 1-2 sample chapters, and
  curriculum vitae
Considers simultaneous submissions:
  Yes, if informed
*Will issue contract on the basis of
  proposal, prospectus, and/or sample
  chapter:* Yes
Style: Chicago; MLA
Special requirements: Length: negotiable;
  prefers electronic manuscripts
Subvention: No

EDITORIAL INFORMATION

*Manuscripts or proposals submitted each
  year:* 500 (estimate)
Manuscripts sent to readers each year:
  100 (estimate)

Manuscripts accepted each year: 25
(estimate)
Number of outside readers: 2 minimum
Author-anonymous submission: No
*Time between submission and publication
decision:* 3-4 months
*Time between decision and return of copy-
edited manuscript:* 2 months
Time between decision and publication:
1 year
Time allotted for reading proof: 4-5
weeks

CONTRACT PROVISIONS

Copyright: Negotiable
Royalty provisions: Negotiable

**PUBLICATION AND DISTRIBUTION
INFORMATION**

Forms of publication: Cloth, paper, elec-
tronic media
Titles published each year: 18
Print run: 1,000-5,000
Number of review copies: 75-150
Distribution area: Worldwide
Time in print: 5 years minimum

**(179)
UNIVERSITY OF MISSOURI PRESS**

2910 LeMone Blvd.
Columbia, MO 65201

Contact: Beverly Jarrett, Director and
Editor in Chief; Clair Willcox, Acqui-
sitions Editor
Established: 1958
Telephone: 314 882-0182
Fax: 314 884-4498

SCOPE

Publishing interests: Literary criticism
and history (primarily American,

British, Spanish, or Latin American
literatures)
*Considers all literary and linguistic
topics:* Yes
Languages published: English

SUBMISSION REQUIREMENTS

Initial contact: Letter of inquiry and
prospectus
Considers simultaneous submissions: No
*Will issue contract on the basis of
proposal, prospectus, and/or sample
chapter:* Rarely
Style: Chicago
Subvention: No

EDITORIAL INFORMATION

*Manuscripts or proposals submitted each
year:* 200 (estimate)
Manuscripts sent to readers each year:
45-50
Manuscripts accepted each year: 15
Number of outside readers: 2
Author-anonymous submission: No
*Time between submission and publication
decision:* 6-8 months
Time between decision and publication:
1 year
Time allotted for reading proof: 3-4
weeks

CONTRACT PROVISIONS

Copyright: Negotiable

**PUBLICATION AND DISTRIBUTION
INFORMATION**

Forms of publication: Cloth, paper
Titles published each year: 15 (estimate)
Print run: 1,200-1,500
Number of review copies: 80-100
Distribution area: Worldwide
Time in print: Indefinitely

(180)
MIT PRESS

55 Hayward St.
Cambridge, MA 02142

Contact: Roger Conover (cultural
studies); Larry Cohen (philosophy);
Amy Pierce (linguistics)
Established: 1963
Telephone: 617 253-1677
Fax: 617 258-6779

SCOPE

Publishing interests: Linguistics;
aesthetics; cultural criticism; philosophy
*Considers all literary and linguistic
topics:* No
Types of works not published: Bibliographies; critical editions; collections
of letters; Festschriften
Languages published: English
Series title(s): Linguistic Inquiry Monographs; Current Studies in Linguistics;
October Books

SUBMISSION REQUIREMENTS

Initial contact: Letter and prospectus
Considers simultaneous submissions: Yes
*Will issue contract on the basis of
proposal, prospectus, and/or sample
chapter:* Sometimes
Style: Chicago
Special requirements: Does not accept
dot-matrix printout
Subvention: Usually not

EDITORIAL INFORMATION

*Manuscripts or proposals submitted each
year:* 100 (estimate)
Manuscripts sent to readers each year: 5
(estimate)
Manuscripts accepted each year: 2
(estimate)

Number of outside readers: 2-4
Author-anonymous submission: Yes
*Time between submission and publication
decision:* 1 month (rejection); 3 months
(acceptance)
*Time between decision and return of copy-
edited manuscript:* 6-8 weeks
Time between decision and publication:
1 year
Time allotted for reading proof: 2 weeks

CONTRACT PROVISIONS

Copyright: Publisher or author

PUBLICATION AND DISTRIBUTION
INFORMATION

Forms of publication: Cloth, paper, elec-
tronic media
Titles published each year: 5 (estimate)
Print run: 2,000-3,000
Number of review copies: 100
Distribution area: Worldwide
Time in print: 8-10 years

(181)
**MODERN HUMANITIES RESEARCH
ASSOCIATION (MHRA)**

Birkbeck College
Malet St.
London WC1E 7HX, England

Contact: D. A. Wells, Honorary Secretary
Established: 1918
Telephone: (0171) 6316103
Fax: (0171) 3833729

SCOPE

Publishing interests: European literatures
(medieval); European literatures
(modern); Slavic literatures; European
languages; Slavic languages

Considers all literary and linguistic topics: Yes
Not interested in proposals on: Pedagogical topics; medical applications of linguistics; library studies; history
Types of works not published: Literary reference works
Languages published: English
Series title(s): MHRA Texts and Dissertations

SUBMISSION REQUIREMENTS

Initial contact: Letter, prospectus, and summary
Considers simultaneous submissions: No
Will issue contract on the basis of proposal, prospectus, and/or sample chapter: No
Style: MHRA
Special requirements: Depends on manuscript
Subvention: Depends on nature of topic

EDITORIAL INFORMATION

Manuscripts accepted each year: 4
Number of outside readers: 2
Author-anonymous submission: Yes
Time between submission and publication decision: 3 months
Time between decision and publication: Up to 2 years
Time allotted for reading proof: 6 weeks

CONTRACT PROVISIONS

Copyright: Publisher
Royalty provisions: 0

PUBLICATION AND DISTRIBUTION INFORMATION

Forms of publication: Cloth, paper
Print run: Varies
Number of review copies: 20
Distribution area: Worldwide
Time in print: Indefinitely

(182)
MODERN LANGUAGE ASSOCIATION OF AMERICA

10 Astor Place
New York, NY 10003-6981

Contact: Joseph Gibaldi, Director, Book Acquisitions and Development
Established: 1883
Telephone: 212 614-6312
Fax: 212 477-9863
E-mail: bookpub@mla.org

SCOPE

Publishing interests: General literature; linguistics; folklore; bibliography; literary research methods; composition; technology and the humanities; reference works; professional topics related to literature and language
Considers all literary and linguistic topics: Yes
Types of works not published: Dissertations; critical editions; collections of letters; biographies; readers; Festschriften
Languages published: English
Series title(s): Approaches to Teaching World Literature; Options for Teaching; Research and Scholarship in Composition; Texts and Translations (works in this series are published in the original language and in an English translation)

SUBMISSION REQUIREMENTS

Initial contact: Letter of inquiry (including discussion of audience)
Considers simultaneous submissions: No
Will issue contract on the basis of proposal, prospectus, and/or sample chapter: No
Style: MLA

Special requirements: Some series have
length restrictions; accepts electronic
manuscripts
Subvention: No

EDITORIAL INFORMATION

*Manuscripts or proposals submitted each
year:* 100 (estimate)
Manuscripts sent to readers each year: 24
Manuscripts accepted each year: 12
Number of outside readers: 2 minimum
Author-anonymous submission: No
*Time between submission and publication
decision:* 1 year
*Time between decision and return of copy-
edited manuscript:* 6 months
Time between decision and publication:
1 year

CONTRACT PROVISIONS

Copyright: Publisher
Royalty provisions: 10%

**PUBLICATION AND DISTRIBUTION
INFORMATION**

Forms of publication: Cloth, paper, elec-
tronic media
Titles published each year: 15
Print run: 1,000-2,000
Number of review copies: 25-50
Distribution area: Worldwide
Time in print: 5 years minimum

**(183)
PRESSES DE L'UNIVERSITE DE
MONTREAL**

C.P. 6128, succ. Centre-Ville
Montreal, PQ H3C 3J7, Canada

Contact: Marie-Claire Borgo, Director;
Marise Labrecque, Editor in Chief
Established: 1962

Telephone: 514 343-6929
Fax: 514 343-2232

SCOPE

Publishing interests: Linguistics; Quebec
literature; critical editions of Quebecois
and French literary works; medieval
studies
*Considers all literary and linguistic
topics:* Yes
Types of works not published: Dissertations; literary encyclopedias
Languages published: French
Series title(s): BNM: Bibliothèque du
nouveau-monde; Collection études
médiévales

SUBMISSION REQUIREMENTS

Initial contact: Letter and manuscript or
letter, outline, and sample chapters
Considers simultaneous submissions: No
*Will issue contract on the basis of
proposal, prospectus, and/or sample
chapter:* No
Special requirements: Requires electronic
manuscript
Subvention: Preferably

EDITORIAL INFORMATION

*Manuscripts or proposals submitted each
year:* 20 (estimate)
Manuscripts sent to readers each year:
10 (estimate)
Manuscripts accepted each year: 2
Number of outside readers: 3
Author-anonymous submission: No
*Time between submission and publication
decision:* 3-6 months
*Time between decision and return of copy-
edited manuscript:* 12-18 months
Time between decision and publication:
1 year
Time allotted for reading proof: 3 weeks

CONTRACT PROVISIONS

Copyright: Publisher
Royalty provisions: 10% of net

PUBLICATION AND DISTRIBUTION INFORMATION

Forms of publication: Paper
Titles published each year: 3
Print run: 1,000-1,500
Number of review copies: 25-30
Distribution area: Francophone Canada and Europe
Time in print: 7 years

(184)
MULTILINGUAL MATTERS

Frankfurt Lodge, Clevedon Hall
Victoria Rd.
Clevedon, Avon BS21 7SJ, England

Imprint(s) and subsidiary firm(s):
  Channel View Publications
Contact: Marjukka Grover
Established: 1980
Telephone: (01275) 876519
Fax: (01275) 343096

SCOPE

Publishing interests: Bilingualism; multi-cultural studies; second-language learning
Considers all literary and linguistic topics: No
Languages published: English
Series title(s): Multilingual Matters; Language and Education Library; Topics in Translation; Bilingual Education and Bilingualism; Modern Languages in Practice

SUBMISSION REQUIREMENTS

Initial contact: Letter, outline, and sample chapters
Considers simultaneous submissions: No
Will issue contract on the basis of proposal, prospectus, and/or sample chapter: No
Style: House
Special requirements: Prefers electronic manuscripts
Subvention: No

EDITORIAL INFORMATION

Manuscripts or proposals submitted each year: 25 (estimate)
Manuscripts sent to readers each year: 20 (estimate)
Manuscripts accepted each year: 15 (estimate)
Number of outside readers: 1
Author-anonymous submission: No
Time between submission and publication decision: 3-6 months
Time between decision and publication: 7-10 months
Time allotted for reading proof: 3 weeks

CONTRACT PROVISIONS

Copyright: Author

PUBLICATION AND DISTRIBUTION INFORMATION

Forms of publication: Cloth, paper
Titles published each year: 20 (estimate)
Print run: 1,000-2,000
Number of review copies: 20-30
Distribution area: Worldwide
Time in print: 4-5 years

(185)
*PRESSES UNIVERSITAIRES DE NANCY

25, rue Baron Louis
54000 Nancy, France

Contact: Jean-Marie Bonnet, Président-Directeur Général
Established: 1976
Telephone: (83) 373765
Fax: (83) 300565

SCOPE

Publishing interests: Linguistics (general, French, English, and American topics); French literature; English literature; American literature; Italian literature; German literature; Slavic literature; drama; literary history
Considers all literary and linguistic topics: Yes
Types of works not published: Bibliographies
Languages published: French; English; German
Series title(s): Phares; Travaux du C.R.A.L.; Textes oubliés; Recherche littéraire; Diagonales; Etudes allemandes; Jalons

SUBMISSION REQUIREMENTS

Initial contact: Letter, outline, and sample chapters
Style: MLA
Special requirements: Accepts electronic manuscripts; provides guidelines for manuscript preparation
Subvention: Not necessarily

EDITORIAL INFORMATION

Manuscripts or proposals submitted each year: 40 (estimate)

Manuscripts sent to readers each year: 6 (estimate)
Manuscripts accepted each year: 20 (estimate)
Number of outside readers: 2
Time between submission and publication decision: 3 months
Time between decision and return of copy-edited manuscript: 2 months
Time between decision and publication: 4-6 months

CONTRACT PROVISIONS

Copyright: Publisher
Royalty provisions: 8% of list

PUBLICATION AND DISTRIBUTION INFORMATION

Forms of publication: Cloth, paper
Titles published each year: 15 (estimate)
Print run: 2,000
Number of review copies: 50
Distribution area: Worldwide
Time in print: 5-10 years

(186)
NATIONAL COUNCIL OF TEACHERS OF ENGLISH

1111 West Kenyon Rd.
Urbana, IL 61801-1096

Contact: Dawn Boyer, Director of Acquisitions; Marlo Welshons, Coordinator of Publications
Established: 1911
Telephone: 217 328-3870
Fax: 217 328-0977
E-mail: ncte@vmd.cso.uiuc.edu

SCOPE

Publishing interests: English-language literature; literary theory; teaching of

literature; literacy; composition
research; teaching of composition;
teaching English as a second language;
professional materials for English
language arts teachers
Considers all literary and linguistic
topics: No
Types of works not published: Dissertations; critical editions; collections of
letters; biographies; readers; literary
reference works; textbooks
Languages published: English
Series title(s): NCTE Research Report
Series; NCTE Classroom Practices
Series; Theory and Research into
Practice Series

SUBMISSION REQUIREMENTS

Initial contact: Letter of inquiry or letter
and prospectus; provides guidelines for
submission
Considers simultaneous submissions:
Yes, if informed
Will issue contract on the basis of
proposal, prospectus, and/or sample
chapter: Yes
Style: MLA; Chicago
Special requirements: Accepts photocopies; requires electronic manuscript;
does not accept dot-matrix printout;
provides guidelines for manuscript
preparation
Subvention: No

EDITORIAL INFORMATION

Manuscripts or proposals submitted each
year: 100 (estimate)
Manuscripts sent to readers each year: 50
(estimate)
Manuscripts accepted each year: 25
(estimate)
Number of outside readers: 3-5
Author-anonymous submission: No
Time between submission and publication
decision: 3-4 months

Time between decision and return of copy-
edited manuscript: 5-10 months
Time between decision and publication:
7-14 months

CONTRACT PROVISIONS

Copyright: Publisher
Royalty provisions: 8% of net (10% after
5,000 copies)

PUBLICATION AND DISTRIBUTION
INFORMATION

Forms of publication: Paper
Titles published each year: 24
Print run: 3,500
Number of review copies: 75
Distribution area: United States
Time in print: Varies

(187)
NCUP

292 Washington Ave. Ext., Suite 107
Albany, NY 12203

Contact: D. Lee Kmieciak
Established: 1983
Telephone: 518 456-2072
Fax: 518 869-8851

SCOPE

Publishing interests: American literature
(seventeeth- through nineteenth-
century); southern American literature;
multiethnic literature; frontier literature;
women's studies; drama; literary
criticism
Considers all literary and linguistic
topics: Yes
Types of works not published: Literary
reference works
Languages published: English; German
Series title(s): Masterworks of Literature

SUBMISSION REQUIREMENTS

Restrictions on authors: Must be English professors for Masterworks series
Initial contact: Letter of inquiry
Considers simultaneous submissions: Yes
Will issue contract on the basis of proposal, prospectus, and/or sample chapter: Yes
Subvention: No

EDITORIAL INFORMATION

Manuscripts or proposals submitted each year: 200
Manuscripts accepted each year: 30 (estimate)
Number of outside readers: 3
Time between submission and publication decision: 1 month
Time between decision and return of copy-edited manuscript: 2 months
Time between decision and publication: 4-6 months
Time allotted for reading proof: 3-4 weeks

CONTRACT PROVISIONS

Copyright: Publisher

PUBLICATION AND DISTRIBUTION INFORMATION

Forms of publication: Paper
Titles published each year: 20
Print run: 600-1,000
Number of review copies: 50-100
Distribution area: Worldwide
Time in print: Varies

Formerly New College and University Press

(188)
UNIVERSITY OF NEBRASKA PRESS

312 North 14th St.
Lincoln, NE 68588-0484

Imprint(s) and subsidiary firm(s): Bison Books; Landmark Editions
Contact: Humanities Editor
Established: 1941
Telephone: 402 472-3581
Fax: 402 472-0308
E-mail: delayton@unlinfo.unl.edu

SCOPE

Publishing interests: English literature (twentieth-century); American literature (twentieth-century); French literature (twentieth-century); German literature (twentieth-century); medieval studies; translations; Native American literature and culture; literary theory
Considers all literary and linguistic topics: Yes
Types of works not published: Festschriften
Prizes and competitions: North American Indian Prose Award
Languages published: English; Latin; Greek; Hopi; Koasati; Arikara
Series title(s): American Indian Lives; European Women Writers; Latin American Women Writers; French Modernist Library; Modern Scandinavian Literature in Translation; Regents Studies in Medieval Culture; Modern German Literature and Culture; Texts and Contexts; Critics of the Twentieth Century; Sources of American Indian Oral Literature; Stages

SUBMISSION REQUIREMENTS

Initial contact: Letter, prospectus, and curriculum vitae

Considers simultaneous submissions:
  Prefers single submission
*Will issue contract on the basis of
  proposal, prospectus, and/or sample
  chapter:* Yes
Style: Chicago
Special requirements: Accepts dot-matrix
  printout and electronic manuscripts;
  provides guidelines for manuscript
  preparation
Subvention: Occasionally

EDITORIAL INFORMATION

*Manuscripts or proposals submitted each
  year:* 600
Manuscripts sent to readers each year:
  120
Manuscripts accepted each year: 50
Number of outside readers: 2 minimum
Author-anonymous submission: No
*Time between submission and publication
  decision:* 5 months
*Time between decision and return of copy-
  edited manuscript:* 3 months
Time between decision and publication:
  14 months
Time allotted for reading proof: 3 weeks

CONTRACT PROVISIONS

Copyright: Varies
Royalty provisions: Varies (from no
  royalties to 15% of list)

**PUBLICATION AND DISTRIBUTION
INFORMATION**

Forms of publication: Cloth, paper, elec-
  tronic media
Titles published each year: 54
Print run: 1,000-2,000
Number of review copies: 150
Distribution area: Worldwide
Time in print: 10 years

(189)
*NELSON-HALL PUBLISHERS

111 North Canal St.
Chicago, IL 60606

Contact: Richard Meade, General
  Manager
Established: 1909
Telephone: 312 930-9446

SCOPE

Publishing interests: Communications;
  popular culture; theater; performing arts
*Considers all literary and linguistic
  topics:* No
Types of works not published: Bibli-
  ographies; collections of letters;
  Festschriften; literary reference books
Languages published: English

SUBMISSION REQUIREMENTS

Initial contact: Letter and prospectus or
  outline
Style: Chicago
Special requirements: Does not accept
  electronic manuscripts
Subvention: No

EDITORIAL INFORMATION

Number of outside readers: 2-4
*Time between submission and publication
  decision:* 1-2 months
Time between decision and publication:
  1 year

CONTRACT PROVISIONS

Copyright: Publisher, generally
Royalty provisions: 10% of net

**PUBLICATION AND DISTRIBUTION
INFORMATION**

Forms of publication: Cloth, paper

Number of review copies: 50-100
Distribution area: United States and
  dependencies; Canada
Time in print: 10-20 years

Specializes in textbooks

(190)
UNIVERSITY OF NEVADA PRESS

Morrill Hall
Mail stop 166
Reno, NV 89557-0076

Contact: Thomas R. Radko, Director
Established: 1961
Telephone: 702 784-6573
Fax: 702 784-1300
E-mail: radko@scs.nevada.edu

SCOPE

Publishing interests: Basque literature;
  Basque culture; western American
  literature; fiction
*Considers all literary and linguistic
  topics:* No
Types of works not published: Unrevised
  dissertations; Festschriften
Languages published: English; Basque
Series title(s): Basque Books Series;
  Western Literature Series

SUBMISSION REQUIREMENTS

Initial contact: Letter and prospectus
Considers simultaneous submissions:
  Yes, if informed
*Will issue contract on the basis of
  proposal, prospectus, and/or sample
  chapter:* Occasionally
Style: Chicago
Special requirements: Requires electronic
  manuscript
Subvention: No

EDITORIAL INFORMATION

*Manuscripts or proposals submitted each
  year:* 30
Manuscripts sent to readers each year:
  15
Manuscripts accepted each year: 5
Number of outside readers: 2 minimum
Author-anonymous submission: No
*Time between submission and publication
  decision:* 2-3 months
*Time between decision and return of copy-
  edited manuscript:* 2 months
Time between decision and publication:
  10 months
Time allotted for reading proof: 1 month

CONTRACT PROVISIONS

Copyright: Publisher
Royalty provisions: 10-15% of net

PUBLICATION AND DISTRIBUTION
INFORMATION

Forms of publication: Cloth, paper
Titles published each year: 5
Print run: 1,500-2,000
Number of review copies: 75-100
Distribution area: Worldwide
Time in print: 10 years minimum

(191)
*UNIVERSITY PRESS OF NEW
ENGLAND

17½ Lebanon St.
Hanover, NH 03755

Contact: Jeanne West, Acquisitions
  Editor (literary, gender, and regional
  studies); Scott Mahler, Editorial
  Director (twentieth-century American
  literature and Jewish studies)
Established: 1970
Telephone: 603 646-3349

Fax: 603 643-1540

SCOPE

Publishing interests: American literature
(eighteenth-, nineteenth-, and twentieth-
century); English literature (eighteenth-,
nineteenth-, and twentieth-century);
French literature (eighteenth-, nine-
teenth-, and twentieth-century); gender
studies (especially involving women of
color); New England studies; literary
criticism; literary theory; cultural
studies
*Considers all literary and linguistic
topics:* Yes
Types of works not published: Unrevised
dissertations; Festschriften; literary
reference works
Languages published: English

SUBMISSION REQUIREMENTS

Initial contact: Letter and prospectus
Style: MLA; Chicago
Special requirements: Length: prefers
200-450 pages; accepts photocopies;
does not accept dot-matrix printout;
encourages submission of electronic
manuscripts; provides guidelines for
manuscript preparation
Subvention: Sometimes

EDITORIAL INFORMATION

*Manuscripts or proposals submitted each
year:* 500 (estimate)
Manuscripts sent to readers each year: 50
(estimate)
Manuscripts accepted each year: 20
(estimate)
Number of outside readers: 2
*Time between submission and publication
decision:* 2-3 months
*Time between decision and return of copy-
edited manuscript:* 2-3 months

Time between decision and publication:
12-18 months

CONTRACT PROVISIONS

Copyright: Negotiable
Royalty provisions: 10% of net (cloth)

PUBLICATION AND DISTRIBUTION INFORMATION

Forms of publication: Cloth, paper
Titles published each year: 14 (estimate)
Print run: 750-3,000
Number of review copies: 50-100
Distribution area: Worldwide
Time in print: Indefinitely

(192)
UNIVERSITY OF NEW MEXICO PRESS

1720 Lomas Blvd., NE
Albuquerque, NM 87131

Contact: Barbara Guth, Editor
Established: 1929
Telephone: 505 277-2346
Fax: 505 277-9270
E-mail: unmpress@carina.unm.edu

SCOPE

Publishing interests: Western American
literature; Chicano literature; Native
American literature
*Considers all literary and linguistic
topics:* No
Types of works not published: Textbooks;
Festschriften; literary reference works
Languages published: English

SUBMISSION REQUIREMENTS

Initial contact: Letter and prospectus
Considers simultaneous submissions: Yes
(proposals); no (manuscripts)

*Will issue contract on the basis of
proposal, prospectus, and/or sample
chapter:* Yes
Style: Chicago
Special requirements: Accepts photocopies or dot-matrix printout; requires
electronic manuscript; provides
guidelines for manuscript preparation
Subvention: No

EDITORIAL INFORMATION

*Manuscripts or proposals submitted each
year:* 25 (estimate)
Manuscripts sent to readers each year: 6
(estimate)
Manuscripts accepted each year: 4
Number of outside readers: 1-3
Author-anonymous submission: No
*Time between submission and publication
decision:* 6 months
*Time between decision and return of copy-
edited manuscript:* 3 months
Time between decision and publication:
12-18 months
Time allotted for reading proof: 4-6
weeks

CONTRACT PROVISIONS

Copyright: Varies
Royalty provisions: 10% of net (cloth);
7.5% of net (paper). First-time authors
and some others are generally asked to
waive royalties on the first printing.

**PUBLICATION AND DISTRIBUTION
INFORMATION**

Forms of publication: Cloth, paper
Titles published each year: 6
Print run: 1,500
Number of review copies: 50-75
Distribution area: United States; United
Kingdom; Canada; Australia; Europe
Time in print: 3-5 years

**(193)
STATE UNIVERSITY OF NEW YORK
PRESS**

SUNY Plaza
Albany, NY 12246-0001

Contact: Carola Sautter, Acquisitions
Editor
Established: 1965
Telephone: 518 472-5031
Fax: 518 472-5038

SCOPE

Publishing interests: Literary theory;
comparative literature; science and
literature; art and literature; psychology
and literature; philosophy and literature;
anthropology and literature; feminist
criticism; feminist theory; minority literatures; Jewish studies
*Considers all literary and linguistic
topics:* No
Types of works not published: Bibliographies; critical editions;
Festschriften; literary handbooks;
literary encyclopedias; literary reference
works
Languages published: English
Series title(s): Intersection: Philosophy
and Critical Theory; The Margins of
Literature; Feminist Criticism and
Theory; Modern Jewish Literature and
Culture; Postmodern Culture; Women
Writers in Translation; The Sublime

SUBMISSION REQUIREMENTS

Initial contact: Letter, outline, and sample
chapter; provides guidelines for
submitting proposals
Considers simultaneous submissions: Yes
*Will issue contract on the basis of
proposal, prospectus, and/or sample
chapter:* Yes
Style: Chicago; MLA (occasionally)

Special requirements: Length: 170-400
  pages
Subvention: Not usually

EDITORIAL INFORMATION

*Manuscripts or proposals submitted each
  year:* 300 (estimate)
Manuscripts sent to readers each year:
  100 (estimate)
Manuscripts accepted each year: 50
  (estimate)
Number of outside readers: 2-4
Author-anonymous submission: No
*Time between submission and publication
  decision:* 4-6 weeks
Time between decision and publication:
  12-18 months
Time allotted for reading proof: 4 weeks

CONTRACT PROVISIONS

Copyright: Publisher; sometimes author
Royalty provisions: Negotiable

**PUBLICATION AND DISTRIBUTION
INFORMATION**

Forms of publication: Cloth, paper
Titles published each year: 60
Print run: 1,200
Number of review copies: 30-50
Distribution area: Worldwide
Time in print: 10-15 years

**(194)
NEW YORK UNIVERSITY PRESS**

70 Washington Square South
New York, NY 10012

Contact: Niko Pfund
Established: 1916
Telephone: 212 998-2575
Fax: 212 995-3833

SCOPE

Publishing interests: Women's studies;
  Middle Eastern literature; gay and
  lesbian studies; Jewish studies; cultural
  studies
*Considers all literary and linguistic
  topics:* Yes
Types of works not published:
  Festschriften
Prizes and competitions: Bobst Library
  Awards
Languages published: English
Series title(s): Gotham Library

SUBMISSION REQUIREMENTS

Initial contact: Letter and prospectus
Considers simultaneous submissions: Yes
*Will issue contract on the basis of
  proposal, prospectus, and/or sample
  chapter:* Yes
Style: Chicago
Special requirements: Accepts camera-
  ready copy; provides guidelines for
  authors
Subvention: No, but accepts subventions
  for highly specialized monographs and
  editions

EDITORIAL INFORMATION

*Manuscripts or proposals submitted each
  year:* 200 (estimate)
Manuscripts sent to readers each year: 25
Manuscripts accepted each year: 20
Number of outside readers: 1-4
Author-anonymous submission: No
*Time between submission and publication
  decision:* 2-12 weeks
*Time between decision and return of copy-
  edited manuscript:* 2-3
Time between decision and publication:
  10-12 months

CONTRACT PROVISIONS

Copyright: Publisher (preferably)

Royalty provisions: Varies

PUBLICATION AND DISTRIBUTION INFORMATION

Forms of publication: Cloth, paper
Titles published each year: 16
Print run: 800-1,500
Number of review copies: 40
Distribution area: Worldwide
Time in print: 5-10 years

**(195)
MAX NIEMEYER VERLAG**

Postfach 2140
72011 Tübingen, Germany

Contact: Karin Wenzel (Marketing);
  Birgitta Zeller (Editorial)
Established: 1870
Telephone: (07071) 98940
Fax: (07071) 989450

SCOPE

Publishing interests: German literature;
  Romance literature; English literature;
  German language; Romance languages;
  English language
Considers all literary and linguistic topics: Yes
Types of works not published:
  Biographies
Languages published: German; English;
  French
Series title(s): Rhetorik-Forschungen;
  Studien und Texte zur Sozialgeschichte
  der Literatur; Studien zur deutschen
  Literatur; Untersuchungen zur
  deutschen Literaturgeschichte;
  Hermaea: Germanistische Forschungen;
  Altdeutsche Textbibliothek;
  Germanistische Arbeitshefte;
  Romanistische Arbeitshefte; Buchreihe
  der Anglia; Studien zur englischen

Philologie; Lexicographica: Series
Maior; Konzepte der Sprach- und
Literaturwissenschaft; Linguistische
Arbeiten; Reihe germanistische
Linguistik; Sprache und Information

SUBMISSION REQUIREMENTS

Initial contact: Letter, outline, and sample
  chapters
Considers simultaneous submissions: No
Will issue contract on the basis of proposal, prospectus, and/or sample chapter: No
Style: House
Subvention: Usually

EDITORIAL INFORMATION

Manuscripts or proposals submitted each year: 300-400 (estimate)
Manuscripts accepted each year: 140
  (estimate)
Number of outside readers: 1-2
Author-anonymous submission: No
Time between submission and publication decision: 3-6 months
Time between decision and publication:
  9-12 months
Time allotted for reading proof: 4-6
  weeks

CONTRACT PROVISIONS

Copyright: Publisher

PUBLICATION AND DISTRIBUTION INFORMATION

Forms of publication: Cloth, paper
Titles published each year: 140
Print run: 500
Number of review copies: 15-20
Distribution area: Worldwide
Time in print: Indefinitely

(196)
EDICIONES DEL NORTE

PO Box 5130
Hanover, NH 03755

Contact: Frank Janney, President
Established: 1979
Telephone: 800 782-5422

SCOPE

Publishing interests: Spanish literature;
  Latin American literature
*Considers all literary and linguistic
  topics:* No
Types of works not published:
  Festschriften; literary handbooks;
  textbooks
Languages published: English; Spanish
Series title(s): Puerta 88; Rama Series;
  Novísimus: New Writers from Latin
  America

SUBMISSION REQUIREMENTS

Initial contact: Letter of inquiry and
  sample chapters
Considers simultaneous submissions: No
*Will issue contract on the basis of
  proposal, prospectus, and/or sample
  chapter:* No
Style: MLA
Special requirements: Accepts camera-
  ready copy; prefers electronic manuscripts
Subvention: Yes

EDITORIAL INFORMATION

*Manuscripts or proposals submitted each
  year:* 75
Manuscripts sent to readers each year: 25
Manuscripts accepted each year: 6
Number of outside readers: 2
Author-anonymous submission: No

*Time between submission and publication
  decision:* 3-6 months
Time between decision and publication: 6
  months
Time allotted for reading proof: 3 months

CONTRACT PROVISIONS

Copyright: Author and publisher
Royalty provisions: 10% of net

PUBLICATION AND DISTRIBUTION
INFORMATION

Forms of publication: Cloth, paper
Titles published each year: 6
Print run: 500
Number of review copies: 30
Distribution area: Worldwide
Time in print: 10 years minimum

(197)
**UNIVERSITY OF NORTH
CAROLINA PRESS**

Box 2288
Chapel Hill, NC 27515-2288

Contact: Sian Hunter White, Assistant to
  the Editor in Chief
Established: 1922
Telephone: 919 966-3561
Fax: 919 966-3829
E-mail: shwhite@email.unc.edu

SCOPE

Publishing interests: American literature;
  American studies; southern American
  studies; southern American literature;
  feminist criticism; English literature
  (nineteenth- and twentieth-century);
  classical literature; folklore; popular
  culture; Romance languages; Germanic
  languages; Romance literature;
  Germanic literature

Considers all literary and linguistic topics: Yes
Types of works not published: Critical editions; Festschriften
Languages published: English
Series title(s): Gender and American Culture; Cultural Studies of the United States; University of North Carolina Studies in the Germanic Languages and Literatures; University of North Carolina Studies in the Romance Languages and Literatures; University of North Carolina Studies in Comparative Literature

SUBMISSION REQUIREMENTS

Initial contact: Letter, outline, and sample chapters, or letter and prospectus
Considers simultaneous submissions: Yes, if notified
Style: Chicago; MLA
Special requirements: Prefers not to receive dot-matrix printout; expects electronic manuscript; provides guidelines for manuscript preparation
Subvention: Occasionally for a highly specialized study

EDITORIAL INFORMATION

Manuscripts or proposals submitted each year: 70 (estimate)
Manuscripts sent to readers each year: 10 (estimate)
Manuscripts accepted each year: 4
Number of outside readers: 2
Author-anonymous submission: No
Time between submission and publication decision: 3-6 months
Time between decision and return of copy-edited manuscript: 3 months
Time between decision and publication: 9 months
Time allotted for reading proof: 3 weeks

CONTRACT PROVISIONS

Copyright: Publisher or author
Royalty provisions: 5% of net on first 1,000 copies, 10% of net on next 4,000 copies, 12-12.5% on next 5,000, and 15% thereafter (cloth); 6% of net (paper)

PUBLICATION AND DISTRIBUTION INFORMATION

Forms of publication: Cloth, paper
Titles published each year: 6
Print run: 1,500-3,000
Number of review copies: 75
Distribution area: Worldwide
Time in print: 5 years minimum

Proposals involving Romance languages or literatures and Germanic languages or literatures should be sent directly to the series editors (Maria Salgado and Paul Roberge, respectively) at the University of North Carolina.

**(198)
UNIVERSITY OF NORTH TEXAS PRESS**

PO Box 13856
Denton, TX 76203

Contact: Frances B. Vick, Director; Charlotte Wright, Editor
Established: 1987
Telephone: 817 565-2142
Fax: 817 565-4590
E-mail: untpress@abn.unt.edu

SCOPE

Publishing interests: Biographies of Texas writers; folklore of Texas
Considers all literary and linguistic topics: Yes

Types of works not published: Bibliographies; critical editions; textbooks; Festschriften; literary reference works
Languages published: English
Series title(s): Texas Writers Series

SUBMISSION REQUIREMENTS

Initial contact: Letter, outline, and sample chapter
Considers simultaneous submissions: No
Will issue contract on the basis of proposal, prospectus, and/or sample chapter: No
Style: Chicago; MLA
Special requirements: Does not accept dot-matrix printout; requires electronic manuscript
Subvention: Not necessarily

EDITORIAL INFORMATION

Manuscripts or proposals submitted each year: 200 (estimate)
Manuscripts sent to readers each year: 5-10 (estimate)
Manuscripts accepted each year: 5-6
Number of outside readers: 2-3
Author-anonymous submission: Yes
Time between submission and publication decision: 10-15 weeks
Time between decision and return of copy-edited manuscript: 5-6 months
Time between decision and publication: 1-2 years

CONTRACT PROVISIONS

Copyright: Negotiable
Royalty provisions: 10% of net

PUBLICATION AND DISTRIBUTION INFORMATION

Forms of publication: Cloth, paper
Titles published each year: 5
Print run: 1,000-3,000
Number of review copies: 50-60

Distribution area: Worldwide
Time in print: 5 years

(199)
NORTHEASTERN UNIVERSITY PRESS

360 Huntington Ave.
272HN
Boston, MA 02115

Contact: Deborah Kops, Editorial Director; John Weingartner, Senior Editor
Established: 1977
Telephone: 617 373-5480
Fax: 617 373-5483

SCOPE

Publishing interests: American literature; African American literature; women's studies
Considers all literary and linguistic topics: No
Types of works not published: Bibliographies; Festschriften; most literary reference books
Languages published: English
Series title(s): Northeastern Library of Black Literature; Northeastern Series in Feminist Theory

SUBMISSION REQUIREMENTS

Initial contact: Letter and prospectus
Considers simultaneous submissions: Yes
Will issue contract on the basis of proposal, prospectus, and/or sample chapter: Yes
Style: Chicago; MLA
Special requirements: Provides guidelines for authors
Subvention: No, but encourages authors to seek publication support

EDITORIAL INFORMATION

Manuscripts or proposals submitted each year: 50
Manuscripts sent to readers each year: 15 (estimate)
Manuscripts accepted each year: 4 (estimate)
Number of outside readers: 2
Author-anonymous submission: Yes
Time between submission and publication decision: 3 months
Time between decision and return of copy-edited manuscript: 6-8 months
Time between decision and publication: 9-10 months

CONTRACT PROVISIONS

Copyright: Author
Royalty provisions: Details supplied upon request

PUBLICATION AND DISTRIBUTION INFORMATION

Forms of publication: Cloth, paper
Titles published each year: 4
Print run: 800-1,000
Number of review copies: 20
Distribution area: Worldwide
Time in print: 5-10 years

(200)
NORTHERN ILLINOIS UNIVERSITY PRESS

De Kalb, IL 60115-2854

Contact: Mary Lincoln, Director and Editor in Chief
Established: 1965
Telephone: 815 753-1826
Fax: 815 753-1845

SCOPE

Publishing interests: American literature; British literature; Slavic literature; French literature; literature in translation
Considers all literary and linguistic topics: Yes
Types of works not published: Bibliographies; readers; Festschriften; collections of previously published essays
Languages published: English

SUBMISSION REQUIREMENTS

Initial contact: Letter and prospectus or letter, prospectus, and sample chapter
Considers simultaneous submissions: Yes (proposals); no (manuscripts)
Will issue contract on the basis of proposal, prospectus, and/or sample chapter: No
Style: Chicago
Subvention: No

EDITORIAL INFORMATION

Manuscripts or proposals submitted each year: 300
Manuscripts sent to readers each year: 20
Manuscripts accepted each year: 5
Number of outside readers: 2
Author-anonymous submission: No
Time between submission and publication decision: 3 months
Time between decision and return of copy-edited manuscript: 3 months
Time between decision and publication: 11 month
Time allotted for reading proof: 3 weeks

CONTRACT PROVISIONS

Copyright: Negotiable
Royalty provisions: 10% on first 3,000 copies, 12.5% on next 3,000, 15% thereafter

PUBLICATION AND DISTRIBUTION
INFORMATION

Forms of publication: Cloth, paper
Titles published each year: 5
Print run: 800-2,000
Number of review copies: 40
Distribution area: Worldwide
Time in print: 10 years

(201)
NORTHWESTERN UNIVERSITY PRESS

625 Colfax St.
Evanston, IL 60208

Contact: Heather Kenny, Editorial
  Assistant
Established: 1958
Telephone: 708 491-5313
Fax: 708 491-8150

SCOPE

Publishing interests: Literary theory;
  literary criticism; drama; east European
  literature; Renaissance literature;
  European literature; theater; South
  American literature; Jewish literature;
  Russian literature
*Considers all literary and linguistic
  topics:* Yes
Types of works not published: Unrevised
  dissertations; bibliographies; literary
  reference works
Languages published: English
Series title(s): Russian Literature and
  Theory; Rethinking Theory; Avant-
  Garde and Modernism

SUBMISSION REQUIREMENTS

Initial contact: Letter and prospectus
Considers simultaneous submissions: Yes
  (proposals); no (manuscripts)

*Will issue contract on the basis of
  proposal, prospectus, and/or sample
  chapter:* No
Style: Chicago
Special requirements: Requires electronic
  manuscript
Subvention: Sometimes

EDITORIAL INFORMATION

*Manuscripts or proposals submitted each
  year:* 500 (estimate)
Manuscripts sent to readers each year: 30
Manuscripts accepted each year: 5
Number of outside readers: 1
Author-anonymous submission: No
*Time between submission and publication
  decision:* 6 months
*Time between decision and return of copy-
  edited manuscript:* 2-8 months
Time between decision and publication:
  1 year

CONTRACT PROVISIONS

Copyright: Publisher
Royalty provisions: Varies

PUBLICATION AND DISTRIBUTION
INFORMATION

Forms of publication: Cloth, paper
Titles published each year: 20 (estimate)
Print run: 500 cloth; 1,500 paper
Number of review copies: 75
Distribution area: Worldwide
Time in print: Indefinitely

(202)
W. W. NORTON

500 Fifth Ave.
New York, NY 10110

Imprint(s) and subsidiary firm(s):
  Liveright

Contact: Julia A. Reidhead, Vice
President and Editor (literatures in
English); Carol Hollas-Zwick, Associate
Editor (composition); Peter J. Simon,
Associate Editor (world literature,
theory, film)
Established: 1923
Telephone: 212 354-5500
Fax: 212 869-0856

SCOPE

Publishing interests: General literature
*Considers all literary and linguistic
topics:* Yes
Types of works not published: Most
dissertations; most literary reference
works; Festschriften
Languages published: English
Series title(s): Norton Critical Editions

SUBMISSION REQUIREMENTS

Initial contact: Letter, prospectus, and
sample chapter
Considers simultaneous submissions: Yes
*Will issue contract on the basis of
proposal, prospectus, and/or sample
chapter:* Varies
Style: Chicago
Special requirements: Varies with project
Subvention: No

EDITORIAL INFORMATION

*Manuscripts or proposals submitted each
year:* 200 (estimate)
Manuscripts sent to readers each year: 20
(estimate)
Manuscripts accepted each year: 3
(estimate)

CONTRACT PROVISIONS

Copyright: Publisher

**PUBLICATION AND DISTRIBUTION
INFORMATION**

Forms of publication: Cloth, paper, electronic media
Titles published each year: 20 (estimate)

**(203)
NORVIK PRESS**

EUR
Univ. of East Anglia
Norwich NR4 7TJ, England

Contact: Janet Garton; James McFarlane
Established: 1987
Telephone: (44) 603 56161
Fax: (44) 603 250599

SCOPE

Publishing interests: Scandinavian
literature
*Considers all literary and linguistic
topics:* No
Languages published: English
Series title(s): Scandinavian Literary
History and Criticism

SUBMISSION REQUIREMENTS

Initial contact: Letter of inquiry
Considers simultaneous submissions: No
*Will issue contract on the basis of
proposal, prospectus, and/or sample
chapter:* No
Style: MLA
Special requirements: Expects electronic
copy (*MS-DOS*)
Subvention: No

EDITORIAL INFORMATION

*Manuscripts or proposals submitted each
year:* 10-15
Manuscripts sent to readers each year:
7-8

Manuscripts accepted each year: 4-5
Number of outside readers: 1
Author-anonymous submission: No
Time between submission and publication
  decision: 6 months
Time between decision and publication:
  1 year
Time allotted for reading proof: 4 weeks

CONTRACT PROVISIONS

Copyright: Author
Royalty provisions: 10% of net

**PUBLICATION AND DISTRIBUTION
INFORMATION**

Forms of publication: Cloth, paper
Titles published each year: 5
Print run: 1,000
Number of review copies: 50
Distribution area: Worldwide
Time in print: Indefinitely

**(204)
UNIVERSITY OF NOTRE DAME
PRESS**

PO Box L
Notre Dame, IN 46556-5010

Contact: Ann Rice, Executive Editor
Established: 1949
Telephone: 219 631-6346
Fax: 219 631-8148

SCOPE

Publishing interests: Religion and
  literature; philosophy; theology; Latino
  studies; Judaic studies; literary
  criticism; Irish studies
*Considers all literary and linguistic
  topics:* No
Types of works not published: Dissertations; bibliographies; critical editions;

collections of letters; textbooks;
  Festschriften; literary encyclopedias
Languages published: English

SUBMISSION REQUIREMENTS

Initial contact: Letter and prospectus
Considers simultaneous submissions: No
Style: Chicago
Subvention: Occasionally

EDITORIAL INFORMATION

*Manuscripts or proposals submitted each
  year:* 100
Manuscripts sent to readers each year: 4
Manuscripts accepted each year: 2-3
Number of outside readers: 2
Author-anonymous submission: No
*Time between submission and publication
  decision:* 3-4 months
Time between decision and publication:
  9-12 months
Time allotted for reading proof: 3 weeks

CONTRACT PROVISIONS

Copyright: Publisher (usually)
Royalty provisions: Escalating scale, 10-
  15% of net (hardcover); 7% of list
  (paper)

**PUBLICATION AND DISTRIBUTION
INFORMATION**

Forms of publication: Cloth, paper
Titles published each year: 2
Print run: 800-1,000
Number of review copies: 35-100
Distribution area: Worldwide
Time in print: 6 years minimum

(205)
NOVA FRONTEIRA

Rua Bambina 25
Botafogo
22251 Rio de Janeiro, Brazil

Imprint(s) and subsidiary firm(s): Nova
  Aguilar
Contact: Sebastião Lacerda, President
Established: 1965
Telephone: (021) 2867822
Fax: (021) 2866755

SCOPE

Publishing interests: Reference books;
  dictionaries; editions of classics
*Considers all literary and linguistic
  topics:* Yes
Languages published: Portuguese

SUBMISSION REQUIREMENTS

Initial contact: Letter and manuscript
*Will issue contract on the basis of
  proposal, prospectus, and/or sample
  chapter:* Rarely
Style: House
Special requirements: Accepts photocopies, dot-matrix printout, camera-
  ready copy, and electronic manuscripts
Subvention: Depends on production cost

EDITORIAL INFORMATION

*Manuscripts or proposals submitted each
  year:* 150-200
Manuscripts sent to readers each year:
  20-30
Manuscripts accepted each year: 20
  (estimate)
Number of outside readers: 5
Author-anonymous submission: No
*Time between submission and publication
  decision:* 1-2 months

*Time between decision and return of copy-
  edited manuscript:* 6 months
Time between decision and publication:
  1 year

CONTRACT PROVISIONS

Copyright: Negotiable
Royalty provisions: 8% on first 3,000
  copies, 10% thereafter

PUBLICATION AND DISTRIBUTION
INFORMATION

Forms of publication: Cloth, paper
Titles published each year: 50 (estimate)
Print run: 3,000-5,000
Number of review copies: 100-150
Distribution area: Brazil; Portugal
Time in print: Varies

(206)
PENERBIT NUSA INDAH

Jl. El Tari
Ende 86318
Flores-NTT, Indonesia

Contact: Henri Daros, Director
Established: 1970
Telephone: (0381) 21502
Fax: (0381) 21645

SCOPE

Publishing interests: Indonesian
  literature; Indonesian language;
  linguistics; psycholinguistics; lexi-
  cology
*Considers all literary and linguistic
  topics:* Yes
Languages published: Bahasa Indonesia
  Malay dialect

SUBMISSION REQUIREMENTS

Initial contact: Letter and manuscript (2 copies)
Considers simultaneous submissions: No
Will issue contract on the basis of proposal, prospectus, and/or sample chapter: No
Subvention: Yes, especially for highly specialized works

EDITORIAL INFORMATION

Manuscripts or proposals submitted each year: 25
Manuscripts sent to readers each year: 2
Manuscripts accepted each year: 8
Number of outside readers: 2-3
Author-anonymous submission: No
Time between submission and publication decision: 3-5 months
Time between decision and return of copy-edited manuscript: 6-8 months
Time between decision and publication: 8-10 months

CONTRACT PROVISIONS

Copyright: Author
Royalty provisions: 10%

PUBLICATION AND DISTRIBUTION INFORMATION

Forms of publication: Paper
Titles published each year: 5
Print run: 2,000
Number of review copies: 10
Distribution area: Indonesia
Time in print: 3-5 years

(207)
OAK KNOLL PRESS

414 Delaware St.
New Castle, DE 19720

Contact: Paul Wakeman, Publishing Manager
Established: 1976
Telephone: 302 328-7232
Fax: 302 328-7276
E-mail: 75047.3320@compuserve.com

SCOPE

Publishing interests: Bibliographies (especially of twentieth-century writers); books about books; printing; bookbinding; papermaking; illustration
Considers all literary and linguistic topics: No
Types of works not published: Critical editions; collections of letters; textbooks; collections of of original essays by different authors
Languages published: English
Series title(s): Winchester Bibliographies of Twentieth Century Authors

SUBMISSION REQUIREMENTS

Initial contact: Letter of inquiry
Considers simultaneous submissions: No
Will issue contract on the basis of proposal, prospectus, and/or sample chapter: Yes
Style: Chicago
Special requirements: Requires electronic copy (*Wordperfect* 5.1 for *MS-DOS*)

EDITORIAL INFORMATION

Manuscripts or proposals submitted each year: 1-2
Manuscripts accepted each year: 1
Number of outside readers: 1
Author-anonymous submission: No
Time between submission and publication decision: 1 month
Time between decision and publication: 6 months
Time allotted for reading proof: 1 month

CONTRACT PROVISIONS

Copyright: Author
Royalty provisions: 10% of gross

PUBLICATION AND DISTRIBUTION
INFORMATION

Forms of publication: Cloth, paper
Titles published each year: 2
Print run: 500
Number of review copies: 20-30
Distribution area: Worldwide
Time in print: 5 years

**(208)
ODENSE UNIVERSITY PRESS**

Campusvej 55
5230 Odense M, Denmark

Contact: Stefan Birkebjerg Andersen
Established: 1973
Telephone: (45) 66 157999
Fax: (45) 66 158126

SCOPE

Publishing interests: Classical studies;
   Scandinavian literature; Scandinavian
   languages; Slavic studies; literature;
   language
*Considers all literary and linguistic
   topics:* Yes
Prizes and competitions: No
Languages published: All languages
Series title(s): Nordica; Odense
   University Studies in Literature; Odense
   University Studies in Scandinavian
   Languages and Literatures

SUBMISSION REQUIREMENTS

Initial contact: Letter of inquiry
Considers simultaneous submissions: Yes

*Will issue contract on the basis of
   proposal, prospectus, and/or sample
   chapter:* No
Subvention: Yes

EDITORIAL INFORMATION

*Manuscripts or proposals submitted each
   year:* 10
Manuscripts sent to readers each year: 5
Manuscripts accepted each year: 5
Number of outside readers: 1-2
Author-anonymous submission: No
*Time between submission and publication
   decision:* Varies
Time between decision and publication:
   Varies
Time allotted for reading proof: Varies

CONTRACT PROVISIONS

Copyright: Author and publisher
Royalty provisions: 15%

PUBLICATION AND DISTRIBUTION
INFORMATION

Forms of publication: Paper
Titles published each year: 15
Number of review copies: 30
Distribution area: Worldwide
Time in print: Indefinitely

**(209)
OHIO STATE UNIVERSITY PRESS**

180 Pressey Hall
1070 Carmack Rd.
Columbus, OH 43210

Imprint(s) and subsidiary firm(s):
   Sandstone
Contact: Charlotte Dihoff, Acquisitions
   Editor
Established: 1957
Telephone: 614 292-6930

Fax: 614 292-2065
E-mail:
  cdihoff@magnus.acs.ohio-state.edu

SCOPE

Publishing interests: Women's studies;
  modern literature; literary theory
Considers all literary and linguistic
  topics: No
Types of works not published: Bibliographies; Festschriften
Languages published: English
Series title(s): Studies in Victorian Life
  and Literature; Theory and Interpre-
  tation of Narrative

SUBMISSION REQUIREMENTS

Initial contact: Letter and prospectus
Considers simultaneous submissions: No
Will issue contract on the basis of
  proposal, prospectus, and/or sample
  chapter: Yes
Style: Chicago
Special requirements: Prefers electronic
  manuscripts
Subvention: Sometimes

EDITORIAL INFORMATION

Number of outside readers: 2
Author-anonymous submission: No
Time between submission and publication
  decision: 3 months
Time between decision and publication:
  1 year
Time allotted for reading proof: 1 month

CONTRACT PROVISIONS

Copyright: Publisher

PUBLICATION AND DISTRIBUTION
INFORMATION

Forms of publication: Cloth, paper
Titles published each year: 10

Print run: 1,000
Distribution area: Worldwide
Time in print: 10 years

(210)
OHIO UNIVERSITY PRESS

Scott Quadrangle
Athens, OH 45701

Imprint(s) and subsidiary firm(s):
  Swallow Press
Contact: Duane Schneider, Director
Established: 1964
Telephone: 614 593-1155
Fax: 614 593-4536
E-mail:
  schneider@ouvaxa.cats.ohiou.edu

SCOPE

Publishing interests: British literature
  (nineteenth-century); American
  literature (nineteenth-century); western
  American literature; African literature
Considers all literary and linguistic
  topics: Yes (literature); no (linguistics)
Types of works not published: Unrevised
  dissertations; critical editions; readers;
  Festschriften
Prizes and competitions: Northeast
  Modern Language Association / Ohio
  University Press Book Award
Languages published: English

SUBMISSION REQUIREMENTS

Initial contact: Letter and prospectus
Considers simultaneous submissions: Yes
Will issue contract on the basis of
  proposal, prospectus, and/or sample
  chapter: No
Style: Prefers Chicago; accepts MLA
Special requirements: Length: prefers 600
  pages maximum; accepts electronic
  manuscripts, photocopies, and

dot-matrix printout; provides guidelines
for manuscript preparation
Subvention: No

EDITORIAL INFORMATION

*Manuscripts or proposals submitted each
   year:* 50 (estimate)
Manuscripts sent to readers each year: 25
   (estimate)
Manuscripts accepted each year: 8
   (estimate)
Number of outside readers: 2
Author-anonymous submission: No
*Time between submission and publication
   decision:* 6 months
*Time between decision and return of copy-
   edited manuscript:* 3 months
Time between decision and publication:
   1 year
Time allotted for reading proof: 3 weeks

CONTRACT PROVISIONS

Copyright: Author
Royalty provisions: 7% of net

**PUBLICATION AND DISTRIBUTION
INFORMATION**

Forms of publication: Cloth, paper
Titles published each year: 14
Print run: 700-1,000
Number of review copies: 50
Distribution area: Worldwide
Time in print: 3-5 years minimum

**(211)
UNIVERSITY OF OKLAHOMA
PRESS**

1005 Asp Ave.
Norman, OK 73019-0445

Contact: Kimberly Wiar, Acquisitions
   Editor

Established: 1928
Telephone: 405 325-5111
Fax: 405 325-5068
E-mail: kwiar@uoknor.edu

SCOPE

Publishing interests: Literary theory;
   literature and science; women's studies;
   women and literature; Native American
   literature; Geoffrey Chaucer; western
   American literature; cultural studies
*Considers all literary and linguistic
   topics:* No
Types of works not published: Disser-
   tations; readers; Festschriften; literary
   handbooks; literary encyclopedias
Languages published: English
Series title(s): Oklahoma Project for
   Discourse and Theory; Oklahoma Series
   in Classical Culture; Civilization of the
   American Indian Series; American
   Indian Literature and Critical Studies;
   Literature of the American West

SUBMISSION REQUIREMENTS

Initial contact: Letter, 2 copies of table of
   contents, sample chapter, and
   curriculum vitae
Considers simultaneous submissions:
   Occasionally
*Will issue contract on the basis of
   proposal, prospectus, and/or sample
   chapter:* Yes
Style: Chicago
Special requirements: Prefers electronic
   manuscripts; provides guidelines for
   manuscript preparation
Subvention: Sometimes

EDITORIAL INFORMATION

*Manuscripts or proposals submitted each
   year:* 120-150 (estimate)
Manuscripts sent to readers each year:
   30-40 (estimate)

Manuscripts accepted each year: 8-10
　(estimate)
Number of outside readers: 2-3
Author-anonymous submission: No
*Time between submission and publication
　decision:* 3-6 months
*Time between decision and return of copy-
　edited manuscript:* 2-4 months
Time between decision and publication:
　12-18 months
Time allotted for reading proof: 10 days

CONTRACT PROVISIONS

Copyright: Publisher
Royalty provisions: 10% of net on first
　5,000 copies, 12.5% on next 5,000,
　15% thereafter (cloth); 5% of list on
　first 10,000 copies, 6% on next 10,000,
　7.5% thereafter (paper)

**PUBLICATION AND DISTRIBUTION
INFORMATION**

Forms of publication: Cloth, paper
Titles published each year: 20 (1994)
Print run: 750-20,000
Number of review copies: 150-300
Distribution area: Worldwide
Time in print: Indefinitely

**(212)
GEORG OLMS VERLAG**

Hagentorwall 7
31134 Hildesheim, Germany

Imprint(s) and subsidiary firm(s): Weid-
　mannsche Verlagsbuchhandlung
Contact: W. Georg Olms; Eberhard
　Mertens
Established: 1945
Telephone: (05121) 15010
Fax: (05121) 150150

SCOPE

Publishing interests: Concordances;
　indexes; bibliographies; Byzantine
　studies; classical studies; English
　literature; American literature; English
　language; folklore; Germanic literature;
　Germanic languages; humanism;
　Renaissance studies; Judaism; Hebrew
　studies; linguistics; manuscripts; Latin
　language (medieval Latin); oriental
　studies; Romance studies; Slavic
　literature; Slavic languages; Spanish
　literature; Portuguese literature; Arabic
　studies
*Considers all literary and linguistic
　topics:* Yes
Languages published: German; English;
　French; Arabic
Series title(s): Auslandsdeutsche Literatur
　der Gegenwart; Deutsche Volksbücher
　in Faksimiledrucken, Reihe B: Unter-
　suchungen zu den Volksbüchern;
　Germanistische Linguistik; Germanisti-
　sche Texte und Studien; Documenta
　Linguistica; Elizabethan Concordance
　Series; Anglistische und amerikanisti-
　sche Texte und Studien; Sprache
　und Computer; Romanistische Texte
　und Studien; Studien zu Sprache und
　Technik

SUBMISSION REQUIREMENTS

Initial contact: Letter of inquiry
Style: MLA
Special requirements: Requires camera-
　ready copy in some cases
Subvention: Yes, for dissertations

EDITORIAL INFORMATION

*Manuscripts or proposals submitted each
　year:* 80 (estimate)
Manuscripts sent to readers each year: 20
　(estimate)

Manuscripts accepted each year: 35
(estimate)
Number of outside readers: 2
*Time between submission and publication
decision:* 1-4 weeks
*Time between decision and return of copy-
edited manuscript:* 2-6 weeks

CONTRACT PROVISIONS

Copyright: Publisher
Royalty provisions: 10%

**PUBLICATION AND DISTRIBUTION
INFORMATION**

Forms of publication: Cloth, paper, elec-
tronic media
Titles published each year: 60 (estimate)
Number of review copies: 25
Distribution area: Worldwide
Time in print: 10 years

**(213)
CASA EDITRICE LEO S. OLSCHKI**

Casella postale 66
50100 Florence, Italy

Contact: Alessandro Olschki
Established: 1886
Telephone: (55) 6530684
Fax: (55) 6530214

SCOPE

Publishing interests: Western European
literature; Italian literature; English
literature; French literature; German
literature; Spanish literature; linguistics
*Considers all literary and linguistic
topics:* No
Types of works not published: Textbooks;
Festschriften; literary handbooks
Languages published: Italian; English;
French; German

Series title(s): Biblioteca dell' "Archivum
Romanicum"; Accademia toscana di
scienze e lettere "La colombaria";
Istituto Nazionale de Studi sul
Rinascimento: Studi e testi; Teatro:
Studi e testi; Saggi di "Lettere italiane";
Strumenti di lessicografia letteraria
italiana; Dantologia; Studi di letteratura
francese; Biblioteca di bibliografia
italiana; Italian medieval and
Renaissance Studies

SUBMISSION REQUIREMENTS

Initial contact: Letter, outline, and sample
chapter
Considers simultaneous submissions: Yes
*Will issue contract on the basis of
proposal, prospectus, and/or sample
chapter:* No
Style: House
Special requirements: Prefers electronic
manuscripts
Subvention: Only for very specialized
works

EDITORIAL INFORMATION

*Manuscripts or proposals submitted each
year:* 90-100
Manuscripts sent to readers each year:
20-30
Manuscripts accepted each year: 33
Number of outside readers: 1
Author-anonymous submission: No
Time allotted for reading proof: 2-3
weeks

CONTRACT PROVISIONS

Copyright: Publisher
Royalty provisions: 10%

**PUBLICATION AND DISTRIBUTION
INFORMATION**

Forms of publication: Cloth, paper

Titles published each year: 33
Print run: 1,000-3,000
Number of review copies: 30
Distribution area: Worldwide
Time in print: Indefinitely

(214)
*OPEN UNIVERSITY PRESS

Celtic Court
22 Ballmoor
Buckingham MK18 1XW, England

PUBLICATION AND DISTRIBUTION
INFORMATION

No longer commissions books in literary
studies.

(215)
OREGON STATE UNIVERSITY
PRESS

101 Waldo Hall
Corvallis, OR 97331-6407

Contact: Jo Alexander, Managing Editor
Established: 1963
Telephone: 503 737-3166
Fax: 503 737-3170

SCOPE

Publishing interests: Pacific Northwest
American literature; Native American
literature of the Pacific Northwest;
nature writing (especially of the Pacific
Northwest)
*Considers all literary and linguistic
topics:* Not usually
Languages published: English
Series title(s): Oregon Literature Series

SUBMISSION REQUIREMENTS

Initial contact: Letter, prospectus, outline,
and sample chapters
Considers simultaneous submissions: No
*Will issue contract on the basis of
proposal, prospectus, and/or sample
chapter:* Rarely
Style: Chicago
Special requirements: Requires electronic
manuscript
Subvention: No

EDITORIAL INFORMATION

*Manuscripts or proposals submitted each
year:* 25 (estimate)
Manuscripts sent to readers each year: 2
Manuscripts accepted each year: 0-1
Number of outside readers: 2
Author-anonymous submission: No
*Time between submission and publication
decision:* 3-9 months
*Time between decision and return of copy-
edited manuscript:* 1-3 months
Time between decision and publication:
1 year

CONTRACT PROVISIONS

Copyright: Negotiable
Royalty provisions: 10-15% after
production costs have been met

PUBLICATION AND DISTRIBUTION
INFORMATION

Forms of publication: Cloth, paper
Titles published each year: 4
Print run: 1,500
Number of review copies: 25-35
Distribution area: Worldwide
Time in print: 20 years

(216)
SCHOOL OF ORIENTAL AND AFRICAN STUDIES (UNIVERSITY OF LONDON)

Thornhaugh St.
Russell Sq.
London WC1H 0XG, England

Contact: M. J. Daly, Publications Officer
Established: 1917
Telephone: (0171) 6372388
Fax: (0171) 4363844
E-mail: md2@soas.ac.uk

SCOPE

Publishing interests: Asian languages; African languages; Asian culture; African culture
Considers all literary and linguistic topics: No
Types of works not published: Readers; literary encyclopedias
Languages published: English
Series title(s): Collected Papers in Asian and African Studies

SUBMISSION REQUIREMENTS

Restrictions on authors: Because of limited funds, usually must be members of the staff or closely associated with the school
Initial contact: Letter and outline
Will issue contract on the basis of proposal, prospectus, and/or sample chapter: No
Style: House
Subvention: No

EDITORIAL INFORMATION

Manuscripts or proposals submitted each year: 10
Manuscripts sent to readers each year: 8
Manuscripts accepted each year: 6

Number of outside readers: 1-2
Author-anonymous submission: No
Time between submission and publication decision: 3-9 months
Time between decision and return of copy-edited manuscript: 2-3 months
Time between decision and publication: 9-12 months

CONTRACT PROVISIONS

Copyright: Author
Royalty provisions: No royalties

PUBLICATION AND DISTRIBUTION INFORMATION

Forms of publication: Paper
Titles published each year: 9
Print run: 300-750
Number of review copies: 10-12
Distribution area: Worldwide
Time in print: 10 years minimum

(217)
*EDITORIAL ORIGENES

Plaza de Tuy, 4
28029 Madrid, Spain

Contact: Eugenio Suárez-Galbán Guerra, Publisher and Director
Established: 1979
Telephone: (91) 2015800

SCOPE

Publishing interests: General literature; linguistics
Considers all literary and linguistic topics: Yes
Languages published: Spanish
Series title(s): Tratados de crítica literaria

SUBMISSION REQUIREMENTS

Initial contact: Letter and prospectus

Style: MLA
Special requirements: Prefers camera-ready copy; accepts electronic manuscripts
Subvention: Sometimes

EDITORIAL INFORMATION

Manuscripts or proposals submitted each year: 80 (estimate)
Manuscripts sent to readers each year: 60 (estimate)
Manuscripts accepted each year: 6
Number of outside readers: 3
Time between submission and publication decision: 6-12 weeks
Time between decision and return of copyedited manuscript: 3 months
Time between decision and publication: 18 months

CONTRACT PROVISIONS

Copyright: Author and publisher
Royalty provisions: 10% (for unsubsidized publications)

PUBLICATION AND DISTRIBUTION INFORMATION

Forms of publication: Cloth
Titles published each year: 29
Print run: 1,000
Number of review copies: 75-100
Distribution area: Europe; North America; South America; Japan
Time in print: Indefinitely

(218)
*VERLAG DER ÖSTERREICHISCHEN AKADEMIE DER WISSENSCHAFTEN

Dr.-Ignaz-Seipel-Platz 2
1010 Vienna, Austria

Contact: Brigitta Nowotny
Established: 1973
Telephone: (0222) 51581
Fax: (0222) 5139541

SCOPE

Publishing interests: General literature; linguistics; folklore
Languages published: German; English

SUBMISSION REQUIREMENTS

Restrictions on authors: Must be members of the Austrian Academy of Sciences

(219)
PRESSES DE L'UNIVERSITE D'OTTAWA / UNIVERSITY OF OTTAWA PRESS

542 King Edward
Ottawa, ON K1N 6N5, Canada

Contact: Suzanne Bossé, Editor in Chief; Thérèse Durdin, Editrice, Publications Françaises
Established: 1936
Telephone: 613 564-2270
Fax: 613 564-9284

SCOPE

Publishing interests: English literature (especially medieval literature); French literature (especially medieval literature); Canadian studies; translation studies
Considers all literary and linguistic topics: Yes
Types of works not published: Dissertations; collections of letters; biographies; collections of original essays; Festschriften; literary handbooks; literary encyclopedias
Languages published: English; French

Series title(s): Reappraisals: Canadian
Writers; Canadian Short Story Library;
Translation Teaching

SUBMISSION REQUIREMENTS

Restrictions on authors: Prefers Canadian
authors
Initial contact: Letter and prospectus
Considers simultaneous submissions: No
*Will issue contract on the basis of
proposal, prospectus, and/or sample
chapter:* No
Style: MLA
Special requirements: Prefers electronic
manuscripts; provides guidelines for
manuscript preparation
Subvention: Usually

EDITORIAL INFORMATION

*Manuscripts or proposals submitted each
year:* 25 (estimate)
Manuscripts sent to readers each year:
15 (estimate)
Manuscripts accepted each year: 7
(estimate)
Number of outside readers: 2
Author-anonymous submission: No
*Time between submission and publication
decision:* 6-8 months
*Time between decision and return of copy-
edited manuscript:* 6 months
Time between decision and publication:
1 year
Time allotted for reading proof: 2-3
weeks

CONTRACT PROVISIONS

Copyright: Publisher
Royalty provisions: 8% for first 500
copies; 10% thereafter

**PUBLICATION AND DISTRIBUTION
INFORMATION**

Forms of publication: Paper, cloth

Titles published each year: 6 (estimate)
Print run: 500-800
Number of review copies: 30
Distribution area: Worldwide
Time in print: 20 years

**(220)
OXFORD UNIVERSITY PRESS**

198 Madison Ave.
New York, NY 10016

Contact: Elizabeth Maguire, Senior
Editor (literature); Cynthia Read, Senior
Editor (linguistics)
Established: 1478 (Oxford); 1896 (New
York)
Telephone: 212 679-7300
Fax: 212 725-2972

SCOPE

Publishing interests: English literature;
American literature; women's literature;
ethnic literatures; gay studies; lesbian
studies
Types of works not published:
Festschriften
Languages published: English
Series title(s): Race and American
Culture; Ideologies of Desire

SUBMISSION REQUIREMENTS

Initial contact: Letter and prospectus
Style: MLA; Chicago
Subvention: No

EDITORIAL INFORMATION

Number of outside readers: 1-2 minimum
Time between decision and publication:
1 year

CONTRACT PROVISIONS

Copyright: Publisher

PUBLICATION AND DISTRIBUTION INFORMATION

Forms of publication: Cloth, paper, electronic media
Titles published each year: 80 (estimate)
Distribution area: Worldwide
Time in print: 3 years minimum

(221)
OXFORD UNIVERSITY PRESS (ENGLISH LANGUAGE TEACHING DIVISION)

Walton St.
Oxford OX2 6DP, England

Contact: Cristina Whitecross, Publishing Manager
Telephone: (44) 865 56767
Fax: (44) 865 56646

SCOPE

Publishing interests: Applied linguistics
Considers all literary and linguistic topics: No
Types of works not published: Dissertations; collections of original essays by different authors
Languages published: English
Series title(s): Oxford Applied Linguistics; Describing English Language

SUBMISSION REQUIREMENTS

Initial contact: Outline and sample chapter
Considers simultaneous submissions: No
Will issue contract on the basis of proposal, prospectus, and/or sample chapter: No
Style: House
Special requirements: Expects electronic copy

Subvention: No

EDITORIAL INFORMATION

Manuscripts or proposals submitted each year: 40
Manuscripts accepted each year: 8
Number of outside readers: 2-6
Author-anonymous submission: No
Time between submission and publication decision: 6 months
Time between decision and publication: 1 year
Time allotted for reading proof: 1 month

CONTRACT PROVISIONS

Copyright: Author
Royalty provisions: 10-16% of net

PUBLICATION AND DISTRIBUTION INFORMATION

Forms of publication: Paper
Titles published each year: 6
Print run: 4,000
Number of review copies: 100
Distribution area: Worldwide
Time in print: Depends on sales

(222)
PARAGON HOUSE

370 Lexington Ave.
New York, NY 10017

Contact: Michael Giampaoli
Established: 1984
Telephone: 212 953-5950
Fax: 212 953-5940
E-mail: gmichael@ix.netcom.com

SCOPE

Publishing interests: Interdisciplinary studies; women's studies; cultural

criticism; literary criticism; philosophy
and literature
*Considers all literary and linguistic
topics:* Yes
Types of works not published: Bibliographies; literary handbooks;
previously published material
Languages published: English

SUBMISSION REQUIREMENTS

Initial contact: Letter and prospectus
Considers simultaneous submissions: Yes
*Will issue contract on the basis of
proposal, prospectus, and/or sample
chapter:* Yes
Style: Chicago
Subvention: No

EDITORIAL INFORMATION

*Manuscripts or proposals submitted each
year:* 30-40
Manuscripts sent to readers each year: 20
Manuscripts accepted each year: 10
Number of outside readers: 2-3
Author-anonymous submission: Yes
*Time between submission and publication
decision:* 2-3 months
Time between decision and publication:
7-9 months
Time allotted for reading proof: 1 month

CONTRACT PROVISIONS

Copyright: Author
Royalty provisions: 10% of net

PUBLICATION AND DISTRIBUTION
INFORMATION

Forms of publication: Cloth, paper
Titles published each year: 4
Print run: 2,500-5,000
Number of review copies: 100-200
Distribution area: Worldwide
Time in print: 4-5 years, depending on
sales

(223)
**UNIVERSITY OF PENNSYLVANIA
PRESS**

Blockley Hall, 13th fl.
418 Service Dr.
Philadelphia, PA 19104-6097

Contact: Jerome E. Singerman (literary
and cultural studies); Patricia Reynolds
Smith (folklore, popular culture, media
studies)
Established: 1922
Telephone: 215 898-6261
Fax: 215 898-0404
E-mail: singerma@pobox.upenn.edu

SCOPE

Publishing interests: English literature;
American literature; medieval literature;
Renaissance literature; Italian literature;
French literature; German literature;
Spanish literature; cultural studies;
women's studies; African American
studies; folklore; fiction (contemporary
American); media studies; popular
culture
*Considers all literary and linguistic
topics:* Yes
Types of works not published: Bibli-
ographies; Festschriften
Languages published: English
Series title(s): Publications of the
American Folklore Society; Penn
Studies in Contemporary American
Fiction; Conduct and Communication
Series; Folklore and Folklife Series;
Lectura Dantis Americana; Middle Ages
Series; New Cultural Studies; Feminist
Cultural Studies, the Media, and
Popular Culture

SUBMISSION REQUIREMENTS

Initial contact: Letter and prospectus or
letter, outline, and sample chapter

Considers simultaneous submissions: Yes

Will issue contract on the basis of proposal, prospectus, and/or sample chapter: Sometimes

Style: Chicago

Special requirements: Length: prefers 200 pages minimum; accepts electronic manuscripts; provides guidelines for manuscript preparation

Subvention: Sometimes

EDITORIAL INFORMATION

Manuscripts or proposals submitted each year: 175 (estimate)

Manuscripts sent to readers each year: 50 (estimate)

Manuscripts accepted each year: 25 (estimate)

Number of outside readers: 2

Author-anonymous submission: No

Time between submission and publication decision: 3-6 months

Time between decision and return of copy-edited manuscript: 2 months

Time between decision and publication: 9-11 month

Time allotted for reading proof: 1 month

CONTRACT PROVISIONS

Copyright: Publisher

Royalty provisions: No royalties for first 1,000 copies, 7% of net on next 1,500, 9% on next 2,500, and 10% thereafter (cloth); no royalties for first 1,000 copies, 5% of net on next 1,500, 7% on next 2,500, and 9% thereafter (paper)

PUBLICATION AND DISTRIBUTION INFORMATION

Forms of publication: Cloth, paper, electronic media

Titles published each year: 23

Print run: 1,000

Number of review copies: 35-50

Distribution area: Worldwide

Time in print: 5-7 years minimum

(224)
PENNSYLVANIA STATE UNIVERSITY PRESS

University Support Bldg., Suite C
820 North University Dr.
Pennsylvania State University
University Park, PA 16802

Contact: Philip Winsor, Senior Editor

Established: 1956

Telephone: 814 865-1327

Fax: 814 863-1408

E-mail: sgt3@psuvm.psu.edu

SCOPE

Publishing interests: General literature; languages

Considers all literary and linguistic topics: Yes

Types of works not published: Unrevised dissertations; bibliographies; Festschriften; literary handbooks and encyclopedias

Series title(s): Literature and Philosophy

SUBMISSION REQUIREMENTS

Initial contact: Letter and prospectus

Considers simultaneous submissions: Negotiable

Will issue contract on the basis of proposal, prospectus, and/or sample chapter: No

Style: MLA

Special requirements: Accepts photo-copies

Subvention: No

EDITORIAL INFORMATION

Manuscripts or proposals submitted each year: 200 (estimate)
Manuscripts sent to readers each year: 125 (estimate)
Manuscripts accepted each year: 8 (estimate)
Number of outside readers: 2 minimum
Author-anonymous submission: No
Time between submission and publication decision: 2-3 months
Time between decision and return of copy-edited manuscript: 2 months
Time between decision and publication: 1 year

CONTRACT PROVISIONS

Copyright: Publisher

PUBLICATION AND DISTRIBUTION INFORMATION

Forms of publication: Cloth, paper
Titles published each year: 60 (estimate)
Print run: 900-1,500
Number of review copies: 50-70
Distribution area: Worldwide
Time in print: Indefinitely

(225)
PERGAMON ELSEVIER SCIENCE LTD.

The Boulevard
Langford Ln.
Oxford OX5 2BJ, England

Contact: Chris Pringle, Publishing Editor
Established: 1948
Telephone: (1865) 843712
Fax: (1865) 843977
E-mail: c.pringle@elsevier.co.uk

SCOPE

Publishing interests: Linguistics; socio-linguistics; philosophy of language; anthropological linguistics; pathology of language; psycholinguistics; phonology; semantics; pragmatics; neurolinguistics; applied linguistics; language teaching
Considers all literary and linguistic topics: Yes (linguistics); no (literature)
Types of works not published: Textbooks
Languages published: English
Series title(s): Language and Communication Library

SUBMISSION REQUIREMENTS

Initial contact: Accepts letter and prospectus; prefers letter, outline, and sample chapters
Considers simultaneous submissions: Yes, if informed
Will issue contract on the basis of proposal, prospectus, and/or sample chapter: Yes
Style: Varies
Special requirements: Provides guidelines for manuscript preparation
Subvention: No

EDITORIAL INFORMATION

Manuscripts or proposals submitted each year: 30 (estimate)
Manuscripts sent to readers each year: 12 (estimate)
Manuscripts accepted each year: 6
Number of outside readers: 1-3
Author-anonymous submission: No, unless requested
Time between submission and publication decision: 4-6 months
Time between decision and return of copy-edited manuscript: 4-5 months
Time between decision and publication: 6-8 months
Time allotted for reading proof: 3 weeks

CONTRACT PROVISIONS

Copyright: Author
Royalty provisions: 10% of net

PUBLICATION AND DISTRIBUTION INFORMATION

Forms of publication: Cloth, paper
Titles published each year: 5
Distribution area: Worldwide
Time in print: Indefinitely

**(226)
PERSEA BOOKS**

60 Madison Ave.
New York, NY 10010

Contact: Karen Braziller, Editorial
 Director
Established: 1975
Telephone: 212 779-7668
Fax: 212 689-5405

SCOPE

Publishing interests: Women's studies;
 biography; general literature
*Considers all literary and linguistic
 topics:* Yes
Types of works not published: Bibliographies; Festschriften
Languages published: English

SUBMISSION REQUIREMENTS

Initial contact: Letter, outline, and sample
 chapters
Considers simultaneous submissions: Yes
Style: Chicago
Subvention: No

EDITORIAL INFORMATION

*Manuscripts or proposals submitted each
 year:* 50-100 (estimate)

Manuscripts accepted each year: 4-5
 (estimate)
*Time between submission and publication
 decision:* 1 month
*Time between decision and return of copy-
 edited manuscript:* 8 months
Time between decision and publication:
 1 year

CONTRACT PROVISIONS

Copyright: Author
Royalty provisions: 8-10% (cloth); 6%
 (paper)

PUBLICATION AND DISTRIBUTION INFORMATION

Forms of publication: Cloth, paper
Titles published each year: 7
Print run: 3,000
Number of review copies: 100
Distribution area: Worldwide
Time in print: 6-10 years

**(227)
PICKWICK PUBLICATIONS**

4137 Timberlane Dr.
Allison Park, PA 15101-2932

Contact: Dikran Y. Hadidian, General
 Editor
Established: 1982
Telephone: 412 487-2159
Fax: 412 487-8862

SCOPE

Publishing interests: Literature and
 religion; Karl Barth; John Calvin;
 theology; church history
*Considers all literary and linguistic
 topics:* No
Types of works not published: Dissertations; biographies

Languages published: English
Series title(s): Pittsburgh Theological Monographs; Princeton Theological Monograph Series

SUBMISSION REQUIREMENTS

Initial contact: Letter, outline, and sample chapter
Style: Chicago
Special requirements: Length: 300 pages of double-spaced camera-ready copy maximum
Subvention: No

EDITORIAL INFORMATION

Manuscripts or proposals submitted each year: 25
Number of outside readers: 1-2
Time between submission and publication decision: 4-6 months
Time between decision and return of copy-edited manuscript: 1 year
Time between decision and publication: 2 years maximum

CONTRACT PROVISIONS

Copyright: Negotiable
Royalty provisions: No royalties

PUBLICATION AND DISTRIBUTION INFORMATION

Forms of publication: Paper
Titles published each year: 5
Print run: 500
Number of review copies: 10-15
Distribution area: Worldwide

(228)
PIERIAN PRESS

Box 1808
Ann Arbor, MI 48106

Contact: C. Edward Wall, Publisher
Established: 1968
Telephone: 313 434-5530
Fax: 313 434-6409

SCOPE

Publishing interests: Bibliographies; directories; reference works; underground press; alternative press
Considers all literary and linguistic topics: No
Types of works not published: Dissertations; critical editions; collections of letters; biographies; readers; collections of essays; Festschriften
Languages published: English

SUBMISSION REQUIREMENTS

Initial contact: Letter, outline, and sample chapter
Style: Chicago
Special requirements: Expects electronic manuscript
Subvention: No

EDITORIAL INFORMATION

Number of outside readers: 2
Author-anonymous submission: No
Time between submission and publication decision: 3-4 months
Time between decision and publication: 1 year

CONTRACT PROVISIONS

Copyright: Negotiable (preferably publisher)
Royalty provisions: 10-15% of net

PUBLICATION AND DISTRIBUTION INFORMATION

Forms of publication: Cloth, paper, electronic media
Print run: 800-2,000

Number of review copies: 100
  (maximum)
Distribution area: Worldwide
Time in print: 10 years maximum

(229)
UNIVERSITY OF PITTSBURGH PRESS

Dept. of English
Duquesne University
Pittsburgh, PA 15282-1703

Contact: Albert C. Labriola
Established: 1936
Telephone: 412 624-7386
Fax: 412 624-7380

SCOPE

Publishing interests: John Milton (and
  related topics); descriptive bibliographies (principally of American
  authors); composition and rhetoric
*Considers all literary and linguistic
  topics:* No
Languages published: English
Series title(s): Pittsburgh Series in Bibliography; Pittsburgh Series in Composition, Literacy, and Culture

SUBMISSION REQUIREMENTS

Initial contact: Letter and prospectus
Style: Chicago; MLA
Special requirements: Accepts photo-
  copies; prefers electronic manuscripts
Subvention: No

EDITORIAL INFORMATION

*Manuscripts or proposals submitted each
  year:* 15 (estimate)
Manuscripts sent to readers each year: 3
  (estimate)

Manuscripts accepted each year: 1
  (estimate)
Number of outside readers: 2
*Time between submission and publication
  decision:* 4-6 months
*Time between decision and return of copy-
  edited manuscript:* 3 months
Time between decision and publication:
  1 year

CONTRACT PROVISIONS

Copyright: Negotiable
Royalty provisions: 12.5% (cloth); 8%
  (paper)

PUBLICATION AND DISTRIBUTION INFORMATION

Forms of publication: Cloth, paper
Titles published each year: 4
Print run: 600-10,000
Number of review copies: 50-70
Distribution area: Worldwide
Time in print: 10 years

(230)
PLAYERS PRESS

PO Box 1132
Studio City, CA 91614-0132

Imprint(s) and subsidiary firm(s): Empire
  Publishing Service
Established: 1965
Telephone: 818 789-4980 (no author
  calls)

SCOPE

Publishing interests: Drama; playwrights;
  theater
*Considers all literary and linguistic
  topics:* No
Languages published: English

SUBMISSION REQUIREMENTS

Initial contact: Letter of inquiry only
Considers simultaneous submissions: No
*Will issue contract on the basis of
proposal, prospectus, and/or sample
chapter:* No
Style: Varies
Special requirements: Requires electronic
copy

EDITORIAL INFORMATION

*Manuscripts or proposals submitted each
year:* 30-100
Manuscripts sent to readers each year:
10-20
Manuscripts accepted each year: 1-10
Number of outside readers: 0
*Time between submission and publication
decision:* 3 months
Time between decision and publication:
6-12 months
Time allotted for reading proof: 1-3
weeks

CONTRACT PROVISIONS

Copyright: Usually author
Royalty provisions: 8-10%

PUBLICATION AND DISTRIBUTION
INFORMATION

Forms of publication: Cloth, paper, elec-
tronic media
Titles published each year: 10
Print run: 2,000-10,000
Number of review copies: 75
Distribution area: Worldwide
Time in print: Indefinitely

(231)
POLEBRIDGE PRESS

2120 Bluebell Dr.
Santa Rosa, CA 95403

Contact: Robert W. Funk
Established: 1981
Telephone: 707 523-1323
Fax: 707 523-1350

SCOPE

Publishing interests: Bible and literature
*Considers all literary and linguistic
topics:* No
Languages published: English

SUBMISSION REQUIREMENTS

Initial contact: Letter of inquiry
Style: Chicago
Subvention: No

EDITORIAL INFORMATION

Number of outside readers: 2-3
Author-anonymous submission: No
*Time between submission and publication
decision:* 3 months
*Time between decision and return of copy-
edited manuscript:* 3 months
Time between decision and publication:
9-12 months

CONTRACT PROVISIONS

Copyright: Author
Royalty provisions: 6-20% of net

PUBLICATION AND DISTRIBUTION
INFORMATION

Forms of publication: Cloth, paper
Distribution area: Worldwide
Time in print: 10-25 years

(232)
PRENTICE-HALL

College Editorial
Englewood Cliffs, NJ 07632

Contact: D. Anthony, Editor in Chief
  (English composition, literature,
  rhetoric)
Established: 1913
Telephone: 201 592-2618
Fax: 201 592-2275

SCOPE

Publishing interests: Rhetoric handbooks;
  composition readers; technical writing;
  advanced composition; linguistics
  (introductory works); anthologies for
  survey courses in world literature,
  women's literature, English literature,
  drama, poetry, short fiction, literary
  criticism
*Considers all literary and linguistic
  topics:* No (publishes college textbooks
  only)
Types of works not published: Dissertations; bibliographies; critical editions;
  collections of letters; biographies;
  collections of original essays;
  Festschriften; literary reference works
Languages published: English
Series title(s): New Century Views

SUBMISSION REQUIREMENTS

Initial contact: Letter, prospectus, and
  sample chapters (and table of contents
  for anthology); provides guidelines for
  submitting a proposal
Considers simultaneous submissions: Yes
*Will issue contract on the basis of
  proposal, prospectus, and/or sample
  chapter:* Yes
Style: Chicago
Special requirements: Provides guidelines
  for authors
Subvention: No

EDITORIAL INFORMATION

*Manuscripts or proposals submitted each
  year:* 80

Manuscripts sent to readers each year: 40
Manuscripts accepted each year: 20
Number of outside readers: 5-10
Author-anonymous submission: Yes, if
  preferred
*Time between submission and publication
  decision:* 2-3 months
*Time between decision and return of copy-
  edited manuscript:* 1-3 years
Time between decision and publication:
  2-4 years

CONTRACT PROVISIONS

Copyright: Publisher
Royalty provisions: Negotiable

PUBLICATION AND DISTRIBUTION INFORMATION

Forms of publication: Cloth, paper
Titles published each year: 20
Distribution area: Worldwide
Time in print: 25 years

(233) PRENTICE-HALL / HARVESTER WHEATSHEAF

Campus 400
Waylands Ave.
Hemel Hempstead HP2 7EZ, England

Contact: Literature Editor
Established: 1988
Telephone: (0442) 881900
Fax: (0442) 252544

SCOPE

Publishing interests: English literature
  (medieval, Renaissance, Restoration,
  Romantic, Victorian, modern, and
  contemporary); American literature;
  poststructuralist theory; postmodernist
  theory; Marxist literary theory; feminist

theory; reader-response theory; literary theory; feminist criticism (English, American, and French literatures); cultural studies; media studies; new literatures in English; colonial studies; postcolonial studies; linguistics and literature; William Shakespeare; interdisciplinary theoretical and critical approaches; Third World literature; black literature

Considers all literary and linguistic topics: Yes

Types of works not published: Dissertations; collections of letters

Languages published: English

Series title(s): Harvester New Critical Introductions to Shakespeare; Feminist Readings; Harvester New Readings; Key Women Writers; Critical Studies of Key Texts; Annotated Critical Bibliographies; Literary Partnerships

SUBMISSION REQUIREMENTS

Initial contact: Letter, outline, sample chapters, curriculum vitae, and samples of any publications related to the proposal; provides guide for authors

Will issue contract on the basis of proposal, prospectus, and/or sample chapter: Yes

Style: MLA; Chicago; Modern Humanities Research Association; house

Special requirements: Accepts electronic manuscripts and camera-ready copy; does not accept photocopies or dot-matrix printout

Subvention: No

EDITORIAL INFORMATION

Number of outside readers: 3

Author-anonymous submission: No

CONTRACT PROVISIONS

Copyright: Negotiable

PUBLICATION AND DISTRIBUTION INFORMATION

Forms of publication: Cloth, paper
Titles published each year: 42 (estimate)
Distribution area: Worldwide

(234)
PRINCETON UNIVERSITY PRESS

41 William St.
Princeton, NJ 08540

Contact: Mary Murrell, Editor
Established: 1905
Telephone: 609 258-4900
Fax: 609 258-6305
E-mail:
    mary-murrell@pupress.princeton.edu

SCOPE

Publishing interests: Russian literature (nineteenth- and twentieth-century); American literature (nineteenth- and early-twentieth-century); Greek literature (modern); Renaissance literature (especially in England and Italy); medicine and literature (especially psychiatry, neuroscience, and literary analysis); gender criticism (especially gender relations); history in literature; modernism (especially T. S. Eliot, Ezra Pound, and H.D. [Hilda Doolittle]); cultural studies; ethnic identity and literature; comparative literature (non-European focus); African American literature; William Blake; W. H. Auden; Vladimir Nabokov; Henry David Thoreau; Fyodor Dostoevsky; women writers

Considers all literary and linguistic topics: No
Types of works not published: Bibliographies; textbooks; Festschriften
Languages published: English
Series title(s): Literature in History; Princeton Studies in Culture/Power/ History; Bollingen Series

SUBMISSION REQUIREMENTS

Restrictions on authors: Authors must have a Ph.D.
Initial contact: Letter and prospectus
Considers simultaneous submissions: Yes
Will issue contract on the basis of proposal, prospectus, and/or sample chapter: Yes
Style: Chicago
Special requirements: Requires electronic manuscript
Subvention: No

EDITORIAL INFORMATION

Manuscripts or proposals submitted each year: 500
Manuscripts sent to readers each year: 75
Manuscripts accepted each year: 25
Number of outside readers: 2
Author-anonymous submission: No
Time between submission and publication decision: 2-3 months
Time between decision and return of copy-edited manuscript: 3 months
Time between decision and publication: 1 year

CONTRACT PROVISIONS

Copyright: Publisher
Royalty provisions: Varies

PUBLICATION AND DISTRIBUTION INFORMATION

Forms of publication: Cloth, paper, electronic media

Titles published each year: 25
Print run: 1,000
Number of review copies: 80-100
Distribution area: Worldwide
Time in print: 10 years

(235)
PUCKERBRUSH PRESS

76 Main St.
Orono, ME 04473

Contact: Constance Hunting, Publisher and Editor
Established: 1971
Telephone: 207 866-4868; 207 581-3832

SCOPE

Publishing interests: Bloomsbury group; Virginia Woolf
Considers all literary and linguistic topics: Yes (literary topics); no (linguistics)
Languages published: English

SUBMISSION REQUIREMENTS

Initial contact: Letter of inquiry or letter and prospectus
Considers simultaneous submissions: Prefers single submission
Will issue contract on the basis of proposal, prospectus, and/or sample chapter: No
Style: House
Special requirements: Does not accept electronic manuscripts
Subvention: No

EDITORIAL INFORMATION

Manuscripts or proposals submitted each year: 12 (estimate)
Manuscripts accepted each year: 1
Number of outside readers: 0

Time between submission and publication decision: 2 months
Time between decision and return of copy-edited manuscript: 6 months
Time between decision and publication: 2 years

CONTRACT PROVISIONS

Copyright: Author
Royalty provisions: 10% of net

PUBLICATION AND DISTRIBUTION INFORMATION

Forms of publication: Paper
Titles published each year: 2
Print run: 500-1,000
Number of review copies: 10
Distribution area: United States
Time in print: 10 years

(236)
PURDUE UNIVERSITY PRESS

1532 South Campus Courts, E
West Lafayette, IN 47907-1532

Contact: Margaret Hunt, Managing Editor
Established: 1960
Telephone: 317 494-2038
Fax: 317 496-2442

SCOPE

Publishing interests: Literary criticism; biography; literary theory; American literature; interdisciplinary approaches to literature; philosophy and literature; science and literature; Indiana authors; English literature; Romance literatures (for series only)
Considers all literary and linguistic topics: Yes (literary); no (linguistics)

Types of works not published: Unrevised dissertations; Festschriften; conference proceedings; bibliographies
Languages published: English
Series title(s): Purdue Studies in Romance Literatures

SUBMISSION REQUIREMENTS

Initial contact: Letter, prospectus, and sample chapters; for Purdue Studies in Romance Literature series, send inquiries directly to the editor, Enrique Caracciolo-Trejo, 1359 Stanley Coulter Hall, Purdue Univ., West Lafayette, IN 47907-1359
Considers simultaneous submissions: Yes (proposals); no (manuscripts)
Will issue contract on the basis of proposal, prospectus, and/or sample chapter: Rarely
Style: Chicago
Special requirements: Length: prefers 150-350 pages in typeset copy; does not consider a manuscript with more than one-third of the text in a language other than English; expects electronic manuscript
Subvention: Only for series

EDITORIAL INFORMATION

Manuscripts or proposals submitted each year: 100 (estimate)
Manuscripts sent to readers each year: 15 (estimate)
Manuscripts accepted each year: 4-5 (estimate)
Number of outside readers: 2-4
Author-anonymous submission: No
Time between submission and publication decision: 2-4 months
Time between decision and return of copy-edited manuscript: 1-2 months
Time between decision and publication: 1 year
Time allotted for reading proof: 1 month

CONTRACT PROVISIONS

Copyright: Publisher
Royalty provisions: 10% of net

PUBLICATION AND DISTRIBUTION INFORMATION

Forms of publication: Cloth, paper
Titles published each year: 2
Print run: 850
Number of review copies: 40
Distribution area: Worldwide
Time in print: Indefinitely

Typically publishes six titles per year

(237)
QUADERNS CREMA-SIRMIO

Valls i Taberner, 8
08006 Barcelona, Spain

Contact: Jaume Vallcorba, Publisher;
  Jordi Cornudella, Editor
Established: 1979 (Quaderns Crema);
  1988 (Sirmio)
Telephone: (93) 2128766; (93) 2123808
Fax: (93) 4182317

SCOPE

Publishing interests: General literature;
  linguistics; Spanish language; Catalan
  language; Romance languages
*Considers all literary and linguistic
  topics:* Yes
Types of works not published: Dissertations; bibliographies; textbooks;
  literary encyclopedias
Languages published: Spanish; Catalan
Series title(s): Biblioteca general; Assaig;
  Assaig minor

SUBMISSION REQUIREMENTS

Initial contact: Letter of inquiry

Considers simultaneous submissions: Yes
*Will issue contract on the basis of
  proposal, prospectus, and/or sample
  chapter:* No
Style: House
Subvention: No

EDITORIAL INFORMATION

*Manuscripts or proposals submitted each
  year:* 150 (estimate)
Manuscripts accepted each year: 20
Number of outside readers: 0
*Time between submission and publication
  decision:* 6 months
*Time between decision and return of copy-
  edited manuscript:* 1 year
Time between decision and publication:
  18 months
Time allotted for reading proof: 2 weeks

CONTRACT PROVISIONS

Copyright: Author
Royalty provisions: 7-10%

PUBLICATION AND DISTRIBUTION INFORMATION

Forms of publication: Cloth, paper
Titles published each year: 15
Print run: 1,000-1,500
Number of review copies: 75
Distribution area: Spain
Time in print: 10 years

(238)
UNIVERSITY OF QUEENSLAND PRESS

PO Box 42
St. Lucia, Queensland 4067, Australia

Contact: Craig Munro, Publishing
  Manager
Established: 1948

Telephone: (07) 3652403
Fax: (07) 365198

SCOPE

Publishing interests: Australian literature; aboriginal literature; literary criticism; literary history
Languages published: English
Series title(s): Studies in Australian Literature; Australian Authors; Black Australian Writing

SUBMISSION REQUIREMENTS

Initial contact: Letter, outline, and sample chapters
Will issue contract on the basis of proposal, prospectus, and/or sample chapter: No
Style: Chicago; house
Special requirements: Accepts photocopies, dot-matrix printout, camera-ready copy, and electronic manuscripts; provides guidelines for manuscript preparation
Subvention: Usually not

EDITORIAL INFORMATION

Manuscripts accepted each year: 40
Number of outside readers: Varies
Author-anonymous submission: No
Time between submission and publication decision: 3 months
Time between decision and return of copy-edited manuscript: 1 year
Time between decision and publication: 18 months

CONTRACT PROVISIONS

Copyright: Author
Royalty provisions: 10% on first 5,000, 12.5% on next 5,000, and 15% thereafter (cloth); 10% (paper)

PUBLICATION AND DISTRIBUTION INFORMATION

Forms of publication: Cloth, paper
Print run: 1,000-2,000
Number of review copies: 20
Distribution area: Australia
Time in print: Indefinitely

(239)
PHILIPP RECLAM JUN. VERLAG

Siemensstr. 32
71254 Ditzingen, Germany

Contact: Stephan Koranyi
Established: 1828
Telephone: (07156) 1630
Fax: (07156) 163197

SCOPE

Publishing interests: World literature; German literature; classical languages
Considers all literary and linguistic topics: Yes
Types of works not published: Dissertations; Festschriften
Languages published: German

SUBMISSION REQUIREMENTS

Initial contact: Letter, outline, and sample chapters
Considers simultaneous submissions: Yes
Will issue contract on the basis of proposal, prospectus, and/or sample chapter: Yes
Subvention: Sometimes

EDITORIAL INFORMATION

Manuscripts or proposals submitted each year: 40-60 (estimate)
Manuscripts accepted each year: 20 (estimate)
Number of outside readers: 0

Time between submission and publication decision: 1 month
Time between decision and return of copy-edited manuscript: 9 months
Time between decision and publication: 8-12 months
Time allotted for reading proof: 1 month

CONTRACT PROVISIONS

Copyright: Publisher
Royalty provisions: 5-10%

PUBLICATION AND DISTRIBUTION INFORMATION

Forms of publication: Cloth, paper
Titles published each year: 100 (estimate)
Print run: 5,000-10,000
Number of review copies: 80-100
Distribution area: Worldwide
Time in print: Indefinitely

(240)
RENAISSANCE ENGLISH TEXT SOCIETY

25 Hunter Hill Dr.
Amherst, MA 01002

Contact: Arthur F. Kinney, President
Established: 1965
Telephone: 413 256-8648
Fax: 413 545-3880
E-mail: afkinney@english.umass.edu

SCOPE

Publishing interests: Old-spelling critical editions of nondramatic works, printed or manuscript, related to the literary or cultural achievement of early modern England (1485-1668)
Considers all literary and linguistic topics: No
Languages published: English

SUBMISSION REQUIREMENTS

Initial contact: Letter and prospectus
Considers simultaneous submissions: Yes
Will issue contract on the basis of proposal, prospectus, and/or sample chapter: No
Style: House
Special requirements: Accepts electronic manuscripts; provides guidelines for manuscript preparation
Subvention: From institutions for long works (more than 400 printed pages)

EDITORIAL INFORMATION

Manuscripts or proposals submitted each year: 12 (estimate)
Manuscripts sent to readers each year: 4-5 (estimate)
Manuscripts accepted each year: 1-3
Number of outside readers: 3
Author-anonymous submission: No
Time between submission and publication decision: 3-9 months

CONTRACT PROVISIONS

Copyright: Publisher
Royalty provisions: No royalties

PUBLICATION AND DISTRIBUTION INFORMATION

Forms of publication: Cloth
Titles published each year: 1
Print run: 800
Number of review copies: 30
Distribution area: Worldwide
Time in print: Indefinitely

After being accepted, an edition must be reviewed by a three-person editorial committee before publication is authorized.

(241)
RICE UNIVERSITY PRESS

Box 1892
Houston, TX 77251

Contact: Susan Bielstein, Humanities
Established: 1982
Telephone: 713 285-5236
Fax: 713 285-5276

SCOPE

Publishing interests: Literary theory;
modernism; contemporary literature;
Latin American literature; African
American literature; Texas literature;
literary history; literary biography
*Considers all literary and linguistic
topics:* Yes
Types of works not published: Readers;
Festschriften
Languages published: English

SUBMISSION REQUIREMENTS

Initial contact: Letter and prospectus
Style: Chicago
Special requirements: Prefers not to
receive dot-matrix printout
Subvention: Sometimes

EDITORIAL INFORMATION

*Manuscripts or proposals submitted each
year:* 200 (estimate)
Manuscripts sent to readers each year:
10 (estimate)
Manuscripts accepted each year: 4
Number of outside readers: 2
*Time between submission and publication
decision:* 2-3 months
*Time between decision and return of copy-
edited manuscript:* 4-6 weeks
Time between decision and publication:
1 year
Time allotted for reading proof: 2 weeks

CONTRACT PROVISIONS

Copyright: Publisher
Royalty provisions: 10% of net minimum;
author often waives royalties on first
500 copies

PUBLICATION AND DISTRIBUTION
INFORMATION

Forms of publication: Cloth, paper
Titles published each year: 3
Print run: 750-2,000
Number of review copies: 40-60
Distribution area: Worldwide
Time in print: Indefinitely

(242)
RODOPI

Keizersgracht 302-304
1016 EX Amsterdam, Netherlands

233 Peachtree St., NE, Suite 404
Atlanta, GA 30303-1504

Contact: Fred van der Zee (literature);
Eric van Broekhuizen (linguistics)
Established: 1966
Telephone: (3120) 227507 (Amsterdam);
404 523-1964 (Atlanta)
Fax: (3120) 380948 (Amsterdam); 404
522-7116 (Atlanta)
E-mail: f.van.der.zee@rodopi.nl;
e.van.broekhuizen@rodopi.nl

SCOPE

Publishing interests: German literature;
English literature; American literature;
Romance literature; Slavic literature;
African literature; African languages
*Considers all literary and linguistic
topics:* Yes
Types of works not published: Literary
handbooks; literary encyclopedias

Languages published: English; German; Spanish; French

Series title(s): Postmodern Studies; Diálogos hispanicos; Chloe: Beihefte zum Daphnis; Teoría literaria: Texto y teoría; Amsterdamer Publikationen zur Sprache und Literatur; DQR Studies in Literature; Rodopi Perspectives on Modern Literature; Costerus; Studies in Slavic Literature and Poetics; Studies in Slavic and General Linguistics; Collection monographique Rodopi en littérature française contemporaine; Language and Computers: Studies in Practical Linguistics; German Monitor; Lier and Boog Studies; Faux titre: Etudes de langue et littérature françaises; European Joyce Studies; Cross Cultures: Readings in the Post-colonial Literatures in English; Approaches to Translation Studies; Portada hispánica; Deutsche Bücher; Cermeil; Foro hispánico; Amsterdamer Beiträge zur älteren Germanistik; Amsterdamer Beiträge zur neueren Germanistik; Avant-Garde Critical Studies; Yearbook of European Studies; CRIN; Amsterdam Monographs in American Studies; Studia Imagologica; Psychoanalysis and Culture; Critical Studies; Leiden Studies in Indo-European; French Literature Series; Internationale Forschungen zur Allgemeinen und Vergleichenden Literaturwissenschaft; Duitse Kroniek; Samuel Beckett Today/*Aujourd'hui*; Dutch Studies in Armenian Language and Literature; Textxet: Studies in Comparative Literature; Orientations; Interactions; Utrecht Studies in Language and Communication; Chiasma

SUBMISSION REQUIREMENTS

Initial contact: Letter and outline

Considers simultaneous submissions: No

Will issue contract on the basis of proposal, prospectus, and/or sample chapter: No

Style: MLA; Chicago

Special requirements: Requires laser-printed camera-ready copy

Subvention: No

EDITORIAL INFORMATION

Manuscripts or proposals submitted each year: 100-200 (estimate)

Manuscripts sent to readers each year: 100-200

Manuscripts accepted each year: 75

Number of outside readers: 1-3

Author-anonymous submission: No

Time between submission and publication decision: 3 months

Time between decision and publication: 3 months

Time allotted for reading proof: 2 weeks

CONTRACT PROVISIONS

Copyright: Publisher

Royalty provisions: No royalties for first printing

PUBLICATION AND DISTRIBUTION INFORMATION

Forms of publication: Cloth, paper

Titles published each year: 75

Print run: 200-1,000

Number of review copies: 10-30

Distribution area: Worldwide

Time in print: 3-6 years

(243)
ROUTLEDGE

11 New Fetter Lane
London EC4P 4EE, England

Contact: Talia Rodgers, Commissioning
Editor for Literature; Julia Hall,
Commissioning Editor for Linguistics
Established: 1988
Telephone: (0171) 8422162 (Rodgers);
(0171) 8422102 (Hall)
Fax: (0171) 8422302
E-mail: trodgers@routledge.com;
jhall@routledge.com

SCOPE

Publishing interests: William Shakespeare; English literature (medieval
through contemporary); literary theory;
feminist criticism; feminist theory;
gender studies; drama; theater studies;
literary reference works; language
reference works; biography (literary);
linguistics; popular literature; cultural
studies; postcolonial studies
*Considers all literary and linguistic
topics:* Yes
Types of works not published: Collections
of letters; Festschriften; biographies;
literary encyclopedias
Languages published: English
Series title(s): New Accents; Routledge
English Texts; Interface; Critics of the
Twentieth Century; New Critical Idiom;
Critical Readers in Theory and Practice

SUBMISSION REQUIREMENTS

Initial contact: Letter and prospectus or
letter, outline, and sample chapter;
provides guidelines for submitting a
proposal
Considers simultaneous submissions: Yes
*Will issue contract on the basis of
proposal, prospectus, and/or sample
chapter:* Yes
Style: House
Special requirements: Provides guidelines
for manuscript preparation
Subvention: No

EDITORIAL INFORMATION

*Manuscripts or proposals submitted each
year:* 360 (estimate)
Manuscripts sent to readers each year: 90
(estimate)
Manuscripts accepted each year: 30
(estimate)
Number of outside readers: 2-3
Author-anonymous submission: No
*Time between submission and publication
decision:* 2-12 weeks
*Time between decision and return of copy-
edited manuscript:* 2-3 months
Time between decision and publication:
10 months
Time allotted for reading proof: 4 weeks

CONTRACT PROVISIONS

Copyright: Author
Royalty provisions: 10% (maximum) of
net (cloth); 7.5% (maximum) of net
(paper)

PUBLICATION AND DISTRIBUTION INFORMATION

Forms of publication: Cloth, paper
Titles published each year: 30 (estimate)
Print run: 400 cloth; 2,000 paper
Number of review copies: 20-30
Distribution area: Worldwide
Time in print: 4-5 years

(244)
ROUTLEDGE

29 West 35th St.
New York, NY 10001

Established: 1986
Telephone: 212 244-3336
Fax: 212 563-2269

SCOPE

Publishing interests: Literary theory;
  feminist criticism; cultural studies;
  history and literature; anthropology and
  literature; new historicism; postcolonial
  studies; psychoanalysis and literature;
  gender studies; William Shakespeare;
  biography; major writers; African
  American literature; Renaissance
  literature; film studies; television
  studies; classical literature
*Considers all literary and linguistic
  topics:* Yes
Types of works not published:
  Festschriften
Languages published: English
Series title(s): The New Ancient World;
  AFI Film Readers; Studies in Culture
  and Communication

SUBMISSION REQUIREMENTS

Initial contact: Letter, prospectus, and
  curriculum vitae
Style: Prefers Chicago; accepts MLA
Subvention: No

EDITORIAL INFORMATION

*Manuscripts or proposals submitted each
  year:* 1,000 (estimate)
Manuscripts sent to readers each year: 75
  (estimate)
Manuscripts accepted each year: 25
  (estimate)
Number of outside readers: 0-4
*Time between submission and publication
  decision:* 3-8 weeks
*Time between decision and return of copy-
  edited manuscript:* 6 weeks
Time between decision and publication: 9
  months

CONTRACT PROVISIONS

Copyright: Negotiable

PUBLICATION AND DISTRIBUTION INFORMATION

Forms of publication: Cloth, paper
Titles published each year: 100 (estimate)
Print run: 1,500-5,000 cloth or 500-700
  cloth plus 2,500-5,000 paper
Distribution area: Worldwide

Routledge is the humanities and social
sciences imprint of Routledge, Chapman,
and Hall.

(245)
RUTGERS UNIVERSITY PRESS

109 Church St.
New Brunswick, NJ 08901

Contact: Leslie Mitchner, Editor in Chief
Established: 1936
Telephone: 908 932-7782
Fax: 908 932-7039

SCOPE

Publishing interests: Women's studies;
  African American studies; American
  literature (especially eighteenth-, nine-
  teenth-, and twentieth-century); English
  literature (especially eighteenth-, nine-
  teenth-, and twentieth-century); interdisciplinary studies; literary theory;
  popular culture; American studies;
  media studies; cultural studies
*Considers all literary and linguistic
  topics:* Yes
Types of works not published: Bibliographies; Festschriften; literary
  reference works
Languages published: English
Series title(s): American Women Writers
  Series; Casebook Series

SUBMISSION REQUIREMENTS

Initial contact: Letter of inquiry
Considers simultaneous submissions: Yes
*Will issue contract on the basis of
proposal, prospectus, and/or sample
chapter:* Yes
Style: Prefers Chicago; accepts MLA
Special requirements: Length: 200 pages
minimum; accepts electronic manuscripts with hard copy; provides
guidelines for manuscript preparation
Subvention: No

EDITORIAL INFORMATION

*Manuscripts or proposals submitted each
year:* 300
Manuscripts sent to readers each year: 25
Manuscripts accepted each year: 27
(some involved advance contracts)
Number of outside readers: 1
Author-anonymous submission: No
*Time between submission and publication
decision:* 2 months maximum
*Time between decision and return of copy-
edited manuscript:* 3-4 months
Time between decision and publication:
11-12 months
Time allotted for reading proof: 2-3
weeks

CONTRACT PROVISIONS

Copyright: Author
Royalty provisions: 5-10% of list or net

**PUBLICATION AND DISTRIBUTION
INFORMATION**

Forms of publication: Cloth, paper
Titles published each year: 25
Print run: 2,000-2,500
Number of review copies: 50
Distribution area: Worldwide
Time in print: 3 years

Books must be well-written and relatively
jargon-free.

**(246)
ST. MARTIN'S PRESS**

257 Park Ave. South
New York, NY 10010

Contact: Garrett Kiely, Director,
Scholarly and Reference Division
Established: 1951
Telephone: 212 982-3900
Fax: 212 777-6359
E-mail: gkiely@adelphi.com

SCOPE

Publishing interests: General literature;
linguistics
*Considers all literary and linguistic
topics:* Yes
Languages published: English
Series title(s): Critical Studies Series;
Insights; Language of Literature;
Modern Novelists; New Casebooks

SUBMISSION REQUIREMENTS

Initial contact: Synopsis, introduction,
table of contents, and sample chapters
Considers simultaneous submissions: Yes
*Will issue contract on the basis of
proposal, prospectus, and/or sample
chapter:* Yes
Style: Chicago
Special requirements: Length: varies by
subject; prefers electronic copy;
provides guidelines for authors
Subvention: No

EDITORIAL INFORMATION

*Manuscripts or proposals submitted each
year:* Several hundred (estimate)

Manuscripts accepted each year: 75
(estimate)
Number of outside readers: 1
Author-anonymous submission: Yes
*Time between submission and publication
decision:* 4-6 weeks
Time between decision and publication: 9
months
Time allotted for reading proof: 1 month

CONTRACT PROVISIONS

Copyright: Author

PUBLICATION AND DISTRIBUTION
INFORMATION

Forms of publication: Cloth, paper
Titles published each year: 75 (estimate)
Print run: 500-1,500
Number of review copies: 20
Distribution area: Worldwide
Time in print: 6-8 years

(247)
ST. PAUL'S BIBLIOGRAPHIES

West End House
1 Step Terrace
Winchester SO22 5BW, England

Contact: R. S. Cross, Chairman
Established: 1981
Telephone: (44) 962 860524
Fax: (44) 962 842409

SCOPE

Publishing interests: Bibliographies
(especially of twentieth-century
writers); history of the book
*Considers all literary and linguistic
topics:* No
Types of works not published: Dissertations; critical editions; collections of
letters; biographies; collections of

original essays by different authors;
Festschriften; literary reference works
Languages published: English
Series title(s): Winchester Bibliographies
of Twentieth-Century Writers

SUBMISSION REQUIREMENTS

Considers simultaneous submissions: No
*Will issue contract on the basis of
proposal, prospectus, and/or sample
chapter:* Sometimes
Special requirements: Length: negotiable;
prefers camera-ready copy
Subvention: If possible

EDITORIAL INFORMATION

*Manuscripts or proposals submitted each
year:* 12
Manuscripts sent to readers each year: 20
Manuscripts accepted each year: 4
Number of outside readers: 3
Author-anonymous submission: No
*Time between submission and publication
decision:* 3 months
Time between decision and publication:
9-10 months
Time allotted for reading proof: 3-4
weeks

CONTRACT PROVISIONS

Copyright: Author
Royalty provisions: 7.5% of gross

PUBLICATION AND DISTRIBUTION
INFORMATION

Forms of publication: Cloth, paper
Titles published each year: 3
Print run: 500-750
Number of review copies: 12
Distribution area: Worldwide
Time in print: Up to 10 years

(248)
***EDITORA DA UNIVERSIDADE DE
SAO PAULO (EDUSP)**

Av. Professor Luciano Gualberto
Travessa J, 374
6° andar
CEP 05508 São Paulo, Brazil

Contact: Carlos Eduardo Machado,
Assistant to the President; Plinio
Martins Filho, Executive Editor
Established: 1962
Telephone: (011) 2116988; (011)
8138837
Fax: (011) 2116988

SCOPE

Publishing interests: American literature;
English literature
*Considers all literary and linguistic
topics:* Yes (literature); no (linguistics)
Types of works not published: Bibli-
ographies; collections of letters;
biographies; literary handbooks; literary
encyclopedias
Languages published: Portuguese
Series title(s): Criação e crítica

SUBMISSION REQUIREMENTS

Initial contact: Letter and prospectus (2
copies)
Special requirements: Expects electronic
manuscript
Subvention: No

EDITORIAL INFORMATION

*Manuscripts or proposals submitted each
year:* 30
Manuscripts sent to readers each year:
21
Manuscripts accepted each year: 8
Number of outside readers: 2

*Time between submission and publication
decision:* 8 months
*Time between decision and return of copy-
edited manuscript:* 5 months
Time between decision and publication:
7-10 months

CONTRACT PROVISIONS

Copyright: Publisher
Royalty provisions: 7-9%

**PUBLICATION AND DISTRIBUTION
INFORMATION**

Forms of publication: Cloth, paper, elec-
tronic media
Titles published each year: 32
Print run: 3,000
Distribution area: Brazil; Portugal

(249)
*K. G. SAUR

Heilmannstr. 15-17
Postfach 71 10 09
8000 Munich 71, Germany

Contact: Klaus G. Saur, President;
Barbara Fischer, Editorial Director
Established: 1948
Telephone: (089) 791040
Fax: (089) 7910499

SCOPE

Publishing interests: Bibliographies;
literary reference works; literary history;
history of linguistics
*Considers all literary and linguistic
topics:* Yes
Types of works not published: Collections
of essays; readers
Languages published: English; German;
French; Italian

SUBMISSION REQUIREMENTS

Initial contact: Letter and outline
Style: House
Subvention: Sometimes

EDITORIAL INFORMATION

*Manuscripts or proposals submitted each
  year:* 50 (estimate)
Manuscripts sent to readers each year: 25
  (estimate)
Manuscripts accepted each year: 25
  (estimate)
Number of outside readers: Varies
*Time between submission and publication
  decision:* 6-8 weeks
Time between decision and publication:
  6-9 months

CONTRACT PROVISIONS

Copyright: Negotiable
Royalty provisions: 10% of list

PUBLICATION AND DISTRIBUTION
INFORMATION

Forms of publication: Cloth, paper, elec-
  tronic media, databases
Titles published each year: 48
Print run: 250-2,000
Number of review copies: 25
Distribution area: Worldwide
Time in print: 20 years

(250)
SCANDINAVIAN UNIVERSITY
PRESS

Box 2959 Tøyen
0608 Oslo, Norway

Contact: Bjørn Gunnar Saltnes, Editor
  (books in English); Lars Audén, Editor
  in Chief
Established: 1950

Telephone: (47) 2 2575400
Fax: (47) 2 2575353

SCOPE

Publishing interests: General literature
*Considers all literary and linguistic
  topics:* Yes
Languages published: Norwegian;
  English; Danish; Swedish

SUBMISSION REQUIREMENTS

Restrictions on authors: Gives priority to
  Scandinavian authors or authors writing
  on subjects related to Scandinavia
Initial contact: Letter and prospectus
*Will issue contract on the basis of
  proposal, prospectus, and/or sample
  chapter:* No
Style: Oxford
Special requirements: Requires electronic
  manuscript
Subvention: Frequently

EDITORIAL INFORMATION

*Manuscripts or proposals submitted each
  year:* 5-10
Manuscripts sent to readers each year: 5
Manuscripts accepted each year: 2-3
Number of outside readers: 1-2
Author-anonymous submission: No
*Time between submission and publication
  decision:* 2-3 months
*Time between decision and return of copy-
  edited manuscript:* 1 month
Time between decision and publication:
  5-6 months
Time allotted for reading proof: 1-2
  weeks

CONTRACT PROVISIONS

Copyright: Publisher
Royalty provisions: 7% of net

PUBLICATION AND DISTRIBUTION
INFORMATION

Forms of publication: Cloth, paper
Titles published each year: 7
Print run: 1,000
Number of review copies: 10-20
Distribution area: Worldwide
Time in print: 10 years

Formerly Norwegian University Press

(251)
SCARECROW PRESS

PO Box 4167
Metuchen, NJ 08840

Contact: Norman Horrocks, Vice
President, Editorial
Established: 1950
Telephone: 908 548-8600
Fax: 908 548-5767

SCOPE

Publishing interests: Reference works on
all literatures and aspects of language
*Considers all literary and linguistic
topics:* Yes
Types of works not published: Critical
editions; collections of letters
Languages published: English
Series title(s): Scarecrow Author Bibliographies

SUBMISSION REQUIREMENTS

Initial contact: Letter of inquiry; letter,
outline, and sample chapters; letter and
prospectus; or letter and full manuscript
Considers simultaneous submissions:
Prefers single submission
*Will issue contract on the basis of
proposal, prospectus, and/or sample
chapter:* Yes

Special requirements: Length: prefers 250
pages minimum; accepts camera-ready
copy; provides guidelines for manuscript preparation
Subvention: No

EDITORIAL INFORMATION

*Manuscripts or proposals submitted each
year:* 250 (estimate)
Manuscripts sent to readers each year: 25
(estimate)
Manuscripts accepted each year: 8
Number of outside readers: 1
Author-anonymous submission: Yes
*Time between submission and publication
decision:* 1-2 months
Time between decision and publication:
6-12 months

CONTRACT PROVISIONS

Copyright: Publisher
Royalty provisions: 10% if typeset by
publisher; 15% if author provides
camera-ready copy

PUBLICATION AND DISTRIBUTION
INFORMATION

Forms of publication: Cloth
Titles published each year: 15
Print run: 750-1,000
Number of review copies: 40
Distribution area: Worldwide
Time in print: 5-8 years

(252)
ERICH SCHMIDT

Gethiner Str. 30G
10785 Berlin, Germany

Contact: Rainer Moritz
Established: 1924

Telephone: (030) 25008560; (030) 25008561
Fax: (030) 25008521

SCOPE

Publishing interests: German literature; German language; Romance literatures; Romance languages; English literature; English language; American literature
Considers all literary and linguistic topics: No
Languages published: German; English
Series title(s): Bibliographien der deutschen Literatur des Mittelalters; Göttinger Beiträge zur internationalen Übersetzungsforschung; Grundlagen der Germanistik; Philologische Studien und Quellen; Texte des späten Mittelalters und der frühen Neuzeit; Grundlagen der Anglistik und Amerikanistik; Grundlagen der Romanistik

SUBMISSION REQUIREMENTS

Initial contact: Letter and outline
Will issue contract on the basis of proposal, prospectus, and/or sample chapter: Yes
Special requirements: Depends on sales expectations
Subvention: Sometimes

EDITORIAL INFORMATION

Manuscripts or proposals submitted each year: 50-100
Manuscripts accepted each year: 20-30
Author-anonymous submission: Yes
Time between submission and publication decision: 1 month
Time between decision and publication: 6 months
Time allotted for reading proof: 1 month

CONTRACT PROVISIONS

Copyright: Publisher

Royalty provisions: Varies

PUBLICATION AND DISTRIBUTION INFORMATION

Forms of publication: Cloth, paper
Titles published each year: 30
Print run: 500-5,000
Number of review copies: 20
Distribution area: Worldwide
Time in print: 20 years

**(253)
SCHOCKEN BOOKS**

201 East 50th St.
New York, NY 10022

Contact: Bonny Fetterman, Senior Editor
Established: 1946
Telephone: 212 572-2559; 212 572-6049
Fax: 212 572-6030

SCOPE

Publishing interests: Judaism; Hebrew literature in translation; Yiddish literature in translation; women's studies; American studies
Considers all literary and linguistic topics: No
Not interested in proposals on: Literary criticism
Types of works not published: Dissertations; textbooks
Languages published: English
Series title(s): Library of Yiddish Classics Series

SUBMISSION REQUIREMENTS

Initial contact: Letter of inquiry or letter and prospectus
Considers simultaneous submissions: Yes

*Will issue contract on the basis of
proposal, prospectus, and/or sample
chapter:* Yes
Style: Chicago
Special requirements: Accepts photocopies; does not accept dot-matrix
printout
Subvention: No

EDITORIAL INFORMATION

*Manuscripts or proposals submitted each
year:* 5,000 (estimate)
Number of outside readers: Varies
*Time between submission and publication
decision:* 6 weeks
Time between decision and publication:
12 months

**PUBLICATION AND DISTRIBUTION
INFORMATION**

Forms of publication: Cloth
Titles published each year: 4
Distribution area: Worldwide
Time in print: 5-10 years

**(254)
SCHOLARS' FACSIMILES AND
REPRINTS**

PO Box 344
Delmar, NY 12054

Contact: Norman Mangouni, Director
Established: 1936
Telephone: 518 439-5978

SCOPE

Publishing interests: Facsimile reprints,
with introductions, of rare or important
books in English literature; American
literature; linguistics; women's studies;
rhetoric (Renaissance through nineteenth-century)

*Considers all literary and linguistic
topics:* Yes
Languages published: English; French;
Caucasian languages
Series title(s): American Linguistics,
1700-1900; Caucasian and Anatolian
Studies; Classical Armenian Texts;
Modern Persian Literature Series; The
Sermon in America, 1620-1800

SUBMISSION REQUIREMENTS

Initial contact: Letter and prospectus
Considers simultaneous submissions:
Prefers single submission
Style: Chicago
Special requirements: Prefers electronic
manuscripts
Subvention: No

EDITORIAL INFORMATION

*Manuscripts or proposals submitted each
year:* 50 (estimate)
Manuscripts sent to readers each year: 30
(estimate)
Manuscripts accepted each year: 20
Number of outside readers: 2
*Time between submission and publication
decision:* 1 month
*Time between decision and return of copy-
edited manuscript:* 1 month
Time between decision and publication: 6
months

CONTRACT PROVISIONS

Copyright: Publisher (usually)
Royalty provisions: No royalties

**PUBLICATION AND DISTRIBUTION
INFORMATION**

Forms of publication: Cloth; microform
Titles published each year: 15
Print run: 200
Number of review copies: 10
Distribution area: Worldwide

Time in print: 25 years minimum

(255)
SCOLAR PRESS

Gower House
Croft Rd.
Aldershot, Hampshire GU11 3HR
England

Contact: Rachel Lynch, Editor
Established: 1972
Telephone: (0252) 331551
Fax: (0252) 344405

SCOPE

Publishing interests: Medieval literature;
   Renaissance literature; English literature
   (Middle English, Renaissance, nine-
   teenth-century); William Shakespeare;
   Andrew Marvell; George Traherne; John
   Milton; critical theory; feminist
   criticism; literary reference works
*Considers all literary and linguistic
   topics:* Yes
Types of works not published: Unrevised
   dissertations; collections of letters
Languages published: English
Series title(s): Critical Thought Series;
   Nineteenth Century Series

SUBMISSION REQUIREMENTS

Initial contact: Letter, outline, and sample
   chapters
Considers simultaneous submissions: Yes
*Will issue contract on the basis of
   proposal, prospectus, and/or sample
   chapter:* Yes
Style: Modern Humanities Research
   Association
Special requirements: Length: negotiable;
   does not accept photocopy; sometimes
   requires camera-ready copy

Subvention: Yes, for extensively illustrated books

EDITORIAL INFORMATION

*Manuscripts or proposals submitted each
   year:* 20 (estimate)
Manuscripts sent to readers each year:
   15 (estimate)
Manuscripts accepted each year: 10-12
   (estimate)
Number of outside readers: 2
Author-anonymous submission: No
*Time between submission and publication
   decision:* 2 months
*Time between decision and return of copy-
   edited manuscript:* 2-3 months
Time between decision and publication: 9
   months
Time allotted for reading proof: 3 weeks

CONTRACT PROVISIONS

Copyright: Author
Royalty provisions: 7.5-10% of net

PUBLICATION AND DISTRIBUTION
INFORMATION

Forms of publication: Cloth, paper
Print run: 600
Number of review copies: 30
Distribution area: Worldwide
Time in print: 3-4 years

(256)
SCOTTISH ACADEMIC PRESS

56 Hanover St.
Edinburgh EH2-2DX, Scotland

Contact: Douglas Grant
Established: 1961
Telephone: (0131) 2257483
Fax: (0131) 2257662

SCOPE

Publishing interests: Gaelic literature; linguistics; general literature; classical literature
Considers all literary and linguistic topics: Yes
Types of works not published: Dissertations; collections of essays; Festschriften; literary reference works
Languages published: English

SUBMISSION REQUIREMENTS

Initial contact: Letter of inquiry
Will issue contract on the basis of proposal, prospectus, and/or sample chapter: No
Style: Chicago
Subvention: Occasionally

EDITORIAL INFORMATION

Manuscripts or proposals submitted each year: 50-60 (estimate)
Manuscripts sent to readers each year: 10-15 (estimate)
Manuscripts accepted each year: 10
Number of outside readers: 1
Author-anonymous submission: No
Time between submission and publication decision: 3 months
Time between decision and publication: 6 months
Time allotted for reading proof: 3 weeks

CONTRACT PROVISIONS

Copyright: Negotiable
Royalty provisions: 10% (cloth); 7.5% (paper)

PUBLICATION AND DISTRIBUTION INFORMATION

Forms of publication: Cloth, paper
Titles published each year: 7

Print run: 1,500
Number of review copies: 25
Distribution area: Worldwide
Time in print: 10-15 years

(257)
UNIVERSITY OF SCRANTON PRESS

Scranton, PA 18510

Imprint(s) and subsidiary firm(s): Ridge Row Press
Contact: Richard W. Rousseau, S.J.
Established: 1987
Telephone: 717 941-7449
Fax: 717 941-4309
E-mail: rousseaur1@udfs.edu

SCOPE

Publishing interests: Theology; religion and literature; Pennsylvania (northeastern) studies; philosophy
Considers all literary and linguistic topics: No
Types of works not published: Textbooks; encyclopedias; literary handbooks
Languages published: English

SUBMISSION REQUIREMENTS

Initial contact: Letter, outline, sample chapter, and SASE
Considers simultaneous submissions: Yes, if informed
Will issue contract on the basis of proposal, prospectus, and/or sample chapter: No
Style: Chicago
Special requirements: Length: 100-350 printed pages; requires electronic copy using major word processing program
Subvention: Yes

EDITORIAL INFORMATION

Manuscripts or proposals submitted each year: 150
Manuscripts sent to readers each year: 40
Manuscripts accepted each year: 8
Number of outside readers: 2
Author-anonymous submission: Yes
Time between submission and publication decision: 3 months
Time between decision and publication: 9 months
Time allotted for reading proof: Flexible

CONTRACT PROVISIONS

Copyright: Publisher
Royalty provisions: 10% of net

PUBLICATION AND DISTRIBUTION INFORMATION

Forms of publication: Cloth; paper
Titles published each year: 12
Print run: 1,000
Number of review copies: 40
Distribution area: Worldwide
Time in print: 5 years if sales drop; otherwise, indefinitely

(258)
SCRIPTA HUMANISTICA

1383 Kersey Lane
Potomac, MD 20854

Contact: Bruno M. Damiani, Publisher
Established: 1973
Telephone: 301 424-9584

SCOPE

Publishing interests: Modern literatures; modern languages
Considers all literary and linguistic topics: Yes

Languages published: All modern languages
Series title(s): Scripta Humanistica

SUBMISSION REQUIREMENTS

Initial contact: Letter and prospectus
Considers simultaneous submissions: No
Will issue contract on the basis of proposal, prospectus, and/or sample chapter: No
Style: MLA
Special requirements: Requires camera-ready copy
Subvention: Yes

EDITORIAL INFORMATION

Manuscripts or proposals submitted each year: 100
Manuscripts sent to readers each year: 40
Manuscripts accepted each year: 10-12
Number of outside readers: 2
Author-anonymous submission: No
Time between submission and publication decision: 4-6 weeks
Time between decision and publication: 4-6 months

CONTRACT PROVISIONS

Copyright: Author or publisher
Royalty provisions: 5% of net

PUBLICATION AND DISTRIBUTION INFORMATION

Forms of publication: Cloth
Titles published each year: 12
Print run: 200-500
Number of review copies: 15-20
Distribution area: Worldwide
Time in print: 5 years

(259)
*MARTIN SECKER AND WARBURG

Michelin House
81 Fulham Rd.
London SW3 6RB, England

Contact: Suzie Yuan
Established: 1910
Telephone: (071) 5819393
Fax: (071) 5898421

SCOPE

Publishing interests: General literature;
  biography; feminist studies
*Considers all literary and linguistic
  topics:* Yes (literature); no (linguistics)
Types of works not published: Dissertations; bibliographies; readers; literary
  reference books
Languages published: English
Series title(s): Writers at Work

SUBMISSION REQUIREMENTS

Initial contact: Letter, prospectus, and
  sample chapters
Subvention: No

EDITORIAL INFORMATION

*Manuscripts or proposals submitted each
  year:* 1,500 (estimate)
Manuscripts sent to readers each year: 50
  (estimate)
Manuscripts accepted each year: 0
  (estimate)
Number of outside readers: 0
*Time between submission and publication
  decision:* 3 weeks
*Time between decision and return of copy-
  edited manuscript:* 14 months
Time between decision and publication:
  18 months

CONTRACT PROVISIONS

Copyright: Author
Royalty provisions: 10% of list (cloth); 5-
  7.5% (paper)

PUBLICATION AND DISTRIBUTION
INFORMATION

Forms of publication: Cloth, paper
Titles published each year: 90 (estimate)
Print run: Varies
Number of review copies: 60-80
Distribution area: Varies
Time in print: 1 year minimum

(260)
M. E. SHARPE

90 Business Park Dr.
Armonk, NY 10504

Imprint(s) and subsidiary firm(s): East
  Gate Books
Contact: Stephen Dalphin, Editorial
  Director
Established: 1958
Telephone: 914 273-1800
Fax: 914 273-2106
E-mail: mes@usa.net

SCOPE

Publishing interests: Asian studies;
  Russian studies; east European studies
*Considers all literary and linguistic
  topics:* No
Languages published: English

SUBMISSION REQUIREMENTS

Initial contact: Letter, outline, sample
  chapters, and curriculum vitae
Considers simultaneous submissions: Yes
*Will issue contract on the basis of
  proposal, prospectus, and/or sample
  chapter:* Possibly

Style: Chicago
Special requirements: Requires electronic
   manuscript (IBM-compatible)
Subvention: No

EDITORIAL INFORMATION

*Manuscripts or proposals submitted each
   year:* 8 (estimate)
Manuscripts sent to readers each year: 6
   (estimate)
Manuscripts accepted each year: 3
   (estimate)
Number of outside readers: 1-2
Author-anonymous submission: No
*Time between submission and publication
   decision:* 1-3 months
*Time between decision and return of copy-
   edited manuscript:* 2 months
Time between decision and publication:
   1 year
Time allotted for reading proof: 2 weeks

CONTRACT PROVISIONS

Copyright: Publisher
Royalty provisions: 10% of net (cloth);
   7.5% (paper)

**PUBLICATION AND DISTRIBUTION
INFORMATION**

Forms of publication: Cloth, paper
Titles published each year: 1
Print run: 750-1,000
Number of review copies: 40
Distribution area: Worldwide
Time in print: 10 years

**(261)
SHEFFIELD ACADEMIC PRESS**

Mansion House
19 Kingfield Rd.
Sheffield S11 9AS, England

Imprint(s) and subsidiary firm(s): JSOT
   Press
Contact: John Jarick (biblical studies);
   Andrew Kirk (literary criticism)
Telephone: (44) 114 2554433

SCOPE

Publishing interests: English literature;
   Thomas Hardy; William Golding
*Considers all literary and linguistic
   topics:* Yes
Types of works not published: Bibli-
   ographies
Languages published: English
Series title(s): Writing on Writing

SUBMISSION REQUIREMENTS

Initial contact: Letter and prospectus
Considers simultaneous submissions: No
*Will issue contract on the basis of
   proposal, prospectus, and/or sample
   chapter:* No
Style: House
Special requirements: Prefers electronic
   copy
Subvention: Sometimes

EDITORIAL INFORMATION

*Manuscripts or proposals submitted each
   year:* 20
Manuscripts sent to readers each year:
   10
Manuscripts accepted each year: 6
Number of outside readers: 1
Author-anonymous submission: No
*Time between submission and publication
   decision:* 10-12 weeks
Time between decision and publication:
   6-9 months
Time allotted for reading proof: 1 month

CONTRACT PROVISIONS

Copyright: Publisher
Royalty provisions: 10% of net

PUBLICATION AND DISTRIBUTION INFORMATION

Forms of publication: Cloth, paper, electronic media
Titles published each year: 6
Print run: 1,000
Number of review copies: 30
Distribution area: Worldwide
Time in print: 5 years

(262)
SHOE STRING PRESS

2 Linsley St.
North Haven, CT 06473-2517

Imprint(s) and subsidiary firm(s): Archon Books; Library Professional Publications
Contact: Diantha C. Thorpe, President
Established: 1952
Telephone: 203 239-2702
Fax: 203 239-2568

SCOPE

Publishing interests: General literature; comparative literature; interdisciplinary studies; English language; American literature
Considers all literary and linguistic topics: Yes
Types of works not published: Unrevised dissertations; collections of essays
Languages published: English

SUBMISSION REQUIREMENTS

Initial contact: Letter and prospectus
Will issue contract on the basis of proposal, prospectus, and/or sample chapter: Yes
Style: Chicago
Special requirements: Provides guidelines for manuscript preparation

Subvention: No

EDITORIAL INFORMATION

Manuscripts or proposals submitted each year: 140
Manuscripts accepted each year: 11
Author-anonymous submission: Yes
Time between submission and publication decision: 1 week minimum

CONTRACT PROVISIONS

Copyright: Author

PUBLICATION AND DISTRIBUTION INFORMATION

Forms of publication: Cloth, paper
Titles published each year: 11
Print run: 1,000
Number of review copies: 65
Distribution area: Worldwide
Time in print: 10-20 years

(263)
SINGAPORE UNIVERSITY PRESS

National Univ. of Singapore
Yusof Ishak House
10 Kent Ridge Crescent
0511 Singapore

Contact: Patricia Tay, Managing Editor
Established: 1971
Telephone: (65) 7761148
Fax: (65) 7740652

SCOPE

Publishing interests: Asian literature; Southeast Asian literature; commonwealth literature; new literatures in English; English as a foreign language; language and culture
Considers all literary and linguistic topics: Yes

Types of works not published: Unrevised dissertations; bibliographies; literary encyclopedias
Languages published: English

SUBMISSION REQUIREMENTS

Restrictions on authors: Gives priority to those affiliated with the National University of Singapore and to Singaporeans
Initial contact: Letter, outline, and sample chapter
Considers simultaneous submissions: Yes, if informed
Will issue contract on the basis of proposal, prospectus, and/or sample chapter: No
Style: House; Chicago
Special requirements: Length: 400 pages (typeset) maximum for single-author volumes, 600 pages for multiple-author volumes; requires camera-ready and electronic copy
Subvention: Yes (at least partial subvention)

EDITORIAL INFORMATION

Manuscripts or proposals submitted each year: 2-4
Manuscripts sent to readers each year: 2-4
Manuscripts accepted each year: 1-2
Number of outside readers: 1
Author-anonymous submission: Yes
Time between submission and publication decision: 4-6 months (plus time for external review)
Time between decision and publication: 6-9 months
Time allotted for reading proof: 1-2 months

CONTRACT PROVISIONS

Copyright: Publisher

Royalty provisions: 10% of net

PUBLICATION AND DISTRIBUTION INFORMATION

Forms of publication: Cloth, paper
Titles published each year: 2
Print run: 500-1,000
Number of review copies: 20
Distribution area: Worldwide
Time in print: Indefinitely

**(264)
SIXTEENTH CENTURY JOURNAL PUBLISHERS**

Dept. of History
University of Missouri
Columbia, MO 65211

Contact: Charles Nauert, General Editor; R. V. Schnucker, Publisher
Established: 1981
Telephone: 314 882-6662

SCOPE

Publishing interests: Renaissance literature (1450-1660)
Considers all literary and linguistic topics: Yes
Languages published: English
Series title(s): Peter Martyr Vermigli Library

SUBMISSION REQUIREMENTS

Initial contact: Letter and complete manuscript
Considers simultaneous submissions: No
Will issue contract on the basis of proposal, prospectus, and/or sample chapter: No
Style: Chicago (13th ed.)
Special requirements: Requires electronic copy

Subvention: No

EDITORIAL INFORMATION

Manuscripts or proposals submitted each year: 3-4
Manuscripts sent to readers each year: 3-4
Manuscripts accepted each year: 1
Number of outside readers: 2
Author-anonymous submission: Yes
Time between submission and publication decision: 3 months
Time between decision and publication: 1 year
Time allotted for reading proof: 1 week

CONTRACT PROVISIONS

Copyright: Publisher
Royalty provisions: 25% of gross after production costs are met

PUBLICATION AND DISTRIBUTION INFORMATION

Forms of publication: Cloth, paper
Titles published each year: 2
Print run: 500-600
Number of review copies: 40
Distribution area: Worldwide
Time in print: Indefinitely

(265)
SLAVICA PUBLISHERS

PO Box 14388
Columbus, OH 43214-0388

Contact: Charles E. Gribble, President
Established: 1966
Telephone: 614 268-4002
Fax: 614 268-0106

SCOPE

Publishing interests: Slavic literature; Slavic languages; Slavic folklore; Baltic literature; Baltic languages; Baltic folklore; east European literature; east European languages; east European folklore; Russian literature; Russian language; Russian folklore
Considers all literary and linguistic topics: No
Types of works not published: Unrevised dissertations
Languages published: English; Slavic languages

SUBMISSION REQUIREMENTS

Initial contact: Letter (prospectus or outline optional)
Considers simultaneous submissions: Prefers single submission
Will issue contract on the basis of proposal, prospectus, and/or sample chapter: Occasionally
Style: Prefers MLA; accepts other standard styles
Special requirements: Accepts dot-matrix printout for evaluation; final copy must be camera-ready
Subvention: No

EDITORIAL INFORMATION

Manuscripts or proposals submitted each year: 100
Manuscripts sent to readers each year: 20
Manuscripts accepted each year: 10-12
Number of outside readers: 1-3
Author-anonymous submission: No
Time between submission and publication decision: 1 week-6 months
Time between decision and publication: 4 months

CONTRACT PROVISIONS

Copyright: Author

Royalty provisions: Varies (usually 10% after production costs have been met)

PUBLICATION AND DISTRIBUTION INFORMATION

Forms of publication: Cloth, paper
Titles published each year: 8
Print run: 500-4,000
Number of review copies: 50-70
Distribution area: Worldwide
Time in print: Indefintely

(266)
COLIN SMYTHE

PO Box 6
Gerrards Cross, Buckinghamshire
SL9 8XA, England

Contact: Colin Smythe
Established: 1966
Telephone: (0753) 886000
Fax: (0753) 886469

SCOPE

Publishing interests: Irish literature (especially 1890-1930); Anglo-Irish literature (especially 1890-1930); biography (Irish)
Considers all literary and linguistic topics: No
Types of works not published: Literary encyclopedias; textbooks
Languages published: English
Series title(s): Irish Literary Studies Series; Irish Drama Selections; Ulster Editions and Monographs; Irish Dramatic Texts; Studies in Contemporary Irish Literature; Princess Grace Irish Library Series; Princess Grace Irish Library Lectures

SUBMISSION REQUIREMENTS

Initial contact: Letter of inquiry; letter and prospectus; or letter, outline, and sample chapter
Considers simultaneous submissions: No
Will issue contract on the basis of proposal, prospectus, and/or sample chapter: No
Style: House
Subvention: Often (depending on subject matter)

EDITORIAL INFORMATION

Manuscripts or proposals submitted each year: 100 (estimate)
Manuscripts sent to readers each year: 20-30 (estimate)
Manuscripts accepted each year: 15
Number of outside readers: 1-2
Author-anonymous submission: Occasionally
Time between submission and publication decision: 9-24 months
Time between decision and publication: 6-18 months

CONTRACT PROVISIONS

Copyright: Author
Royalty provisions: 10% of net (minimum)

PUBLICATION AND DISTRIBUTION INFORMATION

Forms of publication: Cloth, paper
Titles published each year: 20 (estimate)
Print run: 1,200-4,000
Number of review copies: 20-40
Distribution area: Worldwide
Time in print: 10-20 years

(267)
UNIVERSITY OF SOUTH CAROLINA PRESS

Carolina Plaza, 8th fl.
Columbia, SC 29212

Contact: Editor
Established: 1944
Telephone: 803 777-5244
Fax: 803 777-0160
E-mail: warren@uscpress.scarolina.edu

SCOPE

Publishing interests: Rhetoric; women's studies; contemporary literature
Considers all literary and linguistic topics: No
Types of works not published: Festschriften; collections of essays
Languages published: English
Series title(s): Women's Diaries and Letters of the Nineteenth-Century South; Understanding Contemporary American Literature; Understanding Contemporary British Literature; Understanding Modern European and Latin American Literature

SUBMISSION REQUIREMENTS

Initial contact: Letter, outline, sample chapters, and curriculum vitae
Considers simultaneous submissions: No
Style: MLA; Chicago
Special requirements: Accepts electronic manuscripts; provides guidelines for manuscript preparation
Subvention: Sometimes

EDITORIAL INFORMATION

Manuscripts sent to readers each year: 100
Manuscripts accepted each year: 20
Number of outside readers: 2

Author-anonymous submission: No
Time between submission and publication decision: 2 months
Time between decision and return of copy-edited manuscript: 10 months
Time between decision and publication: 1 year

CONTRACT PROVISIONS

Copyright: Publisher
Royalty provisions: 8% of net

PUBLICATION AND DISTRIBUTION INFORMATION

Forms of publication: Cloth, paper
Titles published each year: 12 (estimate)
Print run: 800-2,000
Number of review copies: 50-75
Distribution area: Worldwide
Time in print: 10 years

(268)
SOUTHERN ILLINOIS UNIVERSITY PRESS

PO Box 3697
Carbondale, IL 62902-3697

Contact: John "Rick" Stetter, Director
Established: 1956
Telephone: 618 453-2281
Fax: 618 453-1221

SCOPE

Publishing interests: Literary criticism; composition; rhetoric; feminist studies; science fiction; English literature (modern); American literature (modern); European literature (modern)
Considers all literary and linguistic topics: Yes (literature)
Languages published: English

Series title(s): Ad Feminam: Alternatives;
Crosscurrents / Modern Critiques;
Studies in Writing and Rhetoric;
Landmarks in Rhetoric

SUBMISSION REQUIREMENTS

Initial contact: Letter and prospectus;
provides quidelines for proposals
Considers simultaneous submissions:
Prefers single submission
*Will issue contract on the basis of
proposal, prospectus, and/or sample
chapter:* Yes
Style: Prefers Chicago; accepts MLA
Special requirements: Accepts photocopies; does not accept poor-quality
dot-matrix printout; sometimes requires
electronic manuscripts or camera-ready
copy
Subvention: No

EDITORIAL INFORMATION

*Manuscripts or proposals submitted each
year:* 700 (estimate)
Manuscripts sent to readers each year: 70
(estimate)
Manuscripts accepted each year: 33
Number of outside readers: 2
Author-anonymous submission: No
*Time between submission and publication
decision:* 6 months
*Time between decision and return of copy-
edited manuscript:* 2-3 months
Time between decision and publication:
1 year
Time allotted for reading proof: 2 weeks

CONTRACT PROVISIONS

Copyright: Negotiable
Royalty provisions: Nothing on first 500
copies, 5% on next 500, and 10% on
next 500 (cloth); 5% on first 500 copies,
7.5-10% thereafter (paper)

**PUBLICATION AND DISTRIBUTION
INFORMATION**

Forms of publication: Cloth, paper
Titles published each year: 25 (estimate)
Print run: 1,000
Number of review copies: 50
Distribution area: Worldwide
Time in print: Indefinitely

**(269)
STANFORD UNIVERSITY PRESS**

Stanford, CA 94305-2235

Contact: Helen Tartar, Humanities Editor
(literature); Norris Pope, Associate
Editor (Victorian studies); William W.
Carver, Editor (linguistics)
Established: 1925
Telephone: 415 723-9598
Fax: 415 725-3457

SCOPE

Publishing interests: General literature;
linguistics; Slavic literature; East Asian
literature; literary theory
*Considers all literary and linguistic
topics:* Yes
Types of works not published: Bibli-
ographies; biographies; readers;
Festschriften
Languages published: English
Series title(s): Meridian: Crossing
Aesthetics; *Figurae*: Reading Medieval
Culture

SUBMISSION REQUIREMENTS

Initial contact: Letter and prospectus
Considers simultaneous submissions: No
*Will issue contract on the basis of
proposal, prospectus, and/or sample
chapter:* Yes
Style: House

Special requirements: Prefers not to
receive dot-matrix printout; accepts
electronic manuscripts; provides
guidelines for manuscript preparation
Subvention: No

EDITORIAL INFORMATION

*Manuscripts or proposals submitted each
year:* 500 (estimate)
Manuscripts sent to readers each year: 48
Manuscripts accepted each year: 29
Number of outside readers: 1 minimum
Author-anonymous submission: No
*Time between submission and publication
decision:* 3 months
*Time between decision and return of copy-
edited manuscript:* 6-12 weeks
Time between decision and publication:
12-14 months
Time allotted for reading proof: 1 month

CONTRACT PROVISIONS

Copyright: Publisher
Royalty provisions: 10% of list after the
first 1,000 copies (cloth); 5% of list
(paper)

**PUBLICATION AND DISTRIBUTION
INFORMATION**

Forms of publication: Cloth, paper
Titles published each year: 23 (estimate)
Print run: 800-900 (cloth); 1,500-2,000
(paper)
Number of review copies: 35-65
Distribution area: Worldwide
Time in print: 20 years minimum

Focuses on two major questions in eval-
uating literary studies: How sophisticated
and original is the book's theoretical
framework, the fundamental questions it
asks? How expert are the author's
analyses of specific texts?

**(270)
FRANZ STEINER VERLAG**

Postfach 10 10 61
70009 Stuttgart, Germany

Contact: Vincent Sieveking, Business
Manager
Established: 1949
Telephone: (0711) 2582303
Fax: (0711) 2582390

SCOPE

Publishing interests: German literature;
English literature; Romance literature;
classical Greek literature; Roman
literature; oriental languages; oriental
literature
*Considers all literary and linguistic
topics:* Yes
Types of works not published: Literary
encyclopedias
Languages published: German; English;
French; Spanish; Italian; Latin; Greek
(classical); Arabic; Sanskrit; Chinese
languages
Series title(s): Schriften der mainzer
philosophischen Fakuläts-Gesellschaft
E. V.; Wissenschaftliche Gesellschaft an
der Johann Wolfgang Goethe-
Universität Frankfurt am Main:
Sitzungsberichte; Hermes-
Einzelschriften; Palingenesia;
Forschungen zur antiken Sklaverei;
Heidelberger althistorische Beiträge und
epigraphische Studien; Akademie der
Wissenschaften und der Literatur,
Mainz: Abhandlungen der geistes- und
sozialwissenschaftliche Klasse;
Akademie der Wissenschaften und der
Literatur, Mainz: Abhandlungen der
Klasse der Literatur; Beiträge zur
Literatur des 15.-18. Jahrhunderts;
Deutsche Sprache in Europa und
Übersee; Hydronymia Germaniae;

Mainzer Studien zur Sprach- und Volks-
forschung; Zeitschrift für Dialektologie
und Linguistik: Beihefte; Archivum
Calderonianum; Mainzer romanistische
Arbeiten; Text und Kontext; Unter-
suchungen zur Sprach- und Literatur-
geschichte der romanischen Völker;
Zeitschrift für französische Sprache und
Literatur: Beihefte; Studien zur Rhetorik
des neunzehnten Jahrhunderts;
Hydronymia Europaea; Abhandlungen
für die Kunde des Morgenlandes;
Beiruter Texte und Studien; Freiburger
altorientalische Studien; Münchener
ostasiatische Studien; Tibetan and Indo-
Tibetan Studies; Schriftenreihe des
Südasien-Instituts der Universität
Heidelberg; South Asian Digest of
Regional Writing; South Asian Studies;
Monographien zur indischen
Archäologie, Kunst, und Philologie

SUBMISSION REQUIREMENTS

Initial contact: Letter and prospectus
Considers simultaneous submissions: Yes
Will issue contract on the basis of
  proposal, prospectus, and/or sample
  chapter: No
Subvention: For most books

EDITORIAL INFORMATION

Manuscripts or proposals submitted each
  year: 100 (estimate)
Manuscripts sent to readers each year: 0
  (no outside readers)
Manuscripts accepted each year: 70
  (estimate)
Number of outside readers: 0
Time between submission and publication
  decision: 2-3 months
Time between decision and publication:
  6-8 months (8-10 weeks for camera-
  ready copy)
Time allotted for reading proof: 2 months

CONTRACT PROVISIONS

Copyright: Publisher
Royalty provisions: No royalties for first
  edition

**PUBLICATION AND DISTRIBUTION
INFORMATION**

Forms of publication: Paper
Titles published each year: 70 (estimate)
Print run: 400
Number of review copies: 20
Distribution area: Worldwide
Time in print: 15 years minimum

**(271)
STERLING PUBLISHERS**

L-10, Green Park Ext.
New Delhi 110016, India

Contact: S. K. Ghai, Managing Director
Established: 1964
Telephone: (11) 669560; (11) 660904

SCOPE

Publishing interests: Third World
  literature (especially Asian and African
  literatures); Indian literature in English
Considers all literary and linguistic
  topics: Yes
Types of works not published: Unrevised
  dissertations
Languages published: English

SUBMISSION REQUIREMENTS

Initial contact: Letter and prospectus
Considers simultaneous submissions: No
Will issue contract on the basis of
  proposal, prospectus, and/or sample
  chapter: No
Style: Chicago
Special requirements: Prefers electronic
  manuscripts or camera-ready copy

Subvention: Yes, if available

EDITORIAL INFORMATION

Manuscripts or proposals submitted each year: 50 (estimate)
Manuscripts sent to readers each year: 24 (estimate)
Manuscripts accepted each year: 11
Number of outside readers: 5
Author-anonymous submission: No
Time between submission and publication decision: 3-6 months
Time between decision and return of copy-edited manuscript: 1-2 years
Time allotted for reading proof: 4-6 weeks

CONTRACT PROVISIONS

Copyright: Author
Royalty provisions: 10% of net

PUBLICATION AND DISTRIBUTION INFORMATION

Forms of publication: Cloth, paper
Titles published each year: 6
Print run: 750-1,100
Number of review copies: 75-110
Distribution area: Worldwide
Time in print: 3-4 years

(272)
SUMMA PUBLICATIONS

PO Box 20725
Birmingham, AL 35216

Contact: William C. Carter, Editor in Chief
Established: 1983
Telephone: 205 822-0463
Fax: 205 822-0463

SCOPE

Publishing interests: French literature; French language; francophone literature; comparative literature (involving French); southern American literature
Considers all literary and linguistic topics: No
Not interested in proposals on: South American literature (except francophone writers)
Types of works not published: Unrevised dissertations; literary reference works
Languages published: French; English
Series title(s): Marcel Proust Series; Southern Literary Series

SUBMISSION REQUIREMENTS

Initial contact: Letter of inquiry, prospectus, and (preferably) sample chapter
Considers simultaneous submissions: No
Will issue contract on the basis of proposal, prospectus, and/or sample chapter: No
Style: MLA
Special requirements: Length: 500 pages maximum (exceptions made)
Subvention: Yes, for specialized studies

EDITORIAL INFORMATION

Manuscripts or proposals submitted each year: 15-20 (estimate)
Manuscripts sent to readers each year: 12-13 (estimate)
Manuscripts accepted each year: 8
Number of outside readers: 2-3
Author-anonymous submission: No
Time between submission and publication decision: 3-4 months
Time between decision and return of copy-edited manuscript: 4-5 months

Time between decision and publication: 12-15 months
Time allotted for reading proof: 2-3 months (prefers 2-3 weeks)

CONTRACT PROVISIONS

Copyright: Publisher or author
Royalty provisions: 10-35%

PUBLICATION AND DISTRIBUTION INFORMATION

Forms of publication: Cloth, paper
Titles published each year: 9 (estimate)
Print run: 500-800
Number of review copies: 12-15
Distribution area: Worldwide
Time in print: 7 years minimum

(273)
SUSQUEHANNA UNIVERSITY PRESS

Susquehanna University
Selinsgrove, PA 17870

Contact: Hans Feldmann, Director
Established: 1944
Telephone: 717 372-4175
Fax: 717 372-2745

SCOPE

Publishing interests: British literature; American literature; Pennsylvania German literature; women and literature; film and literature
Considers all literary and linguistic topics: Yes
Not interested in proposals on: Linguistics
Types of works not published: Unrevised dissertations more than three years old; readers; literary handbooks; literary encyclopedias

Languages published: English

SUBMISSION REQUIREMENTS

Initial contact: Letter of inquiry or author and manuscript information form supplied by the publisher
Considers simultaneous submissions: No
Will issue contract on the basis of proposal, prospectus, and/or sample chapter: No
Style: Chicago
Special requirements: Length: normally 200-500 pages; does not accept dot-matrix printout
Subvention: No

EDITORIAL INFORMATION

Manuscripts or proposals submitted each year: 25
Manuscripts sent to readers each year: 20
Manuscripts accepted each year: 4
Number of outside readers: 1-2
Author-anonymous submission: No
Time between submission and publication decision: 4-8 months
Time between decision and publication: 8-12 months

CONTRACT PROVISIONS

Copyright: Publisher
Royalty provisions: 10% after first 800 copies

PUBLICATION AND DISTRIBUTION INFORMATION

Forms of publication: Cloth
Titles published each year: 6
Print run: 800-2,000
Number of review copies: 30-80
Distribution area: Worldwide
Time in print: Indefinitely

(274)
SYRACUSE UNIVERSITY PRESS

1600 Jamesville Ave.
Syracuse, NY 13244-5160

Contact: Cynthia Maude-Gembler,
  Executive Editor
Established: 1943
Telephone: 315 443-5534
Fax: 315 443-5545

SCOPE

Publishing interests: Irish literature;
  medieval literature (especially feminist
  criticism); Renaissance literature (especially feminist criticism); utopian
  literature; Middle Eastern literature
  (twentieth-century); twentieth-century
  literature; Virginia Woolf; New York
  State writers; Native American literature
  (especially of the Northeast)
*Considers all literary and linguistic
  topics:* No
Types of works not published: Unrevised
  dissertations; bibliographies;
  Festschriften; most literary reference
  works
Prizes and competitions: John Ben Snow
  Prize ($1,500 for the best manuscript on
  a New York State topic)
Languages published: English
Series title(s): Irish Studies

SUBMISSION REQUIREMENTS

Initial contact: Letter and prospectus
Considers simultaneous submissions:
  Sometimes
*Will issue contract on the basis of
  proposal, prospectus, and/or sample
  chapter:* Yes
Style: Chicago
Special requirements: Length: prefers 400
  pages maximum; does not accept dot-
  matrix printout; requires electronic

manuscript with author-date system of
documentation; provides guidelines for
manuscript preparation
Subvention: No

EDITORIAL INFORMATION

*Manuscripts or proposals submitted each
  year:* 300 (estimate)
Manuscripts sent to readers each year:
  50-60
Manuscripts accepted each year: 7
Number of outside readers: 2
Author-anonymous submission: No
*Time between submission and publication
  decision:* 3-4 months
*Time between decision and return of copy-
  edited manuscript:* 3 months
Time between decision and publication:
  10-12 months
Time allotted for reading proof: 2 weeks

CONTRACT PROVISIONS

Copyright: Publisher usually
Royalty provisions: 10% of net (cloth);
  7.5% (paper)

PUBLICATION AND DISTRIBUTION
INFORMATION

Forms of publication: Cloth, paper
Titles published each year: 8 (estimate)
Print run: 1,000-1,200
Number of review copies: 50-100
Distribution area: Worldwide
Time in print: 15-20 years

(275)
TEACHERS COLLEGE PRESS

1234 Amsterdam Ave.
New York, NY 10027

Contact: Faye Zucker, Managing Editor
Established: 1904

Telephone: 212 678-3929
Fax: 212 678-4149

SCOPE

Publishing interests: Teaching of
language; teaching of literacy
*Considers all literary and linguistic
topics:* No
Languages published: English
Series title(s): Language and Literacy
Series

SUBMISSION REQUIREMENTS

Initial contact: Letter, prospectus, and
sample chapters (2 copies)
Style: American Psychological Association
Special requirements: Provides guidelines
for manuscript preparation

EDITORIAL INFORMATION

*Manuscripts or proposals submitted each
year:* 50 (estimate)
Manuscripts sent to readers each year: 20
(estimate)
Manuscripts accepted each year: 8
(estimate)
Number of outside readers: 2
Author-anonymous submission: No
*Time between submission and publication
decision:* 3 months
*Time between decision and return of copy-
edited manuscript:* 2 months
Time between decision and publication:
10 months
Time allotted for reading proof: 2-4
weeks

CONTRACT PROVISIONS

Copyright: Publisher
Royalty provisions: 5-7.5% for initial
printing

PUBLICATION AND DISTRIBUTION INFORMATION

Forms of publication: Cloth, paper
Titles published each year: 7
Print run: 2,000-3,500
Number of review copies: 50-100
Distribution area: Worldwide
Time in print: 10 years minimum

(276)
TEMPLE UNIVERSITY PRESS

Broad and Oxford Streets
Philadelphia, PA 19122

Contact: Janet M. Francendese, Executive
Editor
Established: 1969
Telephone: 215 787-8787
Fax: 215 787-4719

SCOPE

Publishing interests: Women's studies;
women writers; African American
women writers; Asian American
literature; Latin American literature;
Native American literature; American
literature (ethnic writers)
*Considers all literary and linguistic
topics:* No
Types of works not published: Bibliographies; Festschriften; readers;
collections of letters; literary reference
works
Languages published: English

SUBMISSION REQUIREMENTS

Initial contact: Letter and manuscript
Considers simultaneous submissions: Yes
*Will issue contract on the basis of
proposal, prospectus, and/or sample
chapter:* No
Style: MLA; Chicago

Special requirements: Accepts electronic manuscripts; does not accept 9-pin dot-matrix printout; provides guidelines for manuscript preparation
Subvention: No

EDITORIAL INFORMATION

Manuscripts accepted each year: 10 (estimate)
Number of outside readers: 2
Author-anonymous submission: No
Time between submission and publication decision: 3-4 months
Time between decision and return of copy-edited manuscript: 2-4 months
Time between decision and publication: 1 year

CONTRACT PROVISIONS

Copyright: Negotiable
Royalty provisions: Varies

PUBLICATION AND DISTRIBUTION INFORMATION

Forms of publication: Cloth, paper
Titles published each year: 5
Print run: 1,000
Number of review copies: 20-50
Distribution area: Worldwide
Time in print: Indefinitely

(277)
UNIVERSITY OF TENNESSEE PRESS

293 Communications Bldg.
Knoxville, TN 37996-0325

Contact: Meredith Morris-Babb, Acquisitions Editor
Established: 1940
Telephone: 615 974-3321
Fax: 615 974-3724

E-mail: utpress@utkvx.utk.edu

SCOPE

Publishing interests: American literature; British literature; English literature; feminist criticism (American literature, English literature, comparative literature, and African American literature); African American literature; Native American literature
Considers all literary and linguistic topics: No
Types of works not published: Bibliographies; readers; Festschriften; literary reference works
Languages published: English
Series title(s): Tennessee Studies in Literature

SUBMISSION REQUIREMENTS

Initial contact: Letter of inquiry; letter and prospectus; or letter, outline, and sample chapter
Considers simultaneous submissions: No
Will issue contract on the basis of proposal, prospectus, and/or sample chapter: Yes
Style: Chicago; house
Special requirements: Length: prefers 200-350 pages; accepts photocopies, camera-ready copy, and electronic manuscripts; does not accept dot-matrix printout; provides guidelines for manuscript preparation
Subvention: Not from author; accepts institutional support for highly specialized publications

EDITORIAL INFORMATION

Manuscripts or proposals submitted each year: 250 (estimate)
Manuscripts sent to readers each year: 30
Manuscripts accepted each year: 6
Number of outside readers: 2

Author-anonymous submission: No
Time between submission and publication decision: 2 months minimum
Time between decision and publication: 10-12 months
Time allotted for reading proof: 1 month

CONTRACT PROVISIONS

Copyright: Publisher
Royalty provisions: Varies (from no royalties for first printing to 10% or more of net)

PUBLICATION AND DISTRIBUTION INFORMATION

Forms of publication: Cloth, paper
Titles published each year: 13
Print run: 1,000-2,500
Number of review copies: 10% of print run
Distribution area: Worldwide
Time in print: 4-5 years

(278)
TEXAS A&M UNIVERSITY PRESS

Drawer C
College Station, TX 77843-4354

Contact: Noel R. Parsons, Editor in Chief
Established: 1974
Telephone: 409 845-1436
Fax: 409 847-8752
E-mail: fdl@tampress.tamu.edu

SCOPE

Publishing interests: Western American literature (nineteenth- and twentieth-century); Texas literature; African American Texas writers; southwestern Mexican American literature; Mexican American Texas writers; women writers; biographies of Texans and southwesterners; linguistic studies of Spanish in Texas and the Southwest
Considers all literary and linguistic topics: No
Not interested in proposals on: Literary theory
Types of works not published: Unrevised dissertations; bibliographies; Festschriften; literary encyclopedias
Languages published: English
Series title(s): Tarleton State University Southwestern Studies in the Humanities

SUBMISSION REQUIREMENTS

Initial contact: Letter and prospectus
Considers simultaneous submissions: No
Will issue contract on the basis of proposal, prospectus, and/or sample chapter: No
Style: Chicago; house
Special requirements: Length: prefers 70,000-90,000 words; accepts photocopies, electronic manuscripts, and camera-ready copy (supply sample of dot-matrix printout before sending); provides guidelines for authors
Subvention: Sometimes (for an exceptionally long book or one with an unusually limited market)

EDITORIAL INFORMATION

Manuscripts or proposals submitted each year: 40-50 (estimate)
Manuscripts sent to readers each year: 9
Manuscripts accepted each year: 7
Number of outside readers: 2
Author-anonymous submission: No
Time between submission and publication decision: 4-5 months
Time between decision and return of copy-edited manuscript: 3-6 months
Time between decision and publication: 12-18 months
Time allotted for reading proof: 3 weeks

CONTRACT PROVISIONS

Copyright: Author
Royalty provisions: 10% of net (cloth);
  7% of net (paper)

PUBLICATION AND DISTRIBUTION INFORMATION

Forms of publication: Cloth, paper, electronic media
Titles published each year: 4
Print run: 1,500
Number of review copies: 70
Distribution area: Worldwide
Time in print: 10-15 years

(279)
TEXAS CHRISTIAN UNIVERSITY PRESS

Box 30783
Fort Worth, TX 76129

Contact: A. T. Row, Editor
Established: 1966
Telephone: 817 921-7822
Fax: 817 921-7333
E-mail: atrow@gamma.is.tcu.edu

SCOPE

Publishing interests: Western American literature; literary criticism
Considers all literary and linguistic topics: No
Types of works not published: Bibliographies; literary encyclopedias; literary reference works
Languages published: English

SUBMISSION REQUIREMENTS

Initial contact: Letter of inquiry
Will issue contract on the basis of proposal, prospectus, and/or sample chapter: Yes

Style: Chicago
Special requirements: Prefers electronic manuscripts; does not accept dot-matrix printout
Subvention: No

EDITORIAL INFORMATION

Manuscripts or proposals submitted each year: 25 (estimate)
Manuscripts sent to readers each year: 5 (estimate)
Manuscripts accepted each year: 2 (estimate)
Number of outside readers: 2
Author-anonymous submission: Yes
Time between submission and publication decision: 6 months
Time between decision and return of copy-edited manuscript: 18 months
Time between decision and publication: 1 year
Time allotted for reading proof: 2 weeks

CONTRACT PROVISIONS

Copyright: Author
Royalty provisions: 10% of net

PUBLICATION AND DISTRIBUTION INFORMATION

Forms of publication: Paper, cloth
Titles published each year: 2
Print run: 2,000
Number of review copies: 60
Distribution area: Worldwide
Time in print: 6-10 years

(280)
UNIVERSITY OF TEXAS PRESS

Editorial Department
PO Box 7819
Austin, TX 78713-7819

Contact: Ali Hossaini, Jr., Sponsoring
Editor (humanities)
Established: 1950
Telephone: 512 471-4278
Fax: 512 320-0668

SCOPE

Publishing interests: Latin American
literature; Latin American languages;
Middle Eastern literature; Native
American literature; Native American
languages; biography; autobiography;
African American literature (Texas);
African American linguistics (Texas);
classical literature; women's studies;
women's literature; Texas literature;
Andean literatures; Andean languages
*Considers all literary and linguistic
topics:* No
Not interested in proposals on: African
literatures; Asian literatures; oceanic
literatures; European literatures
Types of works not published: Unrevised
dissertations; bibliographies;
Festschriften; literary reference works
Languages published: English
Series title(s): Literary Modernism; Pan
American Series in Latin American
Literature

SUBMISSION REQUIREMENTS

Initial contact: Letter, outline, and sample
chapters
Considers simultaneous submissions: Yes
(proposals); no (manuscripts)
*Will issue contract on the basis of
proposal, prospectus, and/or sample
chapter:* No
Style: Chicago
Special requirements: Length: prefers
250-300 pages; does not require
camera-ready copy or electronic manuscripts
Subvention: No

EDITORIAL INFORMATION

*Manuscripts or proposals submitted each
year:* 100
Manuscripts sent to readers each year: 8-
10
Manuscripts accepted each year: 10-15
Number of outside readers: 2
Author-anonymous submission: No
*Time between submission and publication
decision:* 12-18 months
Time allotted for reading proof: 3 weeks

CONTRACT PROVISIONS

Copyright: Publisher
Royalty provisions: No royalty on first
printing

PUBLICATION AND DISTRIBUTION INFORMATION

Forms of publication: Cloth, paper, elec-
tronic media
Titles published each year: 35
Print run: 1,000
Number of review copies: 75-100
Distribution area: Worldwide
Time in print: 5-6 years

(281) TEXAS TECH UNIVERSITY PRESS

PO Box 41037
Lubbock, TX 79409-1037

Contact: Judith Keeling, Acquiring Editor
Established: 1971
Telephone: 806 742-2982
Fax: 806 742-2979

SCOPE

Publishing interests: Classical studies;
eighteenth-century studies; Joseph
Conrad; literature of conflict

Considers all literary and linguistic topics: No

Types of works not published: Dissertations; readers; Festschriften; literary handbooks and encyclopedias; textbooks

Languages published: English

Series title(s): Studies in Comparative Literature

SUBMISSION REQUIREMENTS

Initial contact: Proposal or letter of inquiry

Considers simultaneous submissions: Yes (proposals); no (manuscripts)

Will issue contract on the basis of proposal, prospectus, and/or sample chapter: Sometimes

Style: Chicago

Special requirements: Requires electronic manuscript (_MS-DOS_ diskette)

Subvention: Sometimes

EDITORIAL INFORMATION

Manuscripts or proposals submitted each year: 55 (estimate)

Manuscripts sent to readers each year: 6 (estimate)

Manuscripts accepted each year: 3

Number of outside readers: 2

Author-anonymous submission: No

Time between submission and publication decision: 3-6 months

Time between decision and publication: 1 year

Time allotted for reading proof: 2 weeks

CONTRACT PROVISIONS

Copyright: Negotiable

PUBLICATION AND DISTRIBUTION INFORMATION

Forms of publication: Cloth, paper

Titles published each year: 3 (estimate)

Distribution area: Worldwide

Time in print: Varies

(282)
*THAMES AND HUDSON

500 Fifth Ave.
New York, NY 10110

Contact: Peter Warner, President and Editor; Susan Dwyer, Vice President and Marketing Director

Established: 1977

Telephone: 212 354-3763

Fax: 212 869-0856

SCOPE

Publishing interests: Visual arts and literature; performing arts

Languages published: English

Series title(s): Literary Lives

SUBMISSION REQUIREMENTS

Initial contact: Letter and prospectus

Specializes in art history and archaeology but is interested in serious but nonscholarly works on literary subjects that lend themselves to being illustrated

(283)
THOMAS JEFFERSON UNIVERSITY PRESS

Northeast Missouri State University
MC111L
Kirksville, MO 63501

Contact: R. V. Schnucker, Director

Established: 1984

Telephone: 816 785-4665

Fax: 816 785-4181
E-mail:
ss18%nemomus@academic.nemostate
.edu

SCOPE

Publishing interests: American literature;
literature
*Considers all literary and linguistic
topics:* Yes
Languages published: English
Series title(s): Peter Martyr Vermigli
Library

SUBMISSION REQUIREMENTS

Initial contact: Letter and complete
manuscript (2 copies)
Considers simultaneous submissions: No
*Will issue contract on the basis of
proposal, prospectus, and/or sample
chapter:* No
Style: Chicago (13th ed.)
Special requirements: Requires electronic
copy
Subvention: No

EDITORIAL INFORMATION

*Manuscripts or proposals submitted each
year:* 10
Manuscripts sent to readers each year:
10
Manuscripts accepted each year: 1-2
Number of outside readers: 2
Author-anonymous submission: Yes
*Time between submission and publication
decision:* 3-4 months
Time between decision and publication:
1 year
Time allotted for reading proof: 1 week

CONTRACT PROVISIONS

Copyright: publisher
Royalty provisions: 25% of net after
production costs are met

PUBLICATION AND DISTRIBUTION
INFORMATION

Forms of publication: Cloth, paper
Titles published each year: 5
Print run: 500-600
Number of review copies: 40
Distribution area: Worldwide
Time in print: Indefinitely

(284)
THREE CONTINENTS PRESS

PO Box 38009
Colorado Springs, CO 80937-8009

Contact: Donald E. Herdeck
Established: 1973
Telephone: 719 576-4689

SCOPE

Publishing interests: Non-Western
literatures (including literary criticism,
literary history, biography, and bibliography); sub-Saharan African
literature; Asian literatures; Caribbean
literatures; Latin American literatures;
Middle Eastern literatures; cross-
cultural studies; artistic-intellectual
groups; zeitgeist studies
*Considers all literary and linguistic
topics:* No
Languages published: English
Series title(s): Critical Perspectives;
Time/Place: Artists and Scholars

SUBMISSION REQUIREMENTS

Initial contact: Letter, outline, and sample
chapter (enclose return postage)
Considers simultaneous submissions: Yes
*Will issue contract on the basis of
proposal, prospectus, and/or sample
chapter:* Rarely

THREE

Special requirements: Requires electronic manuscript

EDITORIAL INFORMATION

Manuscripts or proposals submitted each year: 200-300 (estimate)
Manuscripts sent to readers each year: 10 (estimate)
Manuscripts accepted each year: 10-20 (estimate)
Number of outside readers: 1-3
Author-anonymous submission: No
Time between submission and publication decision: 2-3 months
Time between decision and return of copyedited manuscript: 6-12 months
Time between decision and publication: 1-2 years
Time allotted for reading proof: 2 months

CONTRACT PROVISIONS

Copyright: Varies (usually author)
Royalty provisions: 10%

PUBLICATION AND DISTRIBUTION INFORMATION

Forms of publication: Cloth, paper
Titles published each year: 40 (estimate)
Print run: 1,000-2,000
Number of review copies: 50-60
Distribution area: United States; Canada; United Kingdom
Time in print: Indefinitely

**(285)
UNIVERSITY OF TOKYO PRESS**

7-3-1 Hongo
Bunkyo-ku
Tokyo 113, Japan

Contact: Editor, International Publications Department

Established: 1951
Telephone: (03) 3811-0964
Fax: (03) 3814-9458

SCOPE

Publishing interests: English-language translations of Japanese literature
Considers all literary and linguistic topics: No
Types of works not published: Dissertations
Languages published: Japanese; English

SUBMISSION REQUIREMENTS

Initial contact: Letter of inquiry
Considers simultaneous submissions: No
Will issue contract on the basis of proposal, prospectus, and/or sample chapter: No
Style: Chicago
Subvention: Yes

EDITORIAL INFORMATION

Manuscripts or proposals submitted each year: 5
Number of outside readers: 2
Author-anonymous submission: No
Time between submission and publication decision: 6-12 months
Time between decision and return of copyedited manuscript: 3-9 months
Time between decision and publication: 1 year

CONTRACT PROVISIONS

Copyright: Author
Royalty provisions: 6-10%

PUBLICATION AND DISTRIBUTION INFORMATION

Forms of publication: Cloth, paper
Print run: 1,000
Number of review copies: 50

Distribution area: Worldwide
Time in print: 10 years

(286)
UNIVERSITY OF TORONTO PRESS

10 St. Mary St., Suite 700
Toronto, ON M4Y 2W8, Canada

Contact: Ron Schoeffel, Editor in Chief
Established: 1901
Telephone: 416 978-2239
Fax: 416 978-4738

SCOPE

Publishing interests: Canadian literature;
English literature; English language;
Desiderius Erasmus; French literature;
French language; Italian literature;
Italian language; medieval studies;
Renaissance studies; Reformation
studies; Spanish literature; Spanish
language; Ukrainian studies; literary
theory; aesthetic theory; cultural theory;
semiotics
*Considers all literary and linguistic
topics:* No
Types of works not published: Unrevised
dissertations; Festschriften (unless
unified and on important topics)
Languages published: English
Series title(s): University of Toronto
Romance Series; Theory/Culture

SUBMISSION REQUIREMENTS

Initial contact: Letter of inquiry or letter
and prospectus
Considers simultaneous submissions: No
*Will issue contract on the basis of
proposal, prospectus, and/or sample
chapter:* Occasionally
Style: Chicago; MLA

Special requirements: Accepts photocopies and electronic manuscripts; does
not accept dot-matrix printout
Subvention: Generally

EDITORIAL INFORMATION

*Manuscripts or proposals submitted each
year:* 50 (manuscripts only)
Manuscripts sent to readers each year: 50
Manuscripts accepted each year: 15
Number of outside readers: 2 minimum
Author-anonymous submission: No
*Time between submission and publication
decision:* 3-6 months
*Time between decision and return of copy-
edited manuscript:* 2 months
Time between decision and publication:
1 year
Time allotted for reading proof: 4 weeks

CONTRACT PROVISIONS

Copyright: Publisher
Royalty provisions: 5% of net

PUBLICATION AND DISTRIBUTION
INFORMATION

Forms of publication: Cloth, paper
Titles published each year: 25
Print run: 750-1,000
Number of review copies: 25-150
Distribution area: Worldwide
Time in print: 4 years minimum

(287)
TRIGON PRESS

117 Kent House Rd.
Beckenham, Kent BR3 1JJ, England

Imprint(s) and subsidiary firm(s): London
Office; Artsfand

Contact: Roger Sheppard, Projects
  Manager; Judith Dixley, Editorial
  Manager
Established: 1965
Telephone: (44) 81 7780534
Fax: (44) 81 7767525

SCOPE

Publishing interests: American literature;
  English literature; science fiction; bibliographies (literary topics); biography;
  directories of English literature
*Considers all literary and linguistic
  topics:* Yes
Not interested in proposals on: Minority
  groups
Types of works not published: Unrevised
  dissertations; critical editions;
  textbooks; Festschriften
Languages published: English

SUBMISSION REQUIREMENTS

Initial contact: Letter and outline
Considers simultaneous submissions:
  Prefers single submission
*Will issue contract on the basis of
  proposal, prospectus, and/or sample
  chapter:* No
Style: House
Special requirements: Prefers electronic
  copy (Macintosh)
Subvention: Usually not

EDITORIAL INFORMATION

*Manuscripts or proposals submitted each
  year:* 20
Manuscripts accepted each year: 3
Author-anonymous submission: No
*Time between submission and publication
  decision:* 3 months
Time between decision and publication:
  9-12 months
Time allotted for reading proof: 4 weeks

CONTRACT PROVISIONS

Copyright: Author
Royalty provisions: 10% of gross

PUBLICATION AND DISTRIBUTION INFORMATION

Forms of publication: Cloth (primarily)
Titles published each year: 4
Print run: 750-1,000
Number of review copies: 20
Distribution area: Europe
Time in print: 5 years

(288)
*TWAYNE PUBLISHERS

866 Third Ave.
New York, NY 10022

Contact: Lewis DeSimone, Editor; Liz
  Fowler, Editor
Established: 1960

SCOPE

Publishing interests: General literature
  (especially major authors and works);
  children's literature; William Shakespeare; short fiction; literature and
  society; literary theory; genres; novel;
  poetry; short story (topics must fit one
  of the publisher's series)
*Considers all literary and linguistic
  topics:* No
Types of works not published: Dissertations; bibliographies; critical editions;
  collections of letters; readers;
  Festschriften; literary handbooks;
  literary encyclopedias
Languages published: English
Series title(s): Twayne's Masterwork
  Studies; Twayne's Masterwork Studies:
  Children's and Young Adult Literature;
  Twayne's New Critical Introductions to

Shakespeare; Twayne's Studies in Short Fiction; Literature and Society; Twayne's Studies in Literary Theory; Twayne's Studies in Genre; Twayne's Critical History of the Novel; Twayne's Critical History of Poetry; Twayne's Critical History of the Short Story; Twayne's United States Authors Series; Twayne's English Authors Series; Twayne's World Authors Series; Young Adult Authors

SUBMISSION REQUIREMENTS

Restrictions on authors: Preference given to authors with a Ph.D.
Initial contact: Letter and 1-page prospectus
Style: Chicago
Special requirements: Some series have length restriction
Subvention: No

EDITORIAL INFORMATION

Manuscripts or proposals submitted each year: 240 (estimate)
Manuscripts sent to readers each year: 132 (estimate)
Manuscripts accepted each year: 60 (estimate)
Number of outside readers: 1-2
Time between submission and publication decision: 3 months
Time between decision and return of copy-edited manuscript: 3-6 months
Time between decision and publication: 12-18 months

CONTRACT PROVISIONS

Copyright: Negotiable

PUBLICATION AND DISTRIBUTION INFORMATION

Forms of publication: Cloth, paper, electronic media

Titles published each year: 50 (estimate)
Number of review copies: 10
Distribution area: Worldwide
Time in print: 3-30 years

Books must appeal to an undergraduate audience and not be highly specialized.

(289)
*UCA EDITORES

Apartado 01-575
San Salvador, El Salvador

Contact: Rodolfo Cardenal
Established: 1975
Telephone: (503) 240744
Fax: (503) 240288

SCOPE

Publishing interests: Salvadoran literature; Central American literatures
Considers all literary and linguistic topics: No
Types of works not published: Bibliographies; critical editions; Festschriften; literary encyclopedias
Prizes and competitions: Annual National Prize
Languages published: Spanish
Series title(s): Gavidia

SUBMISSION REQUIREMENTS

Initial contact: Letter and manuscript (2 copies)
Subvention: No

EDITORIAL INFORMATION

Manuscripts or proposals submitted each year: 25
Manuscripts sent to readers each year: 4
Manuscripts accepted each year: 5
Number of outside readers: 2

*Time between submission and publication
  decision:* 6 months
*Time between decision and return of copy-
  edited manuscript:* 6 months
Time between decision and publication:
  8-12 months

CONTRACT PROVISIONS

Copyright: Publisher
Royalty provisions: 10%

**PUBLICATION AND DISTRIBUTION
INFORMATION**

Forms of publication: Paper
Titles published each year: 5
Print run: 2,000
Number of review copies: 20
Distribution area: Central America;
  Europe
Time in print: 6 years

Publisher for Universidad
Centroamericana José Simeón Cañas

**(290)
UNIVERSITY PRESS OF AMERICA**

4720 Boston Way
Lanham, MD 20706

Contact: Michelle P. Harris, Acquisitions
  Editor
Established: 1975
Telephone: 301 459-3366
Fax: 301 459-2118

SCOPE

Publishing interests: General literature;
  linguistics
*Considers all literary and linguistic
  topics:* Yes
Languages published: English

SUBMISSION REQUIREMENTS

Initial contact: Publisher's manuscript
  proposal questionnaire, letter of inquiry,
  letter and prospectus, or letter and
  manuscript
Considers simultaneous submissions: Yes
*Will issue contract on the basis of
  proposal, prospectus, and/or sample
  chapter:* Rarely
Style: Chicago
Special requirements: Requires camera-
  ready copy; provides guidelines for
  manuscript preparation
Subvention: Yes

EDITORIAL INFORMATION

*Manuscripts or proposals submitted each
  year:* 100-250
Manuscripts sent to readers each year:
  40-60
Manuscripts accepted each year: 50
  (estimate)
Number of outside readers: 1
Author-anonymous submission: Yes
*Time between submission and publication
  decision:* 8-10 weeks
*Time between decision and return of copy-
  edited manuscript:* Does not copyedit
Time between decision and publication:
  3-6 months

CONTRACT PROVISIONS

Copyright: Varies
Royalty provisions: first 500 copies, no
  royalty; next 500 copies, 5% of net; next
  500 copies, 7% of net; 10% of net
  thereafter

**PUBLICATION AND DISTRIBUTION
INFORMATION**

Forms of publication: Cloth; paper
Titles published each year: 36
Print run: 500-1,000
Number of review copies: 20

Distribution area: Worldwide
Time in print: 5 years

(291)
UNIVERSITY PRESS PLC

Three Crowns Bldg.
Jericho
PMB 5095
Ibadan, Nigeria

Contact: Akin Olajide
Established: 1978
Telephone: (02) 2411356; (02) 2412313
Fax: (02) 412056

SCOPE

Publishing interests: Yoruba literature;
Hausa literature; Igbo literature;
Nigerian literature; Nigerian languages;
Yoruba language; Hausa language; Igbo
language; Efik language; language and
culture
*Considers all literary and linguistic
topics:* Yes
Types of works not published: Critical
editions; collections of letters;
collections of essays; Festschriften;
dissertations
Languages published: English; French;
Yoruba; Igbo; Hausa; Efik
Series title(s): Yoruba Language and
Culture; Igbo Language and Culture;
Hausa Language and Culture

SUBMISSION REQUIREMENTS

Initial contact: Letter of inquiry
Considers simultaneous submissions: No
*Will issue contract on the basis of
proposal, prospectus, and/or sample
chapter:* No
Style: House
Special requirements: Accepts camera-
ready copy

Subvention: Yes

EDITORIAL INFORMATION

*Manuscripts or proposals submitted each
year:* 15 (estimate)
Manuscripts sent to readers each year: 6
(estimate)
Manuscripts accepted each year: 4
(estimate)
Number of outside readers: 2
Author-anonymous submission: Yes
*Time between submission and publication
decision:* 6 months
*Time between decision and return of copy-
edited manuscript:* 2 months
Time between decision and publication: 9
months

CONTRACT PROVISIONS

Copyright: Negotiable
Royalty provisions: 10%

**PUBLICATION AND DISTRIBUTION
INFORMATION**

Forms of publication: Paper
Titles published each year: 4 (estimate)
Print run: 5,000
Number of review copies: 25
Distribution area: Nigeria
Time in print: 2 years

(292)
*UNIVERSITY PUBLISHING CO.

11 Central School Rd.
PO Box 386
Onitsha
Anambra State, Nigeria

Contact: Chairman
Established: 1959
Telephone: (046) 210013

SCOPE

Publishing interests: African literature; Igbo literature; Igbo language; Hausa language; Yoruba language; Efik language
Considers all literary and linguistic topics: Yes
Types of works not published: Readers; literary reference works
Languages published: English; Igbo; Hausa; Yoruba; Efik; Ijo; Nigerian languages; French

SUBMISSION REQUIREMENTS

Initial contact: Letter, outline, and sample chapters or letter and manuscript (2 copies)
Style: MLA
Special requirements: Accepts photocopies, dot-matrix printout, and camera-ready copy; does not accept electronic manuscripts
Subvention: Sometimes

EDITORIAL INFORMATION

Manuscripts or proposals submitted each year: 15 (estimate)
Manuscripts sent to readers each year: 15 (estimate)
Manuscripts accepted each year: 8 (estimate)
Number of outside readers: Several
Time between submission and publication decision: 3 months

CONTRACT PROVISIONS

Copyright: Author and publisher
Royalty provisions: 10%

PUBLICATION AND DISTRIBUTION INFORMATION

Forms of publication: Cloth, paper
Titles published each year: 10

Print run: 5,000-20,000
Distribution area: Africa; United States; western Europe
Time in print: Indefinitely

(293)
UNIVERSITY OF UTAH PRESS

101 University Services Bldg.
Salt Lake City, UT 84112

Contact: Mick Gusinde-Duffy, Acquiring Editor
Established: 1949
Telephone: 801 581-6771
Fax: 801 581-3365

SCOPE

Publishing interests: Western American literature; nature writing; linguistics; Middle East studies
Considers all literary and linguistic topics: No
Types of works not published: Bibliographies; Festschriften
Languages published: English
Series title(s): Studies in Indigenous Languages of the Americas

SUBMISSION REQUIREMENTS

Initial contact: Letter of inquiry; letter and prospectus; letter, outline, and sample chapter; or letter and manuscript
Considers simultaneous submissions: Yes
Will issue contract on the basis of proposal, prospectus, and/or sample chapter: Yes
Style: Chicago, house
Special requirements: Length: 400 manuscript pages maximum
Subvention: No

EDITORIAL INFORMATION

Manuscripts or proposals submitted each year: 100 (estimate)
Manuscripts sent to readers each year: 10
Manuscripts accepted each year: 3
Number of outside readers: 2-4
Author-anonymous submission: No
Time between submission and publication decision: 2 months
Time between decision and return of copy-edited manuscript: 6 months
Time between decision and publication: 1 year
Time allotted for reading proof: 3 weeks

CONTRACT PROVISIONS

Copyright: Negotiable
Royalty provisions: 7.5%

PUBLICATION AND DISTRIBUTION INFORMATION

Forms of publication: Cloth, paper
Titles published each year: 3
Print run: 1,500
Number of review copies: 100
Distribution area: Worldwide
Time in print: 3-5 years

(294)
VANDERBILT UNIVERSITY PRESS

Box 1813, Station B
Nashville, TN 37235

Contact: Charles Backus, Director
Established: 1940
Telephone: 615 322-3585
Fax: 615 343-8823
E-mail: vupress@vanderbilt.edu

SCOPE

Publishing interests: English literature; American literature; southern American literature; Fugitive writers; agrarian writers; French literature; European literature; classical literature
Considers all literary and linguistic topics: Yes (literature)
Types of works not published: Unrevised dissertations; bibliographies; readers; collections of essays; literary reference works; Festschriften
Languages published: English

SUBMISSION REQUIREMENTS

Initial contact: Letter, prospectus, and outline
Considers simultaneous submissions: Yes (prospectus); no (manuscript)
Will issue contract on the basis of proposal, prospectus, and/or sample chapter: Occasionally
Style: Chicago; house
Special requirements: Accepts photocopies
Subvention: Occasionally (for highly specialized or extensively illustrated books)

EDITORIAL INFORMATION

Manuscripts or proposals submitted each year: 40-50
Manuscripts sent to readers each year: 10-20
Manuscripts accepted each year: 5-10
Number of outside readers: 2-3
Author-anonymous submission: No
Time between submission and publication decision: 3-6 months
Time between decision and return of copy-edited manuscript: 3-4 months
Time between decision and publication: 9-12 months

CONTRACT PROVISIONS

Copyright: Author or publisher
Royalty provisions: 10% of net

PUBLICATION AND DISTRIBUTION
INFORMATION

Forms of publication: Cloth, paper
Titles published each year: 4
Print run: 1,000-1,500
Number of review copies: 30
Distribution area: Worldwide
Time in print: 6-8 years minimum

(295)
*VARIORUM REPRINTS

Gower House
Croft Rd.
Aldershot, Hampshire GU11 3HR
England

Contact: John Smedley, Editorial
  Manager
Established: 1980
Telephone: (0252) 331551
Fax: (0252) 344405

SCOPE

Publishing interests: Collections of
  reprinted articles by eminent scholars on
  Byzantine studies; medieval studies;
  Renaissance studies; exploration
*Considers all literary and linguistic
  topics:* Yes
Languages published: English; French;
  German

SUBMISSION REQUIREMENTS

Initial contact: Letter and prospectus
Style: Modern Humanities Research
  Association
Special requirements: Expects camera-
  ready copy

Subvention: Sometimes

EDITORIAL INFORMATION

*Manuscripts or proposals submitted each
  year:* 30 (estimate)
Manuscripts sent to readers each year: 28
  (estimate)
Manuscripts accepted each year: 20
Number of outside readers: 2
*Time between submission and publication
  decision:* 3-4 months
Time between decision and publication:
  10 months

CONTRACT PROVISIONS

Copyright: Author
Royalty provisions: 10% of net

PUBLICATION AND DISTRIBUTION
INFORMATION

Forms of publication: Cloth
Titles published each year: 20
Print run: 400
Number of review copies: 10
Distribution area: Worldwide
Time in print: 4 years

(296)
VERSO

6 Meard St.
London W1V 3HR, England

180 Varick St.
New York, NY 10014

Contact: Malcolm Imne, Commissioning
  Editor
Established: 1970
Telephone: (0171) 4373546; (0171)
  4341704
Fax: (0171) 7340059
E-mail: 100434.1414@compuserve.com

SCOPE

Publishing interests: Women's studies;
Marxist studies; structuralism; post-
structuralism; critical theory; cultural
studies
*Considers all literary and linguistic
topics:* Yes (primarily cultural,
political, historical, or social
perspectives)
Types of works not published: Bibli-
ographies; literary reference works
Languages published: English
Series title(s): Questions for Feminism;
Haymarket Series; Critical Studies in
Latin American and Iberian Culture

SUBMISSION REQUIREMENTS

Initial contact: Letter and prospectus
Considers simultaneous submissions: Yes
Style: House
Subvention: No

EDITORIAL INFORMATION

Number of outside readers: 2
Author-anonymous submission: No
*Time between submission and publication
decision:* 1 month

CONTRACT PROVISIONS

Royalty provisions: 10% (cloth); 7%
(paper)

PUBLICATION AND DISTRIBUTION
INFORMATION

Forms of publication: Cloth, paper
Distribution area: Worldwide

(297)
VICTORIA UNIVERSITY PRESS

Box 600
Wellington, New Zealand

Contact: Fergus Barrowman, Editor
Established: 1975
Telephone: (064) 4955263
Fax: (064) 4955199
E-mail: victoria-press@vuw.ac.nz

SCOPE

Publishing interests: New Zealand
literature; New Zealand languages;
Maori language
*Considers all literary and linguistic
topics:* No
Languages published: English; Maori

SUBMISSION REQUIREMENTS

Initial contact: Letter and prospectus
Considers simultaneous submissions:
Yes, if informed
*Will issue contract on the basis of
proposal, prospectus, and/or sample
chapter:* No
Subvention: Not usually

EDITORIAL INFORMATION

*Manuscripts or proposals submitted each
year:* 20 (estimate)
Manuscripts sent to readers each year:
10 (estimate)
Manuscripts accepted each year: 3
Number of outside readers: 1-2
Author-anonymous submission: No
*Time between submission and publication
decision:* 3-6 months
Time between decision and publication:
1-2 years
Time allotted for reading proof: Varies

CONTRACT PROVISIONS

Copyright: Author
Royalty provisions: 10% of retail

PUBLICATION AND DISTRIBUTION INFORMATION

Forms of publication: Cloth, paper
Titles published each year: 3
Print run: 1,000
Number of review copies: 30
Distribution area: New Zealand
Time in print: Indefinitely

**(298)
UNIVERSITY PRESS OF VIRGINIA**

Box 3608
University Station
Charlottesville, VA 22903

Contact: Cathie Brettschneider,
  Humanities Editor
Established: 1963
Telephone: 804 982-3033
Fax: 804 982-2655

SCOPE

Publishing interests: English literature
  (eighteenth-century, Victorian, modern);
  American literature; African American
  studies; feminist studies; comparative
  cultural studies; New World studies (the
  Americas)
*Considers all literary and linguistic
  topics:* No
Types of works not published:
  Festschriften; literary reference works
Prizes and competitions: Walker Cowen
  Manuscript Prize in Eighteenth-Century
  Studies
Languages published: English
Series title(s): CARAF: Translations of
  Francophone Literature from the
  Caribbean and Africa; Victorian
  Literature and Culture; Feminist Issues:
  Politics, Practice, Theory; Knowledge:
  Disciplinarity and Beyond; Minds of the
  New South; New World Studies

SUBMISSION REQUIREMENTS

Initial contact: Letter and prospectus
Style: Chicago
Special requirements: Does not accept
  dot-matrix printout
Subvention: No

EDITORIAL INFORMATION

*Manuscripts or proposals submitted each
  year:* 69
Manuscripts sent to readers each year:
  14
Manuscripts accepted each year: 11
Number of outside readers: 1-2
Author-anonymous submission: No
*Time between submission and publication
  decision:* 2-4 months
Time between decision and publication:
  9-12 months
Time allotted for reading proof: 1 month

CONTRACT PROVISIONS

Copyright: Publisher

PUBLICATION AND DISTRIBUTION INFORMATION

Forms of publication: Cloth, paper
Titles published each year: 22
Print run: 1,200-1,500
Number of review copies: 30-50
Distribution area: Worldwide
Time in print: 10 years

**(299)
VOLTAIRE FOUNDATION**

99 Banbury Rd.
Oxford OX1 6JX, England

Contact: Andrew Brown
Established: 1970
Telephone: (0865) 284600
Fax: (0865) 284610

SCOPE

Publishing interests: Eighteenth-century
  studies
*Considers all literary and linguistic
  topics:* No
Languages published: English; French

SUBMISSION REQUIREMENTS

Initial contact: Letter and prospectus

(300)
*KARL WACHHOLTZ VERLAG

Postfach 2769
2350 Neumünster, Germany

Contact: Herr Kardel, Verlagsleiter
Established: 1872
Telephone: (04321) 56720
Fax: (04321) 56778

SCOPE

Publishing interests: German literature;
  literature of Schleswig-Holstein;
  northern European literature; German
  language; Plattdeutsch; Frisian language
*Considers all literary and linguistic
  topics:* No
Languages published: German
Series title(s): Kieler Studien zur
  deutschen Literaturgeschichte; Skandi-
  navistische Studien; Kieler Beiträge zur
  Anglistik und Amerikanistik; Kieler
  Beiträge zur deutschen Sprachgeschichte; Sprache und Schrifttum;
  Name und Wort

SUBMISSION REQUIREMENTS

Initial contact: Letter and manuscript
Subvention: Usually

EDITORIAL INFORMATION

*Manuscripts or proposals submitted each
  year:* 10 (estimate)
Manuscripts sent to readers each year: 2
  (estimate)
Manuscripts accepted each year: 2
Number of outside readers: 0
*Time between submission and publication
  decision:* 1-2 months
*Time between decision and return of copy-
  edited manuscript:* 6 months
Time between decision and publication:
  6-12 months

CONTRACT PROVISIONS

Royalty provisions: 6-10% of list

PUBLICATION AND DISTRIBUTION
INFORMATION

Forms of publication: Cloth, paper
Titles published each year: 14
Number of review copies: 3
Distribution area: Worldwide
Time in print: 25 years

(301)
*WAKE FOREST UNIVERSITY
PRESS

PUBLICATION AND DISTRIBUTION
INFORMATION

Now publishes original poetry only.

(302)
UNIVERSITY OF WALES PRESS

6 Gwennyth St.
Cathays
Cardiff CF2 4YD, Wales

Contact: Ned Thomas, Director; Susan
Jenkins, Senior Editor
Established: 1922
Telephone: (0222) 231919
Fax: (0222) 230908

SCOPE

Publishing interests: Welsh literature;
linguistics (Welsh); Celtic studies;
Celtic literature; Celtic languages;
European languages
*Considers all literary and linguistic
topics:* Yes
Languages published: Welsh; English
Series title(s): Writers of Wales

SUBMISSION REQUIREMENTS

Initial contact: Letter of inquiry
*Will issue contract on the basis of
proposal, prospectus, and/or sample
chapter:* Yes
Style: House
Special requirements: Provides guidelines
for manuscript preparation

EDITORIAL INFORMATION

*Manuscripts or proposals submitted each
year:* 60-70
Manuscripts sent to readers each year:
20-30
Manuscripts accepted each year: 6-8
Number of outside readers: 2
Author-anonymous submission: Yes
*Time between submission and publication
decision:* 6 months
*Time between decision and return of copy-
edited manuscript:* 6 months
Time between decision and publication: 6
months

CONTRACT PROVISIONS

Copyright: Author
Royalty provisions: 10%

**PUBLICATION AND DISTRIBUTION
INFORMATION**

Forms of publication: Cloth, paper
Titles published each year: 22
Print run: 500-1,000
Distribution area: Worldwide

**(303)
UNIVERSITY OF WASHINGTON
PRESS**

PO Box 50096
Seattle, WA 98145-5096

Contact: Naomi B. Pascal, Editor in
Chief
Established: 1909
Telephone: 206 543-4050
Fax: 206 543-3932

SCOPE

Publishing interests: Western American
literature; Asian literature; Asian
American literature; Scandinavian
literature; Irish literature; Middle
Eastern literature; Native American
literature; Native American languages;
linguistics (Native American topics)
*Considers all literary and linguistic
topics:* Yes
Types of works not published: Unrevised
dissertations; Festschriften
Languages published: English

SUBMISSION REQUIREMENTS

Initial contact: Letter and prospectus
Considers simultaneous submissions:
Rarely
*Will issue contract on the basis of
proposal, prospectus, and/or sample
chapter:* Occasionally
Style: Chicago

Special requirements: Accepts photocopies and dot-matrix printout; does not
require electronic manuscript
Subvention: No

EDITORIAL INFORMATION

*Manuscripts or proposals submitted each
year:* 200 (estimate)
Manuscripts sent to readers each year:
12 (estimate)
Manuscripts accepted each year: 3
(estimate)
Number of outside readers: 2-3
Author-anonymous submission: No
*Time between submission and publication
decision:* 3-12 months
*Time between decision and return of copy-
edited manuscript:* 2-6 months
Time between decision and publication:
1-2 years
Time allotted for reading proof: 1 month

CONTRACT PROVISIONS

Copyright: Publisher
Royalty provisions: 10% of net (cloth);
5% of net (paper)

**PUBLICATION AND DISTRIBUTION
INFORMATION**

Forms of publication: Cloth, paper
Titles published each year: 6-7 (estimate)
Print run: 1,500-2,500
Number of review copies: 50-100
Distribution area: Worldwide
Time in print: 5 years minimum

**(304)
WAYNE STATE UNIVERSITY PRESS**

The Leonard N. Simons Bldg.
4809 Woodward Ave.
Detroit, MI 48201

Contact: Arthur B. Evans, Director
Established: 1941
Telephone: 313 577-4600
Fax: 313 577-6131
E-mail: abevans@cms.cc.wayne.edu

SCOPE

Publishing interests: German literature
(especially twentieth-century); German
literary theory (especially twentieth-
century); German culture (especially
twentieth-century); Judaica; film
studies; comparative literature
(Renaissance, baroque, Romanticism,
and nineteenth- and twentieth-century);
ethnic literature; African American
literature; Spanish literature (twentieth-
century)
*Considers all literary and linguistic
topics:* Yes
Types of works not published: Unrevised
dissertations; readers; Festschriften
Languages published: English
Series title(s): Latin American Literature
and Culture; *Kritik*: German Literary
Theory and Cultural Studies; African-
American Life Series; Humor in Life
and Letters

SUBMISSION REQUIREMENTS

Initial contact: Letter, prospectus
(including outline), and curriculum vitae
Considers simultaneous submissions:
Prefers single submission
*Will issue contract on the basis of
proposal, prospectus, and/or sample
chapter:* Yes
Style: MLA; Chicago
Special requirements: Length: prefers
under 500 manuscript pages; requires
electronic manuscript; provides questionnaire for prospective authors
Subvention: No

EDITORIAL INFORMATION

Manuscripts or proposals submitted each year: 200 (estimate)
Manuscripts sent to readers each year: 40 (estimate)
Manuscripts accepted each year: 10-15
Number of outside readers: 2
Author-anonymous submission: No
Time between submission and publication decision: 4 months
Time between decision and return of copy-edited manuscript: 3-4 months
Time between decision and publication: 12-15 months
Time allotted for reading proof: 1 month

CONTRACT PROVISIONS

Copyright: Preferably publisher

PUBLICATION AND DISTRIBUTION INFORMATION

Forms of publication: Cloth, paper, electronic media
Titles published each year: 9
Print run: 1,000
Number of review copies: 100
Distribution area: Worldwide
Time in print: 5-10 years

(305)
WESTDEUTSCHER VERLAG

Postfach 5829
65048 Wiesbaden, Germany

Contact: Bernd Schäbler
Established: 1947
Telephone: (0611) 160233
Fax: (0611) 160229

SCOPE

Publishing interests: German literature; literary theory; comparative literature; literary history; linguistic theory; psycholinguistics; discourse analysis; computational linguistics; politics and language; media and language
Considers all literary and linguistic topics: No
Languages published: German; occasionally English
Series title(s): Kulturwissenschaftliche Studien zur deutschen Literatur; Psycholinguistische Studien; Konzeption empirische Literaturwissenschaft

SUBMISSION REQUIREMENTS

Initial contact: Letter, outline, and sample chapters
Considers simultaneous submissions: Yes
Special requirements: Prefers camera-ready copy; provides guidelines for manuscript preparation
Subvention: Usually not

EDITORIAL INFORMATION

Manuscripts or proposals submitted each year: 40-50 (estimate)
Manuscripts accepted each year: 15-20 (estimate)
Number of outside readers: 0
Time between submission and publication decision: 2-4 months
Time between decision and publication: 4-12 months
Time allotted for reading proof: 2-3 weeks

CONTRACT PROVISIONS

Copyright: Publisher
Royalty provisions: 4-6% of net

PUBLICATION AND DISTRIBUTION INFORMATION

Forms of publication: Paper

Titles published each year: 12-15
  (estimate)
Print run: 400-2,000
Number of review copies: 12-50
Distribution area: Germany; Austria;
  Switzerland
Time in print: Indefinitely

(306)
UNIVERSITY OF WESTERN
AUSTRALIA PRESS

University of Western Australia
Nedlands, Western Australia 6009
Australia

Contact: Ian Drakeford, Manager; Janine
  Drakeford, Acquisitions Editor
Established: 1954
Telephone: (09) 3803670
Fax: (09) 3801027

SCOPE

Publishing interests: General literature
*Considers all literary and linguistic
  topics:* Yes
Languages published: English

SUBMISSION REQUIREMENTS

Initial contact: Letter, outline, and sample
  chapter (with bibliography)
Considers simultaneous submissions: No
*Will issue contract on the basis of
  proposal, prospectus, and/or sample
  chapter:* No
Style: House
Special requirements: Accepts photocopies, camera-ready copy, and electronic manuscripts; provides guidelines
  for manuscript preparation
Subvention: Sometimes

EDITORIAL INFORMATION

*Manuscripts or proposals submitted each
  year:* 60-80 (estimate)
Manuscripts sent to readers each year:
  15-20 (estimate)
Manuscripts accepted each year: 1
Number of outside readers: 2
Author-anonymous submission: No
*Time between submission and publication
  decision:* 3-4 months
*Time between decision and return of copy-
  edited manuscript:* 1-3 months
Time between decision and publication:
  3-6 months

CONTRACT PROVISIONS

Copyright: Author
Royalty provisions: 10%

PUBLICATION AND DISTRIBUTION
INFORMATION

Forms of publication: Cloth, paper
Titles published each year: 1-2 (estimate)
Print run: 1,200-1,500
Number of review copies: 20-30
Distribution area: Worldwide
Time in print: 8-10 years

(307)
*WHITSTON PUBLISHING CO.

PO Box 958
Troy, NY 12181

Contact: Jean Goode, President
Established: 1969
Telephone: 518 283-4363

SCOPE

Publishing interests: American literature;
  English literature; collections of essays
  on authors; bibliographies; poetry;
  studies of single authors

Considers all literary and linguistic topics: Yes
Types of works not published: Dissertations
Languages published: English

SUBMISSION REQUIREMENTS

Initial contact: Letter and prospectus
Style: MLA
Special requirements: Accepts electronic manuscripts
Subvention: No

EDITORIAL INFORMATION

Manuscripts or proposals submitted each year: 150 (estimate)
Manuscripts sent to readers each year: 20 (estimate)
Manuscripts accepted each year: 10 (estimate)
Number of outside readers: 1
Time between submission and publication decision: 1-12 months
Time between decision and return of copy-edited manuscript: Does not copyedit manuscripts
Time between decision and publication: 1-3 years

CONTRACT PROVISIONS

Copyright: Author
Royalty provisions: No royalties for the first 500 copies, 10% of net on next 500, 12.5% on next 1,000, and 15% thereafter

PUBLICATION AND DISTRIBUTION INFORMATION

Forms of publication: Cloth
Titles published each year: 15 (estimate)
Print run: 500
Number of review copies: 40
Distribution area: Worldwide
Time in print: Indefintely

(308)
WILFRID LAURIER UNIVERSITY PRESS

Wilfrid Laurier University
75 University Ave. West
Waterloo, ON N2L 3C5, Canada

Contact: Sandra Woolfrey, Director and Senior Editor
Established: 1974
Telephone: 519 884-0710, ext. 6123
Fax: 519 725-1399
E-mail: wlupress@mach1.wlu.ca

SCOPE

Publishing interests: Canadian literature; American literature; British literature; European literature; commonwealth literature; ethnic studies; nineteenth-century literature; twentieth-century literature; life writing
Considers all literary and linguistic topics: Yes (literature)
Types of works not published: Unrevised dissertations; bibliographies; Festschriften; literary reference works
Languages published: English
Series title(s): The Library of the Canadian Review of Comparative Literature

SUBMISSION REQUIREMENTS

Restrictions on authors: Usually must be Canadian residents eligible for government or other subvention funds
Initial contact: Letter, outline, and sample chapter
Style: MLA; Chicago
Special requirements: Accepts camera-ready copy and electronic manuscripts; provides guidelines for manuscript preparation
Subvention: Yes

EDITORIAL INFORMATION

*Manuscripts or proposals submitted each
year:* 12 (estimate)
Manuscripts sent to readers each year: 4
Manuscripts accepted each year: 3
Number of outside readers: 2
Author-anonymous submission: No
*Time between submission and publication
decision:* 4-6 months
*Time between decision and return of copy-
edited manuscript:* 3-6 months
Time between decision and publication:
1 year

CONTRACT PROVISIONS

Copyright: Publisher
Royalty provisions: 0-15% of net

**PUBLICATION AND DISTRIBUTION
INFORMATION**

Forms of publication: Cloth, paper
Titles published each year: 1
Print run: 750-1,000
Distribution area: Worldwide
Time in print: 8 years

**(309)
UNIVERSITÄTSVERLAG C.
WINTER**

Hans Bunte-Str. 18
69123 Heidelberg, Germany

Contact: Eilert Erfling, Geschäftsführer
Telephone: (06221) 770260
Fax: (06221) 770269

SCOPE

Publishing interests: Classical literature;
classical languages; English literature;
American literature; English language;
Romance literature; Romance
languages; Indo-European languages;

German literature; German language;
oriental literature; oriental languages;
Slavic literature; Slavic languages
*Considers all literary and linguistic
topics:* Yes
Languages published: German; English;
French; Russian
Series title(s): Abhandlungen der Heidel-
berger Akademie der Wissenschaften:
Philosophische-historische Klasse;
Anglistische Forschungen; Anglistik
und Englischunterricht; Indoger-
manische Bibliothek; Beihefte zum
Euphorion; Beihefte zum Gymnasium;
Beiträge zur Geschichte der Literatur
und Kunst des 18. Jahrhunderts;
Beiträge zur neueren Literatur-
geschichte; Beiträge zur ukrainischen
Literaturgeschichte; Bibliothek der klas-
sischen Altertumswissenschaften;
Britannica et Americana; Editiones
Heidelbergenses; Frankfurter Beiträge
zur Germanistik; Germanische
Bibliothek; Heidelberger Forschungen;
Middle English Texts; Neue Bremer
Beiträge; Probleme der Dichtung; Reihe
Siegen: Beiträge zur Literatur- und
Sprachwissenschaft; Studia Linguarum
Africae orientalis; Studia Romanica;
Studien zum Frühneuhochdeutschen;
Sprachgeschichte; Sprache, Literatur,
und Geschichte: Studien zur Linguistik/
Germanistik

SUBMISSION REQUIREMENTS

Initial contact: Letter and outline
Considers simultaneous submissions:
Prefers single submission
*Will issue contract on the basis of
proposal, prospectus, and/or sample
chapter:* No
Style: MLA
Special requirements: Prefers camera-
ready copy
Subvention: Sometimes

EDITORIAL INFORMATION

Manuscripts or proposals submitted each year: 220 (estimate)
Manuscripts sent to readers each year: 50
Manuscripts accepted each year: 65
Number of outside readers: 1
Author-anonymous submission: No
Time between submission and publication decision: 1 month
Time between decision and publication: 4-12 months
Time allotted for reading proof: 2 months

CONTRACT PROVISIONS

Copyright: Publisher
Royalty provisions: 0-10%

PUBLICATION AND DISTRIBUTION INFORMATION

Forms of publication: Cloth, paper
Titles published each year: 75
Number of review copies: 20-30
Distribution area: Worldwide
Time in print: 30 years

**(310)
UNIVERSITY OF WISCONSIN PRESS**

114 North Murray St.
Madison, WI 53715

Contact: Allen N. Fitchen, Director (film studies, literary criticism, regional studies); Rosalie Robertson, Senior Acquisitions Editor (African studies, African American studies, classics, literary criticism and theory, cultural studies, women's studies)
Established: 1937
Telephone: 608 262-4928
Fax: 608 262-7560

SCOPE

Publishing interests: Literary theory; classics; women's studies; African studies; American literature; science and literature; autobiography (of Americans); film studies; Native American studies
Considers all literary and linguistic topics: Yes
Types of works not published: Festschriften; unrevised dissertations
Languages published: English
Series title(s): Wisconsin Project on American Writers; Wisconsin Studies in American Autobiography; Science and Literature; Rhetoric of the Human Sciences; Wisconsin Studies in Classics; Wisconsin Studies in Film

SUBMISSION REQUIREMENTS

Initial contact: Letter and prospectus
Considers simultaneous submissions: Yes
Style: Chicago; MLA
Subvention: No

EDITORIAL INFORMATION

Manuscripts or proposals submitted each year: 500 (estimate)
Manuscripts sent to readers each year: 100 (estimate)
Manuscripts accepted each year: 20 (estimate)
Number of outside readers: 2 minimum
Author-anonymous submission: No
Time between submission and publication decision: 3-5 months
Time between decision and publication: 1 year

CONTRACT PROVISIONS

Copyright: Negotiable
Royalty provisions: 5% of list minimum

PUBLICATION AND DISTRIBUTION INFORMATION

Forms of publication: Cloth, paper
Titles published each year: 20
Print run: 1,200-1,500
Number of review copies: 35-75
Distribution area: Worldwide
Time in print: Indefinitely

(311)
*WOMEN'S PRESS

34 Great Sutton St.
London EC1V 0DX, England

Contact: Ros de Lanerolle
Established: 1978
Telephone: (071) 2513007
Fax: (071) 6081938

SCOPE

Publishing interests: Feminist studies; black writers; Third World writers; women writers; biography
Considers all literary and linguistic topics: No
Languages published: English

SUBMISSION REQUIREMENTS

Initial contact: Letter and prospectus
Special requirements: Length: prefers 100,000 words maximum

EDITORIAL INFORMATION

Number of outside readers: Varies
Time between submission and publication decision: 2-3 months
Time between decision and return of copy-edited manuscript: 3-6 months
Time between decision and publication: 9-15 months

CONTRACT PROVISIONS

Copyright: Author
Royalty provisions: 10% of list (cloth); 7.5% (paper)

PUBLICATION AND DISTRIBUTION INFORMATION

Forms of publication: Cloth, paper
Titles published each year: 2
Print run: 3,000 minimum
Number of review copies: 50-250
Distribution area: Worldwide
Time in print: Indefintely

Manuscript must be suitable for a general market.

(312)
YALE UNIVERSITY PRESS

92A Yale Station
New Haven, CT 06520

Contact: Jonathan Brant, Senior Editor
Established: 1908
Telephone: 203 432-0960
Fax: 203 432-2397
E-mail: yupress@yalevm

SCOPE

Publishing interests: General literature
Considers all literary and linguistic topics: Yes
Types of works not published: Festschriften
Languages published: English
Series title(s): Yale French Studies; Elizabethan Club Series; Yale Studies in English (independent submissions not accepted for series)

Initial contact: Letter of inquiry or letter and prospectus; does not accept unsolicited manuscripts
Considers simultaneous submissions: Yes
Will issue contract on the basis of proposal, prospectus, and/or sample chapter: Yes
Style: Chicago
Special requirements: Length: prefers 200-400 pages; accepts photocopies; does not accept dot-matrix printout
Subvention: No

EDITORIAL INFORMATION

Manuscripts or proposals submitted each year: 700-1,000 (estimate)
Manuscripts sent to readers each year: 50 (estimate)
Manuscripts accepted each year: 15-20 (estimate)
Number of outside readers: 1 minimum
Author-anonymous submission: Yes
Time between submission and publication decision: 3-5 months
Time between decision and return of copy-edited manuscript: 2-3 months
Time between decision and publication: 1 year

CONTRACT PROVISIONS

Copyright: Publisher

PUBLICATION AND DISTRIBUTION INFORMATION

Forms of publication: Cloth, paper
Titles published each year: 25 (estimate)
Print run: 1,500-2,000
Number of review copies: 125-200
Distribution area: Worldwide
Time in print: 5 years minimum

(313)
YORK PRESS

PO Box 1172
Fredericton, NB E3B 5C8, Canada

Contact: S. Elkhadem
Established: 1975
Telephone: 506 458-8748
Fax: 506 458-8748
E-mail: ifr@unb.ca

SCOPE

Publishing interests: General literature; comparative literature; Arabic literature
Considers all literary and linguistic topics: Yes
Types of works not published: Unrevised dissertations; readers
Languages published: English; German; Spanish; French; Arabic
Series title(s): Authoritative Studies in World Literature; Arabic Literature and Scholarship

SUBMISSION REQUIREMENTS

Initial contact: Letter, outline, and sample chapters (including introduction, conclusion, and bibliography)
Considers simultaneous submissions: No
Will issue contract on the basis of proposal, prospectus, and/or sample chapter: No
Style: MLA; house
Special requirements: Length: prefers 200 pages (approximately 50,000 words) maximum
Subvention: No

EDITORIAL INFORMATION

Manuscripts or proposals submitted each year: 50 (estimate)
Manuscripts sent to readers each year: 18

Manuscripts accepted each year: 8
Number of outside readers: 2
Author-anonymous submission: Yes
Time between submission and publication decision: 3 months
Time between decision and return of copy-edited manuscript: 3 months
Time between decision and publication: 9 months
Time allotted for reading proof: 2 weeks

CONTRACT PROVISIONS

Copyright: Negotiable
Royalty provisions: 10%

PUBLICATION AND DISTRIBUTION INFORMATION

Forms of publication: Paper
Titles published each year: 6
Print run: 500
Number of review copies: 35
Distribution area: Worldwide
Time in print: 10 years

(314)
ZANICHELLI EDITORE

Via Irnerio 34
40126 Bologna, Italy

Contact: Federico Enriques, General Manager
Established: 1859
Telephone: (051) 293236
Fax: (051) 293311; (051) 249782
E-mail: zanichelli@bologna.nettuno.it

SCOPE

Publishing interests: Italian literature; Italian language; Latin language
Considers all literary and linguistic topics: No

Types of works not published: Dissertations; bibliographies; critical editions; collections of essays; Festschriften
Languages published: Italian

SUBMISSION REQUIREMENTS

Initial contact: Letter, outline, and sample chapter
Style: House
Special requirements: Provides guidelines for manuscript preparation
Subvention: No

EDITORIAL INFORMATION

Manuscripts or proposals submitted each year: 12 (estimate)
Manuscripts sent to readers each year: 6 (estimate)
Manuscripts accepted each year: 4 (estimate)
Number of outside readers: 1-2
Time between submission and publication decision: 3 months
Time between decision and return of copy-edited manuscript: 4 months
Time between decision and publication: 14 months

CONTRACT PROVISIONS

Copyright: Publisher
Royalty provisions: 6-10%

PUBLICATION AND DISTRIBUTION INFORMATION

Forms of publication: Cloth, paper
Titles published each year: 8 (estimate)
Print run: 3,000
Number of review copies: 100
Distribution area: Italy; Switzerland
Time in print: 8 years

(315)
HANS ZELL PUBLISHERS

PO Box 56
Oxford OX1 2SJ, England

Contact: Hans Zell
Established: 1975
Telephone: (1865) 511428
Fax: (1865) 311534

SCOPE

Publishing interests: Bibliographies;
biographical reference works; literary
reference works
*Considers all literary and linguistic
topics:* No
Types of works not published: Dissertations; critical editions; collections of
letters; collections of essays
Languages published: English

SUBMISSION REQUIREMENTS

Initial contact: Letter, outline, and sample
chapters
Considers simultaneous submissions: Yes
*Will issue contract on the basis of
proposal, prospectus, and/or sample
chapter:* Yes
Style: Chicago

Special requirements: Expects electronic
manuscript
Subvention: No

EDITORIAL INFORMATION

*Manuscripts or proposals submitted each
year:* 10
Manuscripts sent to readers each year: 3
Manuscripts accepted each year: 3
Number of outside readers: 1-2
Author-anonymous submission: Yes
*Time between submission and publication
decision:* 4-6 months
Time between decision and publication:
6-18 months
Time allotted for reading proof: 3 weeks

CONTRACT PROVISIONS

Copyright: Publisher
Royalty provisions: 12.5% of net

PUBLICATION AND DISTRIBUTION
INFORMATION

Forms of publication: Cloth, electronic
media
Titles published each year: 4
Print run: 800
Number of review copies: 25
Distribution area: Worldwide
Time in print: 5 years

Appendix

The following publishers, listed in the first edition of the *Directory*, have since ceased operation: Aberdeen University Press, Adler Publishing, Amana Books, American Classical College Press, Academische Uitgeverij Amersfoort, Atlantis-Verlag, Bodley Head, Foris, NC Press, Undena, and the University of Waterloo Press.

The publishers in the field of language and literature listed below were invited to submit information for this edition of the *Directory* but did not return the initial questionnaire or respond to subsequent letters or telephone calls.

ABC-CLIO
PO Box 1911
Santa Barbara, CA 93116-1911

Edizioni Abete
Via Prenestina 685
00155 Rome
Italy

Abhinav Publications
E-37 Hauz Khas
New Delhi 110016
India

Academic Press
24-28 Oval Road
Camden Town
London NW1 7DX
England

Editura Academiei Române
Calea 13 Septembrie nr. 13
76117 Bucharest
Romania

Mario Adda Editore
Via Tanzi 59
70121 Bari
Italy

Addison-Wesley Longman Publishing Co.
One Jacob Way
Reading, MA 01867-3999

African Universities Press
305 Herbert Macaulay St.
Yaba
PO Box 3560
Lagos
Nigeria

Editions L'Age d'Homme-La Cité
10 rue de Genève
1003 Lausanne
Switzerland

Agora-Verlag
Grunewald Str. 53
10825 Berlin
Germany

Aguilar
Ave. Universidad 757
03100 Mexico
Mexico

Ajanta Publications
1 UB Jawahar Nagar
Delhi 110007
India

Akademie Verlag
Mühlenstr. 33-34
13187 Berlin
Germany

Akademiförlaget i Göteborg
Box 1503
402 23 Göteborg
Sweden

Akademisk Forlag
Store Kannikestr. 8
1169 Copenhagen
Denmark

Akros Publications
18 Warrender Park Terrace
Edinburgh EH9 1EF
Scotland

Alekh Prakashan
V-8 Navin Shahdara
Delhi 110032
India

ALFA
Postbus 26
5360 AA Grave
Netherlands

Editorial Alfa
Defense 599-3° piso
1065 Buenos Aires
Argentina

Editorial Alhambra
Fernandez de la Hoz 9
28010 Madrid
Spain

Editorial Alianza
Juan Ignacio Luca de Tena 15
28027 Madrid
Spain

Uitgeverij Ambo
Prinses Marielaan 8
Postbus 308
3740 AH Baarn
Netherlands

Amistad Press
Time and Life Bldg.
Rockefeller Center
1271 Avenue of the Americas
New York, NY 10020

Ankur Publishing House
Uphaar Cinema Bldg.
Green Park Ext.
New Delhi 110016
India

Editions Anthropos
49 rue Héricart
75015 Paris
France

Universidad de Antioquia
Divisíon Publicaciones
Apdo Aéreo 1226
Calle 67 No. 53-108
Medellín, Antioquia
Colombia

APA (Academic Publishers Associated)
Postbus 122
3600 AC Maarssen
Netherlands

Appletree Press
19 Alfred St.
Belfast BT2 8DL
Northern Ireland

Argalia Editore
Via S. Donato 148c
61029 Urbino
Italy

Argument Verlag
Rentzelstr. 1
20146 Hamburg
Germany

Artemis und Winkler
Hackenstr. 5
Postfach 330120
80331 Munich
Germany

Editions Arthaud
26 rue Racine
75006 Paris
France

Aschendorffsche Verlagsbuchhandlung
Postfach 1124
48135 Münster
Germany

Asian Educational Services
PO Box 4534
New Delhi 110016
India

Association for Scottish Literary Studies
c/o Dept. of English
Univ. of Aberdeen
Aberdeen AB9 2UB
Scotland

Atheneum Publishers
866 Third Ave.
New York, NY 10022

Atlantic Monthly Press
841 Broadway
New York, NY 10003

Aubier-Montaigne
13 quai Conti
75006 Paris
France

Aufbau-Verlag
Postfach 193
10105 Berlin
Germany

August House Inc.
Box 3223
Little Rock, AR 72203

Editions d'Aujourd'hui
Plan de la Tour
83120 Sainte-Maxime
France

K. P. Bagchi
286 B B Ganguli St.
Calcutta 700012
India

Bahri Publications
PO Box 4453
New Delhi 110019
India

Baker Books
Box 6287
Grand Rapids, MI 49516

Bani Mandir
Rani Bari Panbazer
Guwahati 781001
India

Bantam Doubleday Dell
1540 Broadway
New York, NY 10036

Lillian Barber Press
Box 232
New York, NY 10163

Bar Ilan University Press
Bar Ilan University
Ramat Gan 52900
Israel

Barnes and Noble Books
120 Fifth Ave., 4th fl.
New York, NY 10011

Basic Books
10 East 53rd St.
New York, NY 10022

Batsford
4 Fitzhardinge St.
London W1H 0AH
England

Casa Editrice Luigi Battei
Str. Cavour 5/C
43100 Parma
Italy

Bayard Presse
Départment Livre
3 rue Bayard
75393 Paris Cedex 08
France

Editores Bedout
Calle 61 No. 51-04
Apdo Aéreo 760
Medellín, Antioquia
Colombia

Belfond
216 blvd St-Germain
75007 Paris
France

Instituto Nacional de Bellas Artes
Paseo de la Reforma y Campo Marte Atras
    del Auditorio Nacional
Bosque de Chapultepec
Dirección General
Modulo A
Lázaro Cárdenas 2
2do piso
11580 Miguel Hidalgo
Mexico

Société d'Edition les Belles Lettres
95 blvd Raspail
75006 Paris
France

Editorial Andrés Bello
Av. Ricardo Lyon 946
Casilla de Correo 4256
Providencia, Santiago
Chile

Bialik Institute
PO Box 92
Jerusalem 93469
Israel

Bibliographisches Institut
Querstr. 18
04103 Leipzig
Germany

Bihar Hindi Granth Akademi
Premchand Marg
Rnagar
Patna 800003
India

A. & C. Black
35 Bedford Row
London WC1R 4JH
England

Black Rose Books
3981 St. Laurent Blvd.
8th fl., Suite 888
Montreal, Quebec H2W 1Y5
Canada

Nakladatelství Blok
Rooseveltova 4
65700 Brno
Czech Republic

Bloodaxe Press
PO Box 1SN
Newcastle upon Tyne NE99 1SN
England

Bloomsbury Publishing
2 Soho Sq.
London W1V 5DE
England

Bob Jones University Press
1700 Wade Hampton Blvd.
Greenville, SC 29614

Böhlau-Verlag
Theodor-Heuss Str. 76
51149 Cologne
Germany

Editrice Bompiani
Via Mecenate 91
20138 Milan
Italy

Presses Universitaires de Bordeaux
Domaine Universitaire
Université de Bordeaux III
33405 Talence Cedex
France

Borgo Press
Box 2845
San Bernardino, CA 92406

Christian Bourgois Editeur
Presses de la Cité
12 ave de l'Italie
75013 Paris
France

Bovolenta Editore
Via Belletti 14
44100 Ferrara
Italy

Boxwood Press
183 Ocean View Blvd.
Pacific Grove, CA 93950

Marion Boyars Publishers
237 East 39th St.
New York, NY 10016

Brandon Book Publishers
Cooleen, Dingle
Co. Kerry
Ireland

Editora Brasiliense
AV Marques De Sao Vincente 1771
01139-003 São Paulo
Brazil

Editions de l'Université de Bruxelles
Ave Paul Héger 26
1050 Brussels
Belgium

Büchse der Pandora Verlags
Postfach 2820
35538 Wetzlar
Germany

Bulzoni Editore
Via dei Liburni 14
00185 Roma
Italy

Helmut Buske Verlag
Richardstr. 47
22081 Hamburg
Germany

Editorial Calicanto
Alsina 722
Buenos Aires
Argentina

Canadian Institute of Ukrainian Studies
Slavic Dept.
University of Toronto
21 Sussex Ave.
Toronto, ON M5S 1A1
Canada

Canterbury University Press
Private Bag 4800
Christchurch
New Zealand

Aristide D. Caratzas, Publisher
Box 210
30 Church St.
New Rochelle, NY 10802

Carnegie Mellon University Press
Box 21, 4902 Forbes Ave.
Pittsburgh, PA 15213-3799

Carolina Academic Press
700 Kent St.
Durham, NC 27701

Carroll & Graf Publishers
260 Fifth Ave.
New York, NY 10001

Edizioni Casagrande
Postfach 1291
Bellinzona
Switzerland

Frank Cass
Newbury House
890-900 Eastern Ave.
Newbury Park, Ilford
Essex IG2 7HH
England

Cassell
Wellington House
125 The Strand
London WC2R 0BB
England

Ediciones Cátedra
Juan Ignacio Luca de Tena 15
28027 Madrid
Spain

Pontifica Universidad Católica de Ecuador
Centro de Publicaciones
Ave 12 de Octubre y Carríon
Apdo 17-01-2184
Quito
Ecuador

CEDAM
Via Jappelli 5/6
35121 Padua
Italy

Celuc Libri
Via Santa Valeria 5
20123 Milan
Italy

Center for Applied Linguistics
1118 22nd St., NW
Washington, DC 20037

Centro Editor
Salta 38-3° Piso
1074 Buenos Aires
Argentina

Champ Libre/Ivrea
1 place Paul-Painlevé
75005 Paris
France

Chanakya Publications
F10/14 Model Town
Delhi 110009
India

S. Chand
Ram Nagar
New Delhi 110055
India

Chelsea House Publishers
300 Park Ave. South, 6th fl.
New York, NY 10010

Chiron Publications
400 Linden Ave.
Wilmette, IL 60091

Editorial Ciordia
San Luis 2569/71
1056 Buenas Aires
Argentina

Editrice Ciranna-Roma
Via Capograssa 1115
04010 Borgo S Michele (Latina)
Italy

Cistercian Publications
WMU Sta.
Kalamazoo, MI 49008

City Lights Books
261 Columbus Ave.
San Francisco, CA 94133

Claassen-Verlag
Postfach 100555
31105 Hildesheim
Germany

CLEUP
Via Prati 19
35122 Padua
Italy

Editrice CLUEB
Via Marsala 24
40126 Bologna
Italy

CLUT Editrice
Corso Duca degli Abruzzi 24
10129 Turin
Italy

CNRS Editions
20-22 rue St-Armand
75015 Paris
France

Editions Complexe
24 rue de Bosnie
1060 Brussels
Belgium

Concourse Press
Box 8265
Philadelphia, PA 19101

Constable and Co.
3 The Lanchesters
162 Fulham Palace Rd.
London W6 9ER
England

Coronado Press
Box 3232
Lawrence, KS 66046

Editorial Costa Rica
Apdo. 10010
San José
Costa Rica

J. G. Cotta'sche
Rotebühlstr. 77
70178 Stuttgart
Germany

Thomas Y. Crowell Publishers
c/o Harper and Row
10 East 53rd St.
New York, NY 10022

Editorial Cultural
Calle Robles 51
Río Piedras, PR 00925

Current Books
Round West
Trissur
Kerala 680001
India

John Daniel Publishers
Box 21922
Santa Barbara, CA 93121

Dan Kook University Press
San 8 Hannam-dong
Yongsan-gu
Seoul 140-714
Republic of Korea

Dante University of America Press
Box 843
17 Station St.
Brookline Village, MA 02147

Dar es Salaam University Press
PO Box 35182
Dar es Salaam
Tanzania

Davidsfonds
Blyde Inkomststr. 79-81
3000 Leuven
Belgium

Deakin University Press
Deakin University
336 Glenferne Road
Malvern, Victoria 3144
Australia

Dejaie
1154 chaussée de Dinant
5100 Namur
Belgium

Delacorte Press
1540 Broadway
New York, NY 10036

J. M. Dent
91 Clapham High St.
London SW4 7TA
England

Izdatelstvo Detskaya Literatura
Malyi Cherkaskij pereulok 1
103720 Moscow
Russia

André Deutsch
105 Great Russell St.
London WC1B 3LJ
England

Dharma Publishing
2910 San Pablo Ave.
Berkeley, CA 94702

Ediciones Diálogo
Calle Brasil 1391
Asunción
Paraguay

John Donald Publishers
138 Saint Stephen St.
Edinburgh EH3 5AA
Scotland

Doaba House
1688 Nai Sarak
Delhi 110006
India

Sociedad Editorial Dominicana
Apdo 559
Calle Ramón Santana 2B
Santo Domingo
Dominican Republic

Dover Publications
31 East 2nd St.
Mineola, NY 11501

Livraria Duas Cidades
Rua Bento de Freitas 158
01220-000 São Paulo
Brazil

Dublin Institute for Advanced Studies
10 Burlington Road
Dublin 4
Ireland

Duculot
Fond Jean-Pacques 4
1348 Louvain-la-Neuve
Belgium

Dustbooks
Box 100
Paradise, CA 95967

Dutton/Signet
375 Hudson St.
New York, NY 10014

East African Educational Publishers
PO Box 45314
Nairobi
Kenya

Editorial Edicol
Murcia 2 esq Actipan 45
Col Insurgentes Mixcoac
Apdo 19-376
03920 Mexico
Mexico

Editorial Universitaria
Estafeta Universitaria
Universidad de Panamá
Panama 4
Panama

Editorial Universitaria
Maria Luisa Santander 0447
Casilla 10220
Santiago
Chile

Eichborn Verlag
Kaiserstr. 66
60329 Frankfurt am Main
Germany

Giulio Einaudi Editore
Via Biancamano 2
10100 Turin
Italy

Editorial Universitaria de la Universidad
El Salvador
Ciudad Universitaria
Apdo 1703
San Salvador
El Salvador

N. G. Elwert Verlag
Postfach 1128
35001 Marburg an der Lahn
Germany

Erel
St-Sebastiaanstr. 16
8400 Ostend
Belgium

EUDEBA
(Editorial Universitaria de Buenos Aires)
Ave Rivadavia 1571-73
1033 Buenos Aires
Argentina

EUNSA
Plaza de los Sauces 1-2
Apdo 396
31080 Barañain
Spain

Ewha Woman's University Press
11-1 Daehyeon-dong
Seodaemun-gu
Seoul 120-170
Republic of Korea

Faber & Faber Ltd.
3 Queen Sq.
London WC1N 3AU
England

Familia et Patria
Handzamestr. 155
8120 Kortemark-Handzame
Belgium

Farrar, Straus & Giroux
19 Union Sq. West
New York, NY 10003

Faxon Co.
15 Southwest Park
Westwood, MA 02090

Giangiacomo Feltrinelli Editore
Via Andegari 6
2021 Milan
Italy

Howard Fertig Inc., Publisher
80 East 11th St.
New York, NY 10003

Editions Fides
165 rue Deslauriers
Saint-Laurent, PQ H4N 2S4
Canada

Wilhelm Fink
Ohmstr. 5
80802 Munich
Germany

Firebrand Books
141 The Commons
Ithaca, NY 14850

Ediciones de la Flor
Gorriti 3695
1172 Buenos Aires
Argentina

Fonds Mercator
Meir 85
2000 Antwerp
Belgium

Foreign Languages Press
24 Baiwanzhuang Road
Beijing 100037
People's Republic of China

Foreign Language Teaching &
    Research Press
19 Xiganhuan Beilu
Beijing 100081
People's Republic of China

Presses Universitaires de France
108 blvd Saint-Germain
75006 Paris
France

Free Press
866 Third Ave.
New York, NY 10022

Fromm International Publishing
560 Lexington Ave.
New York, NY 10022

Verlag A. Fromm
Postfach 1948
49009 Osnabrück
Germany

Editorial Galerna
Characas 3741
1425 Buenos Aires
Argentina

Gallaudet University Press
800 Florida Ave., NE
Washington, DC 20002

Editions Gallimard
5 rue Sébastien-Bottin
75007 Paris
France

Casa García
Pellegrini 41
Resistencia Chaco
Argentina

Editrice Garigliano
Via Aligerno 91/93
03043 Cassino
Italy

Garzanti Editore
Via Senato 25
20121 Milan
Italy

Genesis Publications
51 Lynwood
Guildford GU2 5NY
England

Georg et Cie
Chemin de la Mousse 46
1225 Chêne-Bourg
Switzerland

Editrice Giannotta
Viale Regina Margherita 2/e-2/f
95125 Catania
Italy

Glendale Press
4 Haddington Terrace
Sandycove
Co. Dublin
Ireland

David R. Godine, Publisher
9 Lewis St.
Lincoln, MA 01773

Gomer Press
Wind St.
Llandysul
Dyfed SA44 4BQ
Wales

Gordian Press
Box 40304
85 Tompkins St.
Staten Island, NY 10304

Gower Publishing
Gower House
Croft Rd.
Aldershot
Hants GU11 3HR
England

Universidad de Granada
Collegio Maximo
Campus Universitario de Cartuja
18071 Granada
Spain

Jean Grassin Editeur
Port-en-Dro
BP75
56340 Carnac
France

Gregg Publishing
Gower House
Croft Rd.
Aldershot
Hants GU11 3HR
England

Presses Universitaires de Grenoble
BP 47 Campus St Martin d'Hères
38040 Grenoble Cedex 09
France

Grosset & Dunlap
200 Madison Ave.
New York, NY 10016

Groupe Expansion
25 rue Leblanc
75842 Paris Cedex 15
France

Grove Press
841 Broadway
New York, NY 10003-4793

Editorial Guadalupe
Mansila 3865
Piso 1°
1425 Bueno Aires
Argentina

Universidad de Guayaquil
Dpto de Publicaciones
Chile 900
Guayaquil
Ecuador

Gyldendal Norsk Forlag
Sehestedsgt. 4
Postboks 6860
St. Olaf
0130 Oslo
Norway

Gyldendalske Boghandel
Klareboderne 3
1029 Kobenhavn
Denmark

Hachette
83 ave Marceau
75116 Paris
France

Hale & Iremonger
19 Eve St.
Erskineville, NSW 2043
Australia

Hamish Hamilton
27 Wright's Lane
London W8 5TZ
England

Peter Hammer Verlag
Postfach 200693
42209 Wuppertal
Germany

Hansa Verlag
Postfach 1480
25804 Husum
Germany

Harcourt Brace & Co.
6277 Sea Harbor Dr.
Orlando, FL 32821

Harlan Davidson / Forum Press
773 Glenn Ave.
Wheeling, IL 60090-6000

Literaturverlag Karlheinz Hartmann
Rodheimer Str. 17
61381 Friedsrichsdorf im Taunus
Germany

Ernst Hauswedell
Rosenbergstr. 113
Postfach 140155
70193 Stuttgart
Germany

Haworth Press
10 Alice St.
Binghamton, NY 13904-1580

Haymon-Verlag
Kochstr. 10
2336020 Innsbruck
Austria

Heinemann Educational
Halley Ct.
Jordan Hill
Oxford OX2 8EJ
England

Heinle & Heinle Publishers
20 Park Plaza
Boston, MA 02116

Henssel Verlag
Glienicker Str. 12
14109 Berlin
Germany

Verlag Herder
Hermann-Herder-Str. 4
79104 Freiburg im Breisgau
Germany

Heritage Publishers
32 Prakash Apts.
5 Ansari Road
New Delhi 110002
India

Editions de l'Herne
41 rue de Verneuil
75007 Paris
France

HES Publishers
Westrenen Tunrdÿk
3997 MS 'tGoy-Houten Utrecht
Netherlands

Anton Hiersemann Verlag
Rosenbergstr. 113
Postfach 140155
70193 Stuttgart
Germany

Hill & Wang
19 Union Sq. West
New York, NY 10003

Hodder & Stoughton
338 Euston Rd.
London NW1 3BH
England

Hong Kong University Press
University of Hong Kong
139 Pokfulam Rd.
Hong Kong

Houghton Mifflin
222 Berkeley St.
Boston, MA 02116

Howard University Press
1240 Randolph St., NE
Washington, DC 20017

Max Hueber Verlag
Postfach 1142
85729 Ismaning
Germany

Indian Books Centre
40/5 Shakti Nagar
Delhi 110007
India

Infoboek
Roosterputstr. 34
2450 Meerhout
Belgium

Editrice Innocenti
Via Zara 36
38100 Trento
Italy

Institute for Polynesian Studies
Brigham Young University
Laie, HI 96762

Intercultural Press
Box 700
Yarmouth, ME 04096

Hid Islenzka Bókmenntafélag
Sidumula 21
108 Reykjavík
Iceland

Izdatelstvo Iskusstvo
3 Schinovsky Lane
Moscow 103009
Russia

Japadre Editore
Corso Federico II 49
67100 L'Aquila
Italy

Jewish Publication Society
1930 Chestnut St.
Philadelphia, PA 19103-4599

Editorial Juventud
Plaza Murillo 519
Casilla de Correo 1489
La Paz
Bolivia

Karoma Publishers
2509 North Campbell Ave.
Suite 45
Tucson, AZ 85719

Kerala University
Dept. of Publications
Thiruvananthapuram 695034
Kerala
India

Keter Publishing House
Industrial Zone
Givat Shaul B
PO Box 7145
Jerusalem 91071
Israel

Akadémiai Kiadó
Prielle K u 19-35
1117 Budapest
Hungary

Suomalaisen Kirjallisuuden Seura
PL 259
00171 Helsinki
Finland

Editions Klincksieck
8 rue de la Sorbonne
75005 Paris
France

Vittorio Klostermann
Postfach 900601
60446 Frankfurt
Germany

Wolters Kluwer Academic Publishers
Spuiboulevard 50
PO Box 989
3300 AZ Dordrecht
Netherlands

Izdatelstvo Kniga
ul Gorkovo 50
125047 Moscow
Russia

Alfred A. Knopf Inc.
201 East 50th St.
New York, NY 10022

Kodansha America
114 5th Ave.
New York, NY 10011

W. Kohlhammer
Hessbrühlstr. 69
70565 Stuttgart
Germany

Verlag Königshausen und Neumann
Postfach 6007
97010 Würzburg
Germany

Korea University Press
1-2 Anam-dong 5-ga
Seongbug-gu
Seoul 136-701
Republic of Korea

Karin Kramer Verlag
Postfach 440417
12004 Berlin
Germany

Kyung Hee University Press
1 Hueki-dong
Dongdaemun-gu
Seoul 131-050
Republic of Korea

University of Lagos Press
PO Box 132
Unilag
Akoka
Lagos
Nigeria

Lapis Press
2058 Broadway
Santa Monica, CA 90904

Giuseppe Laterza Editore
Piazza Umberto 154
70121 Bari
Italy

Il Lavoro Editoriale
Via Piave 32
60124 Ancona
Italy

Leiden University Press
Postbus 9000
2300 PA Leiden
Netherlands

Lerner
Calle 8A No. 68A-41
PO Box 8304
Santafé de Bogotá Cundinamarca
Colombia

Casa Editrice Le Lettere
Costas San Giorgio 28
50125 Florence
Italy

Lettres Modernes
67 rue du Cardinal Lemoine
75005 Paris
France

Leuven University Press
Krakenstr. 3
3000 Leuven
Belgium

Liber Verlag
Postfach 2946
55019 Mainz
Germany

Libraries Unlimited
Box 6633
Englewood, CO 80155-6633

Library of Social Science
320 East 42nd St., Suite 1602
New York, NY 10017

Licosa
Via Duca di Calabria 1/1
50125 Florence
Italy

Presses Universitaires de Liège
Domaine Universitaire-Sart-Tilman
Bâtiment 8, bte 27
4000 Liège
Belgium

Liguori Editore
Via Mezzocannone 19
80134 Naples
Italy

Little, Brown
34 Beacon St.
Boston, MA 02108

Liverpool University Press
Senate House
Liverpool L69 3BX
England

Le Livre de Poche
43 quai de Grenelle
75905 Paris Cedex 15
France

Loffredo Editore
Via Consalvo 99
80126 Naples
Italy

Carlos Lohlé
Tacuarí 1516
1139 Buenos Aires
Argentina

Longwood (Imprint of Simon & Schuster.
  See below)

Editorial Losada
Moreno 3362/64
1209 Buenos Aires
Argentina

Presses Universitaires de Lyon
86 rue Pasteur
69365 Lyon Cedex 07
France

Macmillan Canada
29 Birch Ave.
Toronto, ON M4V 1E2
Canada

McGraw-Hill
1221 Ave. of the Americas
New York, NY 10020

Magnes Press
Hebrew University
PO Box 7695
Jerusalem 91076
Israel

Maisonneuve et Larose
15 rue Victor-Cousin
75005
Paris
France

University of Malta Press
University of Malta
Administration Bldg.
Msida M5 D06
Malta

Ateneo de Manila University Press
PO Box 154
1099 Manila
Philippines

Aldo Marino Editore
Via Firenze 182/188
95128 Catania
Italy

Mercier Press
5 French Church St.
PO Box 5
Cork
Ireland

Mestre Jou
CP 24090
05089 São Paulo
Brazil

Metamorphous Press
Box 10616
Portland, OR 97210-0616

Universidad Nacional Autónoma de México
Torre 11 de Humanidades P14
Ciudad Universitaria
04510 Mexico
Mexico

Milella Editore
Viale Risorgimento 1
73100 Lecce
Italy

Minard
45 rue de St André
14123 Fleury/Orne
France

Minerva Publications
96 Jalan Dato' Bandar
Tunggal
70000 Seremban
Negeri Sembilan
Malaysia

Editions Modernes Média
21 rue du Cardinal-Lemoine
75005 Paris
France

Arnaldo Mondadori Editore
Via Mondadori
20090 Segrate (Milan)
Italy

Editora Moraes
Rua Ministro Godoy 1036 Perdizes
05015-001 São Paulo
Brazil

Mosaic Press
Box 1032
Oakville, ON L6J 5E9
Canada

Moscow University Press
ul Gertsena 5-7
103009 Moscow
Russia

Società Editrice Il Mulino
Str Maggiore 37
40125 Bologna
Italy

Munksgaard International Publishers
Nørre Søgade 35
PO Box 2148
1016 Copenhagen
Denmark

John Murray Publishers
50 Albemarle St.
London W1X 4BD
England

Presses Universitaires de Namur
Rempart de la Vierge 8
5000 Namur
Belgium

Gunter Narr Verlag
Dischingweg 5
72070 Tübingen
Germany

University of Natal Press
PO Box X01
Scottsville 3209
South Africa

Izdatelstvo Nauka
Profsoyuznaya ul 90
117864 Moscow
Russia

Ediciones Universidad de Navarra
Plaza de los Sauces, 1-2
Apdo 396
31010 Barañain
Spain

Newbury House Publishers
10 East 53rd St.
New York, NY 10022

NeWest Publishers
10359 82nd Ave., Suite 310
Edmonton, AB T6E 1Z9
Canada

New South Wales University Press
32 Botany St.
PO Box 1
Randwick, NSW 2031
Australia

New Writers' Press
13 Thorndale Lawn
Artane
Dublin 5
Ireland

Nistri-Lischi Editori
Via XXIV Maggio 28
56123 Pisa
Italy

Nizet
3bis pl de la Sorbonne
75005 Paris
France

La Nuova Italia Editrice
Via Codignola
50018 Casellina (Firenze)
Italy

Oberbaum Verlag
Friedelstr. 6
12047 Berlin
Germany

Odense University Press
Campusvej 55
5230 Odense M
Denmark

Oleander Press
17 Stansgate Ave.
Cambridge CB2 2QZ
England

Omnigraphics
Penobscot Bldg.
Detroit, MI 48226

Editorial Orion
Sierra Mojada 325
Col Lomas de Chapultepec
CP 11000 Mexico 10, DF
Mexico

Oryx Press
4041 North Central Ave.
Suite 700
Phoenix, AZ 85004-3397

University of Otago Press
56 Union St.
Dunedin
New Zealand

Editorial Oveja Negra
Carrerra 14 No 79-17
Bogotá, Colombia

Oxford University Press Australia
Academic Div.
Commissioning Editor
253 Normanby Road
South Melbourne
Australia

Editorial Paidós
Defensa 599-1° piso
1065 Buenos Aires
Argentina

Pallas Editora e Distribuidora
Rua Frederico de Albuquerque 44
Higienópolis
21050-840 Rio de Janeiro RJ
Brazil

G. B. Palumbo Editore
Via Ricasoli 59
90139 Palermo
Italy

Pankaj Publications
3 Regal Bldg.
Connaught Circus
New Delhi 110001
India

Panstwowe Wydawnictwo Rolnicze i Leśne
al Jerozolimskie 28
00-024 Warsaw
Poland

Pantheon
201 East 50th St.
New York, NY 10022

Paragon House Publishers
370 Lexington Ave.
New York, NY 10017

Parimal Prakashan
Parimal Bldg.
Khadkeshwar
Aurangabad 431001
India

Park Street Press
1 Park St.
Rochester, VT 05767

Passigli Editori
Via di Doccia 5
50135 Florence
Italy

Editorial Patria
Ave San Lorenzo 160
Col Esther Zuno de Echeverria-I
09860 Mexico DF
Mexico

Pàtron Editore
Via Badini 12
40050 Quarto Inferiore
Bologna
Italy

Editions Payot
106 blvd Saint-Germain
75006 Paris
France

Editora Paz e Terra
Rua do Triunfo 177
01212-010 São Paulo
Brazil

Pehuén Editores
Antonio Varas 1476
Casilla 10460
Santiago
Chile

Penguin Books
27 Wright's Lane
London W8 5TZ
England

Editions Phébus
12 rue Grégoire-de-Tour
75006 Paris
France

University of the Philippines Press
Gonzales Hall
Dilliman
Quezon City 3004
Philippines

Editions Picard
82 rue Bonaparte
75006 Paris
France

Editions Picollec
47 rue Auguste-Lançon
75013 Paris
France

Pinter Publishers
Wellington House
125 The Strand
London WC2R 0BB
England

Plenum Publishing
233 Spring St.
New York, NY 10013

Editorial Plus Ultra
Callao 575
1055 Buenos Aires
Argentina

Politikens Forlag
Vestergade 26
1456 Copenhagen K
Denmark

Pontifical Institute of Mediaeval Studies
59 Queens Park Crescent East
Toronto, ON M5S 2C4
Canada

Popular Prakashan
4648/1 Ansari Rd. 21
Daryagani
New Delhi 110002
India

Ediciones José Porrúa Turanzas
Cea Bermúdez 10
28003 Madrid
Spain

Clarkson Potter
201 East 50th St.
New York, NY 10022

Guido Pressler Verlag
Auf dem Strifft
52393 Hürtgenwald
Germany

Procultura
Av 25C No 3-97
Apdo Aéreo 044700
Santafé de Bogotá Cundinamarca
Colombia

Prometheus Books
59 John Glenn Dr.
Buffalo, NY 14228

University of Puerto Rico Press
Apdo. 23322
Estación UPR
San Juan, PR 00931-3322

Les Presses de l'Université du Québec
2875 boul Laurier
Ste-Foy, PQ G1V 2M3
Canada

Quelle und Meyer Verlag
Postfach 4747
65037 Wiesbaden
Germany

Rajpal & Sons
1590 Madarasa Rd.
Kashmere Gate
Delhi 110006
India

Ramsay Head Press
15 Gloucester Place
Edinburgh EH3 6EE
Scotland

Random House
201 East 50th St.
New York, NY 10022

Raven Arts Press
2 Brookside
Dundrum Road
Dundrum
Dublin 14
Ireland

RCS Rizzoli Libri
Via Mecenate 91
20128 Milan
Italy

Redcliffe Press
49 Park St.
Bristol BS1 5NT
England

Editiore Riuniti
Piazza Vittorio Emanuele
00185 Rome
Italy

Rosenkilde & Bagger
Postboks 2184
1017 Copenhagen K
Denmark

Rupa and Co.
PO Box 12333
15 Bankim Chatterjee St.
Calcutta 700073
India

Saarbrücker Druckerei und Verlag
Postfach 102745
66027 Saarbrücken
Germany

Verlag Otto Sagner
Hess Str. 39/41
80798 Munich
Germany

SAIE Editrice
Corso Regina Margherita 2
10153 Turin
Italy

Ediciones Universidad de Salamanca
Espana 51
Apdo 325
37080 Salamanca
Spain

Salem Press
580 Sylvan Ave.
Englewood Cliffs, NJ 07632

San Diego State University Press
San Diego State University
San Diego, CA 92182-8141

Universidad Nacional Mayor de San Marcos
Ave República de Chile 295
Apdo 454
Lima 1
Peru

Universidad Autónoma de Santo Domingo
Ciudad Universitaria
Apdo 1355
Santo Domingo
Dominican Republic

Sasta Sahitya Mandal
N-77 Connaught Circus
New Delhi 110001
India

Dr. A. Schendl
Karlsgasse 15
Postfach 29
1041 Vienna
Austria

Verlag Lambert Schneider
Postfach 100123
70826 Gerlingen
Germany

Schocken Publishing House
24 Nathan Yelin Mor St.
PO Box 2316
Tel Aviv 61022
Israel

Scholarly Resources
104 Greenhill Ave.
Wilmington, DE 19805-1897

Scholars Press
Box 15399
Atlanta, GA 30333

Verlag für Schöne Wissenschaften
Unterer Zielweg 36
4143 Dornach 2
Switzerland

Ferdinand Schöningh
Postfach 2540
33055 Paderborn
Germany

Salvatore Sciascia
Corso Umberto 1111
93100 Caltanissetta
Italy

SBD Enterprises
4422-23 Nai Sarak
Delhi 110006
India

Seoul National University Press
56-1 Sinlim-dong
Gwanag-gu
Seoul 151-742
Republic of Korea

Editions du Seuil
27 rue Jacob
75006 Paris
France

Shambhala Publications
Horticultural Hall
300 Massachusetts Ave.
Boston, MA 02115

Sharda Prakashan
33/1 Bhul Bhullian Road
Mehrauli
New Delhi 110030
India

Sidgwick & Jackson
18-21 Cavaye Place
London SW10 9PG
England

Siglo XXI de España Editores
Plaza 5
28043 Madrid
Spain

Sigo Press
50 Grove St.
Salem, MA 01970

Simon & Pierre
2181 Queen St. East, Suite 301
Toronto, ON M4E 1E5
Canada

Simon & Schuster
Simon & Schuster Bldg.
1230 Ave. of the Americas
New York, NY 10020

Sinclair-Stevenson
Michelin House
81 Fulham Road
London SW3 6RB
England

Institut d'Etudes Slaves
9 rue Michelet
75006 Paris
France

Slovensky Spisovatel
Laurinská 2
81367 Bratislava
Slovakia

Societäts-Verlag
Postfach 10081
60327 Frankfurt
Germany

Sogang University Press
1 Shinsu-dong
Mapo-ku
Seoul 121-742
Republic of Korea

Editorial Sopena
Moreno 957-7° piso
Dept 2
1091 Buenos Aires
Argentina

Southern Methodist University Press
314 Fondren Library West
Dallas, TX 75275

Izdatelstvo Sovetskii Pisatel'
ul Vorovskovo 11
121069 Moscow
Russia

Volker Spiess
Postfach 303046
10730 Berlin
Germany

Springer-Verlag
Jachenplatz 4-6
1201 Vienna
Austria

Station Hill Press
Station Hill Road
Barrytown, NY 12507

Sterling Publishing Co.
387 Park Ave.
New York, NY 10016

Stern-Verlag
Postfach 101053
40001 Düsseldorf
Germany

Stocker Verlag
Hofg 5
Postfach 438
8011 Graz
Austria

Stoddart
34 Lesmill Road
Don Mills, ON M3B 2T6
Canada

Edizioni di Storia e Letteratura
Via Lancellotti 18
00186 Rome
Italy

Sudamericana
Humberto 531/55
1103 Buenos Aires
Argentina

Suhrkamp Verlag
Lindenstr. 29-35
Postfach 4229
60019 Frankfurt
Germany

Swets en Zeitlinger
Heereweg 347b
Postbus 825
2160 SZ Lisse
Netherlands

Texas Western Press
University of Texas
El Paso, TX 79968-0633

Jan Thorbecke Verlag
Postfach 546
72488 Sigmaringen
Germany

Ticknor & Fields
215 Park Ave. South
New York, NY 10003

Tilgher-Genova
Via AAssarotti 52
16122 Genoa
Italy

Tokai University Press
2-27-4 Tomigaya
Shibuya-ku
Tokyo 151
Japan

Tuduv Verlagsgesellschaft
Postfach 340163
80098 Munich
Germany

Charles E. Tuttle, Inc.
153 Milk St., 5th fl.
Boston, MA 02109

Edizioni Unicopli
Via Soperza 13
20127 Milan
Italy

Union College Press
College Grounds
Schenectady, NY 12308

Editura Univers
Piata Presei Liberel 1
79739 Bucharest
Romania

La Universal
Calle Jenaro Sanjines 538
Casilla de Correo 2888
La Paz
Bolivia

Verlag Urachhaus
Postfach 131053
70190 Stuttgart
Germany

Utah State University Press
Logan, UT 84322-7800

UTB
Breitweisenstr. 9
Postfach 801124
70511 Stuttgart
Germany

Ediciones Universitarias de Valparaíso
12 De Febrero 187
Valparaíso
Chile

Vandenhoeck & Ruprecht
37070 Göttingen
Germany

Vani Prakashan
4697/5
21-A Daryaganj
New Delhi 110002
India

Vikas Publishing House
576 Masjid Road
Jangpura
New Delhi 110014
India

Viking-Penguin
375 Hudson St.
New York, NY 10014

Virago Press
The Rotunda
42-43 Gloucester Crescent
London NW1 7PD
England

Vita e Pensiero
Largo Gemelli 1
20123 Milan
Italy

Vrie Universiteit Boekhandel
De Boelelaan 1105
1018 HV Amsterdam
Netherlands

Wadsworth Inc.
10 Davis Dr.
Belmont, CA 94002

Washington State University Press
Cooper Publications Bldg.
Washington State University
Pullman, WA 99164-5910

Water Row Press
Box 438
Sudbury, MA 01776

John Wiley & Sons
605 Third Ave.
New York, NY 10158

H. W. Wilson Co.
950 University Ave.
Bronx, NY 10452

Wissenschaftliche Buchgesellschaft
Hindenburgstr. 40
Postfach 100110
64295 Darmstadt
Germany

Witwatersrand University Press
36 Jorissen St.
Braamfontein 2001
South Africa

Wolfhound Press
68 Mountjoy Sq.
Dublin 1
Ireland

Women's Press
34 Great Sutton St.
London EC1V 0DX
England

Yeshiva University Press
500 West 185th St.
New York, NY 10033-3201

YMCA Press
11 rue de la Montagne Ste.-Geneviève
75005 Paris
France

Yonsei University Press
134 Shinchon-dong
Seodaemun-ku
Seoul 120-749
Republic of Korea

Index to Publishing Interests

Index to Imprints and Subsidiary Firms

Index to Series Titles

Index to Editorial Personnel

Index to Languages of Publication
Other Than English